Powerful, Profitable Software Products

You hold in your hands a comprehensive guide to creating a flourishing software development practice – one that makes a powerful impact with the software it builds. This guide describes the unique aspects of creating software-based products. It also lays out the clear practical guidance that's necessary to construct and evolve a modern practice. This includes hiring, structuring teams properly, writing good code, leveraging test-driven development, designing architecture, automating development processes with DevOps techniques, and – importantly – leading teams through the disruptive change that each of these can represent. Further, the first principles upon which these practices rest will be elaborated so that the reader can readily adapt the already practical techniques to the broadest possible set of real-world situations.

Kyle Rowland brings an incredibly rich and diverse base of experience to TechMentor and its clients. He has spent more than 20 years delivering software solutions across a broad set of industries – from Defense Department to Financial Services, from Telecommunications to Big Data Analytics, and just about everything in between. Leading and building across such a broad set of problem domains and team approaches have given him both an uncommon depth of technical expertise and a unique perspective into the generalized problems that plague all of software development. More importantly though, it's given him a solid grasp of the fundamental principles and techniques that underpin the most powerful and effective solutions to these problems – solutions he's personally used to lead organizations from near stand-still to highly productive. Most importantly, Kyle has a deep-seated passion to move you and your organization to the next level – believing thoroughly that disciplined, small steps in the right direction change people, that change organizations, that change the world.

Powerful, Profitable Software Products
The Executive Guidebook

Kyle Rowland

CRC Press
Taylor & Francis Group
Boca Raton London New York

CRC Press is an imprint of the
Taylor & Francis Group, an **informa** business

Designed cover image: Shutterstock images

First edition published 2025
by CRC Press
2385 NW Executive Center Drive, Suite 320, Boca Raton FL 33431

and by CRC Press
4 Park Square, Milton Park, Abingdon, Oxon, OX14 4RN

CRC Press is an imprint of Taylor & Francis Group, LLC

ISBN: 978-1-032-46670-5 (hbk)
ISBN: 978-1-032-46672-9 (pbk)
ISBN: 978-1-003-38275-1 (ebk)

DOI: 10.1201/9781003382751

Typeset in Sabon
by KnowledgeWorks Global Ltd.

To Kathy ("Mom") Rowland –

Whether it was including me in the process of buying the family computer or hitting the mall with me to pick up my first compiler – your consistent support, hunger for tech, and modeling of adaptability made me the geek I am today.

Contents

Chapter 1

Introduction

Building software is a unique challenge among our endeavors to be useful to one another. This unique challenge begets unique solutions – solutions that are both far from intuitive and simultaneously deeply gratifying to leverage.

The book you hold in your hand – whether paper, pixel, or e-ink, on tablet, desktop, or e-reader – will start from the very beginning. We will build up a deep understanding about the unique nature of software development and inquire into the challenges that it creates. From those first principles, we will build up a set of tools and techniques that can be applied to most effectively – most impactfully – build great software. Ultimately, a roadmap will emerge – one that will provide a path to rapidly, painlessly, and effectively take an idea from conception to solving real problems and creating real value.

Before we begin, I'd like to share a story that taught me a core lesson about the nature of software development.

It was a crisp pacific northwest morning. I'd made it through several hours of music classes and of course an hour of physics. The physics class was the first "period" of the day, and the time when most normal North Kitsap High School students were only beginning to shake off the sleep of the night before. I, however, had been playing jazz for an hour or so prior to that. There's nothing like the bang of the drum-set hitting the back of your head while participating in an escalating volume war (my weapon was the trumpet) to get the blood flowing in the early morning. I'm not sure still whether it was helpful or harmful toward bringing my burgeoning mental capacities online for the day.

At any rate, I had survived that usual routine and my treat was spending time in the computer lab. For the rural area I grew up and lived in, it was nicely endowed. The whole lab was connected with a Novell Netware network, whose capabilities seemed endless. Most of the machines were 386s (DXs – not the weaker SX model). For our final year here, the school even snagged a couple of the latest generation machines which were being called "Pentiums." We fought over who got to use them – though we weren't really sure what difference they made to any of the computing we were doing.

A couple of my friends and I had been programming and using Bulletin Board Systems (or BBSes as we called them) and just generally enjoying computers for much of our young lives. We chatted with others in the area over

DOI: 10.1201/9781003382751-1

BBSes that could have as many as four simultaneously connected users (wow!). We even waded into the deep waters of the Internet and Internet Relay Chat (IRC). This allowed us to chat with people all over the world – frequently with dozens of people at a time. In today's world, when this kind of communication is the norm, it's hard to explain the frontier expanding impact of this new kind of communication. It was a powerful thing for a kid – like me – that had grown up not communicating with anyone outside a 20- or 30-mile radius of his own home.

This, in my mind, was the killer app of the computer itself. It was going to allow us to communicate with many people, all over the globe – in real-time.

So on this crisp morning – after the usual routine – I got to talking with a friend of mine, Kevin Fleming. We decided we needed to challenge each other. The winner of the challenge would be the one that built the best chat program that ran on the computers and network in the lab. It also had to be a TSR (terminate and stay resident program) – so that our fellow students could bring it up and hide it in the case a teacher walked by. This was in the days of DOS programs and single-threaded operating systems. Multitasking in this manner wasn't commonplace, so this would be a valuable feature. It would be particularly so for our socialite classmates that didn't want their social activities to negatively impact their grade.

We coded and coded. I took my cues from IRC and built a full-screen, colorless chatting system. Kevin, who had been telling me he was developing a (text-based) windowing system, with colors, applied his new windowing library in service of his chat program. His program had a small (colorful) popup chat window, while mine colorlessly took control of the whole screen. His looked and felt better. He buried me.

After I saw how much better his approach was, I threw mine out and started working on his. Everyone in the class eventually started using it to chat.

As I mentioned as I got into this story, our challenge taught me an important and powerful lesson about the nature of software development. No matter how long we've been in the game, the point is to create things that are useful for people. Though it wasn't really our focus, we ended up meeting the desire of our classmates to connect and maybe to avoid doing their work at times.

Meeting a perceived need or desire is the same fundamental thing that we do in the "grown-up" world. Since then, we've had web pages with guestbooks, MySpace, and Facebook. Similarly, starting with the storied "dot-com boom," Amazon, eBay, and its generation of innovators made a lot of headway in buying and selling with computers.

Through that early period and beyond, even the most technical among us haven't taken full notice of the significant change software was (and is) bringing to commerce. Yes, with the dot-com era, we began to buy and sell things with computers. The more subtle and more powerful change is in what represents value to people. In prior days, that was almost always a physical product, even if the real value came from ideas (as is the case with a book).

Now, increasingly, ideas and their physical representations can be divorced, and economic activity focused most powerfully on the idea.

We can invent, we can create new value, and we can be useful to people in new ways directly through ideas. This is the software revolution.

SOFTWARE AS BUSINESS

As a society, the way we bring any kind of usefulness to each other is through reciprocity. I can spend my time, expertise, and energy creating something of value for you in hopes that you will do the same for me. In this way, I don't have to become an expert in everything that is useful to me while still having access to it. This, of course, is called business.

The end of my use of the High School computer lab came in the mid-1990s as I graduated.

Following that graduation, there was a boom of business built around software. It was an exciting time. General acceptance of the usefulness of computers and their networks began to drive the maturity of supporting tools and techniques. Understanding of the web, even by those that weren't natively interested in tech, flourished. People gradually started communicating and carrying on commerce in a more compucentric fashion.

Enabling all of this was software.

The business world throughout the end of the 20th century was beginning to recognize the uniqueness of software along with its unique problems. Many businesses stuck their heads in the sand and some still are. But the exploding need for software and the resulting exploding number of software developers at the turn of the millennium made it all but impossible to ignore the problem.

The following score of years has not seen any slowing of this explosion – and thus the problems have become increasingly clear. The solutions exist but take some time to learn, not only because they are complicated and counterintuitive but because they cut across widely divergent skill sets. And since the number of developers is increasing so rapidly, the knowledge is still somewhat diffuse.

And so here we are – looking closely at the nature of this unique endeavor, and then building up the tooling and techniques from first principles so that we can be truly useful to each other using this beautiful medium – software.

THE MAP AND THE TERRAIN

As Stephen Covey points out, if you're looking to tour Chicago but you're using a map of Detroit, you're going to run into problems [1].

There is an underlying reality that we interact with – the actual terrain. Though we can only think and communicate about it using models (paradigms, to use Covey's parlance), the more accurate the model, the more useful it will be as a tool to interact with that reality. Having a map of Chicago will ensure that we are able to make better choices in terms of streets to follow and turns to make in our tour of Chicago. A map of Detroit will be less useful.

So, our first task is to truly understand the terrain to develop a map that is as close as we can make it to that terrain. And then once we have that clear for ourselves, we can build up tools and techniques around that.

As we look to develop this map (or model), we need to begin by asking ourselves pointed questions. What is the nature of software development? Why do we see the same problems bubbling up in diverse organizations conducting software development? What are their causes? Do the problems and their causes have any connections?

One of the first pieces of the model that we need to put in place goes well outside the bounds of software development – back to our definition and understanding of business.

BUSINESS AND ENTREPRENEURSHIP

Earlier, we discussed the nature of being useful to our fellow human beings. We do it through reciprocal relationships – I have something you want, you have something I want, and so we exchange. We both come out ahead because we value what the other has more than what we must give in exchange for it.

To be useful to others, we build up a capacity for producing the things others value. That can mean buying equipment, or investigating ideas, or it can mean getting targeted training so that we can carry out specific actions that people value.

Whatever form this takes, that capacity is called "capital" [2].

This is the common understanding of business. That we accumulate capital, meet a need, and collect an appropriate return based on the law of reciprocity.

That definition is a good working one under normal circumstances. But when we start considering our unique brand of capital, viz. computer software, this abstract view loses a few details that turn out to be very relevant.

When we consider business, we imagine that at some point in the past, an entrepreneur had the idea about what desire or need might be met, then in a discrete move, set up a business to do that thing. At the time that the business is up and operating profitably, we no longer consider it to be an entrepreneurial venture; we consider it to be a simple machine that meets the need and provides a return.

The detail that we're glossing over here is the idea that we know in any certain sense what is going to meet a particular concrete need that a real customer has. In reality, we deal with probabilities based on our own insights and past experience meeting peoples' needs. Whether the specific individual Joe Smith will choose to value the bicycle we build more than the money he might trade to get it, we don't know precisely. We've observed a widely held need in the past and have insight about the human condition such that we can make an informed prediction that some individuals may choose to meet their need with our product.

To step back for a second, we should define entrepreneurship. Entrepreneurship is simply the act of making a prediction about the future desires of people such that the entrepreneur will take the personal risk of accumulating the appropriate capital in the hopes of meeting that need [3].

This activity is constantly happening in every business. Even if it has become a rote process, that engages little cognitive effort.

This rote process – this rut that business organizations fall into – is such a powerful pattern that even before software turned things upside down, many have fallen prey to it.

This is illustrated by Clayton Christensen with a story about the early evolution of the computer hard drive. As drives got progressively smaller and more portable, each generation was championed by an organization who made the innovation and then seemingly got stuck, unable to take the innovation to the next rung on the ladder [4].

Christensen asks the question:

> Why was it that firms that could be esteemed as aggressive, innovative, customer-sensitive organizations could ignore or attend belatedly to technological innovations with enormous strategic importance? In the context of the preceding analysis of the disk drive industry, this question can be sharpened considerably. The established firms were, in fact, aggressive, innovative, and customer-sensitive in their approaches to sustaining innovations of every sort. But the problem established firms seem unable to confront successfully is that of downward vision and mobility, in terms of the trajectory map. Finding new applications and markets for these new products seems to be a capability that each of these firms exhibited once, upon entry, and then apparently lost. It was as if the leading firms were held captive by their customers, enabling attacking entrant firms to topple the incumbent industry leaders each time a disruptive technology emerged [4].

The answer is this – the abstract view of a business neglects the concrete reality that all businesses continue to be fundamentally entrepreneurial even once they are successfully bringing in a profit. The leisureliness of both communication and the general transacting of business in prior decades has made ignoring this while still reaping a livelihood possible. As speed has increased and the cost of entry to do any kind of business has decreased, this has become decreasingly viable.

Attempting to work in software without coming to terms with this "continuous entrepreneurship" will always result in a short-lived venture.

And to be fair – for most leaders and businesspeople creating value through software – an intuitive grasp of this reality has become common.

Stating it explicitly though will help us to have the solid theoretical foundation necessary on which to build our tactical framework. Leveraging this framework will then provide the utmost value through our software development efforts.

So to boil this down to something, we can easily remember:
Every business is continuously entrepreneurial.

BUSINESS, ENTREPRENEURSHIP, AND SOFTWARE

This gets particularly interesting when we begin to use software to meet needs.

Classically, the entrepreneurial cycle is as follows. It begins with making a prediction about what need may exist at some point in the future. After this initial idea, the entrepreneur calculates whether he will be able to build up the capital to meet that need at the point it exists. If he is able, he begins to build up the appropriate capital until the time comes to meet the need, at which point he does so and collects his return.

With physical capital such as buildings or pencils or bicycles, there is a great deal of effort put into the physical realization of every unit that a human being potentially derives value from. Someone must assemble each and every bicycle in order for it to have the potential to meet a need.

This meant that a majority, a vast majority, of the labor to provide the ultimate value came from that physical realization. Defining the idea of the bicycle clearly enough that it might be physically produced is the other important work, but relative to the physical production, it is the smaller effort.

That is to say, the entrepreneurial effort of anticipating the need with a sufficiently defined product was dwarfed by the effort it took to put it into a useful form for each of the "end-users."

Software reverses that entirely.

As Pete McBreen says in *Software Craftsmanship*, "the production process for software is trivially easy – just copy a disk or CD" [5]. Today, it's even easier; there's not even any intermediate media involved – just issue the command to copy the code to a cloud environment.

That is to say, in the software world, the nature of things dictates that we spend energy almost entirely on invention rather than on "production" (the realization of the product for the individual). That invention work includes discovering the problem, envisioning a solution, and specifying the precise details of that solution. That's not to say those are serially performed activities, but that they are aspects of any invention whatsoever. Whether it's the light bulb, the automobile, or the iPhone, when we seek to find a new way to help a human work through a problem we must do these things.

That last step in most other inventions is a paper-only activity – sketching out how the product will actually be built. In software development, the paper becomes the product automatically. That is, the program code immediately and trivially becomes the system that serves the person.

What all of this means is that we must be very careful about the model we use for software development (and any metaphor that we might use to uphold that model). Treating invention like "production" is a recipe for disaster. It assumes invention has already been accomplished and that there is a clearly designated path from beginning to end. Following from this assumption is that very little communication other than a simple checklist (and basic management) is needed to keep team members in step. Both of these assumptions are obviously false if applied to invention itself.

So, the inescapable, and unspeakably important conclusion is that software development is core to the entrepreneurial activities that an organization engages in. This, further, and quite practically, implies that there should be small and very closely connected communication networks among the broader team involved in the organization's invention. That is, those that are working to shape the capital being created should ideally be on the same day-to-day working group, and that working group should be as small as possible.

To be more concrete, we will dig deeper into how an entrepreneur anticipates a need.

For now, we don't have time machines or any communication mechanisms that can circumvent the space-time continuum. Our insights about what someone might find useful are always guesses. We can apply varying degrees of rigor to our guesses but what we are trying to do, in essence, is predict the future emotional state of members of our fickle species.

So how can we accomplish something that – on face of it – seems impossible? There are three general approaches to this:

1. We can have a flash of insight. Our cognitive capabilities are sometimes quite beyond our grasp to explicitly understand. We can reason things out without explicitly working through every step of logic. We can pick a right answer without "learning" a particular thing – or without having the conscious experience of working it out. However, these mysterious mental mechanics work; we have this powerful capability that we tend to refer to as intuition.
2. We can use a posteriori analysis. That is, we can make a guess based on related observations. There are two ways to do this. The first is by conducting an experiment – creating something that might meet a need and see how well it meets needs. The second is by analyzing how existing software has met the needs of people.
3. We can create the need. By pointing out situations that may be less than satisfactory, and framing them clearly, we can help to create the sense of need within people.

Though in practice, we wouldn't use just one of these. It is more likely that each of them would be useful to varying degree, depending on the specifics of the problem being addressed.

To reiterate though, our target is to formulate a correct map of the world – a mental model that accurately describes the reality of things. When we do this, our software development efforts will be more effective.

So to bring it all together, we remember from the earlier discussion that software development is core to the entrepreneurialism of the organization, and because of this it should share a day-to-day working group with the company's other entrepreneurial aspects. Further, actual working groups should be small.

If we look closely at the three tools for anticipating needs that we unpacked above, we will notice something interesting. In modern practice, each of the three tends to be isolated organizationally.

Number 1 (flashes of insight) tends to be isolated in senior leadership or even just in the CEO in an early stage startup. Number 2 (experimentation) tends to be isolated in the "Product" department. And number 3 (creating a need) tends to be isolated in the "Marketing" department.

This method for sharing responsibility is why mental model is so important. To decompose responsibility in this manner accepts (however implicitly) the faulty model that assumes software development to be akin to the act of physical realization ("production" as we were calling it earlier). As we said, and as is borne out by the experience of so many organizations over the past several decades, this faulty model brings with it powerful problems. It's the map of Detroit in our hands as we attempt to navigate Chicago.

As we build out a comprehensive model, the idea that software development is invention is foundational. Further, it is one of several ideas that must be well-understood in order to best be delivering real value to people.

In our efforts along these lines, we will dig deeply into the principles that underpin this complicated work of organizations that develop software. We will build up a framework that will elucidate these principles and instruct in how to best put them to use. We will follow that by building a software-development-specific leadership approach on this foundation. Once this is in place, we'll lay out the specific skill areas that every software developer should be competent and be growing in. After this, we'll illustrate how this full model applies to real-life engineering organizations – particularly as they are seeking to improve.

We'll finish by boiling everything down to a generalized guideline that will allow any engineering organization to quickly analyze where it is at and make the steps necessary to move forward.

WORKS CITED

1. S. Covey, The 7 Habits of Highly Effective People, 1989.
2. F. A. Hayek, The Pure Theory of Capital, 1941.
3. L. v. Mises, Human Action, 1949.
4. C. M. Christensen, The Innovator's Dilemma, 1997.
5. P. McBreen, Software Craftsmanship: The New Imperative, Addison-Wesley, Boston, 2001.

Section I

Groundwork

Chapter 2

The problem

Creating software is creating value for people.

In business, it's easy to view the return that we pursue as the primary goal. This is something to be cautious about. Making a living – putting a roof over our heads and food on our table – is important. Optimizing for return above all else can, however, lead to poor short-term choices – choices that ultimately lead to smaller long-term returns.

Jim Collins shows that an unrelenting focus on excellence for its own sake separates the companies that make his "Good to Great" leap from those that don't [1]. That is to say, one might not be able to see the direct line connecting the extra effort refining the product (or service) and a specific return. Making that effort, though, makes the organization incrementally more successful. Ultimately through this, it brings the best returns. In our terms, focusing on the value that we are creating with our software and maximizing the effort toward that end will ensure that our businesses are the most successful, most profitable software creators they can be.

Creating the most value for people will be our north star as we dive deeply into how to build software most effectively. We must keep our focus on this target as we build up our mental model. We will use this mental model to fashion the tools we need to win with software. As we go through this effort, you will notice that we will return to our north star regularly. This reflects how truly important it is to always start there as we seek to build the best organizations that we can.

As we begin, we need to recognize that attaining and maintaining clarity is a primary concern with our model. There is an overabundance of bad information and advice available. Clarity will help us to avoid the perspective-warping, productivity-damaging effect of that low-quality advice.

Bad information comes into the industry through two primary vectors.

First, it can come from the fact that the leaders and engineers building software today are typically under quite a bit of pressure. Under pressure like this, it is common to reach for the first answer available. Often, this answer is then verified against only a few data points. That is, the individual leader or engineer has only seen and responded to a given circumstance (even framed

DOI: 10.1201/9781003382751-3

generally) – at most – a handful of times. This is "hasty generalization" – a common problem in our young industry.

Second, bad information can come from hype. Because our industry is so young we change at a break-neck pace. Many of us have come up at a time when there have been months or even days between the old tools and the new shiny ones that replace them. There is almost always a new tool, technique, or thought to be excited about – and there is often very little time to consider the idea as it flies by.

Understanding the unchanging principles of software development and being able to readily apply them will help us to wade through this information overload. Moreover, it will help us to pick out the ideas that really matter, even when they're new to us or when only sparse information is available. This will be true whether we're talking about git, "the cloud" or Kubernetes; Agile or Waterfall; Rust, Python or C++.

Once we have our mental model clearly in view, the next thing to do will be to use that model to develop concrete tools and techniques. Eventually, we will use these as a guide through our execution.

If it isn't clear yet, the challenge with software development is one of thinking. First, it's important to do as much thinking before the crisis as possible. We must develop generalized thinking tools before they're needed. It is equally important, though, to be able to think clearly and accurately during the crisis – when the pressure is on.

The former we will do in the coming chapters. You will continue this important work as you develop tools yet more specific to your context. The latter is a matter of thoroughly understanding the principles and having practice applying them.

THE ULTIMATE PROBLEM

Software is invention. Further, it is invention performed by groups.

These groups are often – out of necessity – oddly shaped.

Involved in these groups are people with deep technical knowledge and skill – in things such as programming languages, algorithms, or distributed computing. There are also folks that are masters of the intricate work of creating a friendly product that pleases human beings. And of course, there are business-minded people that are thoroughly versed in balancing the resources being invested against the future return being sought.

To work well, all of these types of people must trust each other, communicate well, and stay aligned with the same set of ultimate goals. They must also group themselves in ways that are most productive but can at times be counterintuitive and uncomfortable.

I've often compared the act of software development to writing a piece of music ... with a team of people ... as it is being played.

This ultimate problem is very unique – quickly defying the metaphors that are so often used to explain it.

FIRST THINGS FIRST

As mentioned earlier, clarity is job one. With respect to that, our target is to build a bullet-proof theoretical platform with which to approach software development.

It is important to recognize – as we begin – that there are many organizations that have invested heavily in providing businesses with menus of answers – specific sets of actions. These menu items purport to result in optimal software delivery. "Conduct these meetings and your software development will be successful." "Use this tool and your software development will be successful."

In almost every case, these pre-canned answers come without any attempt at attaching themselves to underlying principles. They often lack recognition that there are, in fact, underlying principles. In any domain, a solution without an accurate theoretical framework is fraught with danger because minute changes in context can undermine the validity of the tactical approach.

In music – for example – practitioners study a theoretical framework to ensure the adaptability and integrity of their performances. Even artists in less-complicated genres understand constructs like chords and timing, and leverage frameworks that, at least roughly, define their relationships.

No advisor or consultant – no matter how brilliant – can provide a tactical solution that will always work in every context. Such a solution simply doesn't exist.

Even still, a search for improved methods is underway in the software world. The results of the search have been positive. The quality of the "menus of answers" has improved dramatically.

The reason for the improvement is the increased proximity between the pre-canned answers and the underlying principles. In past decades, we've had menus of answers that were quite out of alignment with reality. That is changing.

This positive move has been made empirically.

Though it hasn't been particularly coordinated. Throughout the industry, we simply share the interest of improving how we create software. As we try different approaches or techniques, we make a note of the things that work. We then share this information with one another.

Since the sample sizes have been large (and dramatically increasing as we speak) – the breadth of this type of empirical approach is superior to the narrower one mentioned earlier. Gathering data in the heat of battle in a single organization simply doesn't offer the quantity examples from which to make helpful generalizations.

While industry-wide empiricism is obviously superior to that of a single organization, we've still been lacking one important thing. We haven't been trying to extract principles – we've focused primarily on extracting tactics.

Getting at the principles is important because it makes our approach more adaptable. Adaptability is particularly important when the pressure is on.

When we're not under pressure, we can take the time to think and to figure out how to meet whatever the need is. We can even run some experiments in controlled environments. When we are under pressure – things need to just work, we must be practiced in whatever our technique is.

To repeat this important point, adaptability, an absolutely essential characteristic, comes from understanding principle and from having practice in its application.

ENTREPRENEURSHIP AND SOFTWARE, REPRISE

To start, we need to step back to some of what we covered in the first chapter.

We really need to get our heads around the nature of entrepreneurialism. This may seem like a departure from thinking about software development, but understanding this gets to the heart of how building software systems really works. More importantly, it gets at the principles we can be using to improve our ability in this arena.

Entrepreneurialism is the act of predicting a need that someone will have, building up the capability to meet that need, and then meeting it in exchange for a return.

For that return to be reaped, both the entrepreneur and the customer must feel that they are gaining from the transaction. "Feel" is an important word here – because a lot of time, we make abstractions out of supply and demand, and the other components of the economic machine – we try to treat this need-meeting activity like a natural science. Add two grams of substance X, mix it with one liter of liquid Y, and then out proceed the fully formed business machine. In reality, though, all business is made up of countless transactions for which every involved party is satisfied by their exchange. The term "satisfied" – like "feel" – illustrates the absolute subjectivity of the overall activity – the aggregation of which doesn't magically extract an objectively quantifiable reality.

To get into the position to be able to meet someone's needs, the entrepreneur must collect resources that will be put to use to meet those needs. This may mean raising and slaughtering chickens to meet a need for meat. It may mean gathering supplies and labor to build a house to meet a need for shelter. It may mean gathering training and paying for a commute to meet an employer's need for labor.

The resources that we gather to meet someone else's needs are known as capital.

Entrepreneurialism again is predicting a need, gathering capital, and then meeting the need in exchange for a return.

Historically, capital has been looked at as a very physical thing. Sometimes, it is money, sometimes factories, sometimes iron ore, but almost exclusively it has been something physical.

This means that after the entrepreneur has decided how to meet a need, there is an expensive, time-consuming, and ongoing effort to turn that idea into a physical reality. This is true whether that is a factory or iron ore or housing.

As we mentioned in the first chapter, the idea about the need to meet is often looked at as a small portion of the business. Regular "business operations" tend to refer to the process of realizing the idea and meeting the need.

The reason physical realization like this is valuable is because, as with any other economic exchange, the people buying the thing that this realization brought into reality valued a certain amount of money less than they valued the physical product being created.

Eliminating realization

One fascinating thing that we need to examine is what software does to physical realization as a necessary part of meeting needs. The fact is that it all but eliminates it [2].

No one planned this widespread transition. Three simultaneous pressures have added up to and resulted in it.

Action as information

A number of classes of valuable action have been converted to information. This is a general feature of software. This is its purpose.

For many years now, computers have come with keyboards and monitors; they've offered storage, allowed alphanumeric input, and communicated with a visual display of information.

Everything from personal budgeting to cooking recipe storage fell into the general class of problems solved by such a lightly endowed computer. Things we used to do with pen and paper are now conducted more quickly and repeatably while simultaneously taking up less physical space.

More and more useful input and output options are becoming available. This makes more and more general classes of problems solvable with information rather than physical things. In the late 1990s and early 2000s, music became information instead of a physical artifact. In our current day, with the advent of 3D printing, the factory is becoming virtual as people print Halloween masks, machine gears, and even firearms.

Doing useful things with information means we can exchange that ability with others.

In my younger years, we spent time trading files over Bulletin Board Systems (the BBSes mentioned earlier). They included everything from communication utilities to databases and other useful pieces of "Action as Information" – that is, computer programs.

Today, we can download an "app" for a mobile phone in under a minute that provides absolutely remarkable value – from brainstorming tools to project management software.

Rapid transfer rate increase

Computers and computer networks have increased in speed rapidly over the last several decades. All information is more readily, more speedily, and more cheaply transferred wherever it is that it needs to go.

The faster the exchange rate gets, the more complex the data and the action can be that we share.

Economics

As things become easier and cheaper to create, they represent a less valuable need. This is because competitors can offer a lower price for the exchange as their cost to produce the thing drops. Alternatively, the individual that would have otherwise exchanged for the met need might meet the need for themselves.

Putting all of this together, software has turned many traditional industries and need-meeting opportunities into "Action as Information," so that simply by using a computer program, I can get the same value as if I had bought the physical representation. Further, because the methods for exchanging information are constantly getting faster, we've long since made physical realization trivially cheap and inexpensive for many, many use-cases, and we continue to do the same for others as the months and years tick by.

The basic forces of economics add to this to make physical realization a target for elimination as it becomes less valuable in every domain. And of course, the cost to produce many physical realizations doesn't drop – so all around, treating the physical realization (in certain domains) as a part of the need being met becomes untenable to the entrepreneur.

I was just reminiscing about one of my favorite stores at our local mall from years ago – Software, Etc. I was explaining to my wife – who isn't the computer geek that I am – that we actually used to go to the mall and pay for boxed software. I even remember buying my first C/C++ compiler at that particular store – Borland's Turbo C++.

The boxes had (actually printed) manuals and floppy disks – the physical realization of a computer program.

A compiler was already "Action as Information," but the increased rate of information transfer over the coming years combined with economic forces quickly eliminated boxed software along with the brick-and-mortar stores dedicated to such products.

This confluence of forces has conspired to eliminate physical realization in much of modern-day business.

Idea capital

How is the elimination of physical realization important?

To get at that, we must go back again to the entrepreneurial process with a slightly more detailed eye.

Again, the first, most important part of running a business is finding a potential need to meet and planning how to meet it.

Classically, this is viewed as something of a one-time event – often as separate from the actual business. Boiled down to a few words, it was often viewed as the act of creating the business.

So while finding a need and meeting it is really an ongoing task, the need can be so constant that little thought is needed to plan for it. As Christensen points out [3], this is a bit of a recipe for disaster, software development notwithstanding. An organization's ability to forecast a need and seek to meet it can atrophy, and their customers can disappear as newer organizations meet additional needs that the existing organization didn't seek out.

But what we want to look closely at is the activity of predicting a need and devising the approach to meet it.

In a traditional small business, this activity might be as simple as noticing the excessive line at an existing coffee shop, and recognizing that there is a need for fast, high-quality coffee that isn't being met. The approach to meeting it might be finding a location to rent, hiring staff, and preparing for regularly ordering the raw ingredients for the coffee. The rest of the business would likely only involve physical realization (e.g., making and serving the coffee) or perhaps some light tweaking of the original idea (who doesn't like a pumpkin spice latte in the Fall).

In the software world, where neither you nor any of your competitors need spend anything in terms of either time or money on physical realization, the one that spends resources on constantly refining and evolving the need and its approach will be the one that the customer will continue to do business with.

Traditionally, creating the idea about the need and the solution is something a company founder and a small group of trusted friends and colleagues might engage in. In the software world, anyone who writes code or influences its creation is participating in that exact same process.

This is because every single line of code represents thinking about the problem and how to solve it and to a certain extent the existence of that line of code even begins to bounce these ideas against reality.

For example, if in writing your code you recognize the need for many database transactions, and that the cost of those database transactions will reduce your margin unacceptably, you've gained valuable (entrepreneurial) information about your approach.

One way that we can think of this is that as we begin to discard large efforts of physical realization, what we are left with is our efforts to uncover needs that can be met and the ways that we can meet them. Our physical capital is replaced by the intellectual capital represented by our need-meeting ideas.

This is what software is. It represents, down to the finest, most concrete detail how we might, in reality, meet a particular need. It is more concrete than historical need-meeting ideation because it's quickly clear when an approach won't work in reality, because the software won't work or the people using it immediately know that it doesn't do what's needed once they see it.

So as businesses that are seeking to meet a need – the primary form of capital generated is the insight gained as we seek to meet the need. Businesses heavy in physical realization build up this kind of capital as well – it's just proportionally smaller, because such heavy focus is placed on realization.

Importantly, in such a case, it's not just our organization focusing our resources on physical realization – so the bar for anticipating new needs is lower, meaning the risk of not focusing on entrepreneurial activities is lower (though not eliminated).

THE PRIMACY OF SPEED

To restate it – all business is entrepreneurial. All the time. Business is about finding a need and meeting it. Because the same need is met repeatedly and habitually doesn't mean the same basic process isn't being followed.

In fact, businesses are frequently caught flat-footed when they lose sight of this truth – they spend so much of their time and resources physically realizing one idea, that they haven't developed a capacity (let alone a habit) for predicting and meeting other needs.

Viewed right-side-up, the operational side of physically realizing ideas should be subordinate to the organization's ability to predict needs and go about meeting them.

Looked at closely, we see an important truth.

This truth is that, to increase the value of the needs we meet, we need to move faster – in particular, we need to move through need-and-solution-finding cycle faster.

Why is this? There are two reasons.

Experimentation

All attempts to meet a need are a guess at the future need of another individual. This is inherently subjective and unpredictable. Experimentation aligns the organization more accurately to the need it is meeting.

Time preference

Any product or service exchanged today will be considered more valuable than the same performed a week from now [4]. This is a matter of human nature – we simply value a met need today more than the same need met in the future.

To say it again, to bring more value to our need-meeting endeavors as businesses (read: entrepreneurs), we must be focused on simply meeting those needs sooner rather than later. We need to move faster.

Because the bulk of the time and resource commitment in most businesses has been to make physical realization of the idea, the primary way organizations have attempted to increase the value they deliver is by reducing the amount of time it takes to realize things physically.

We should note that this primarily operates on the "time preference" side in increasing speed, since if physical realization is the focus, organizations rarely do much to take feedback back into their need-predicting thought process.

SPEED UP IDEA CAPITAL CREATION

So top to bottom, delivery speed is primary to any business (from idea about the need to meet to the point where that plan is carried out and the need is met). Further, for many needs, particularly those where software is already at the core, physical realization has been all but eliminated.

That is to say, the only opportunity to intentionally affect the value of the software creating organization's need-meeting activity is to optimize the creation of ideas about meeting the need.

That is to say – *speed is everything*.

FASTER SOFTWARE DELIVERY

So, the real question then is "how do we deliver software faster?!"

The answer is straightforward – we must eliminate any time spent during the course of software development that doesn't add to its value.

Software development, as we mentioned, is invention – it's a creative, intellectual activity performed together by groups of people.

Because of this, the working methods, communication habits, and general shape of the team or teams involved in the effort are the spot to look for speed improvements.

These are the sole entry-points for delivery deceleration. Focus your efforts exclusively on this space to improve speed – and through speed, value – and through value, the impact you have on the world and the return you gain for your efforts.

To clarify this further, and to arm ourselves to begin solving for speed, we will look at the various combinations of players on a software team and the general areas of challenge that they bring along with them.

In many ways, this may mirror the actual evolution of a real software development team, though the point of this discussion is to understand the impact that the various players have on delivery speed.

Single person, building for their own use

This scenario might seem trivial on the surface. Given our focus on business and how it reflects our action as humans to seek to meet the needs of others, perhaps it is.

Though even with one person developing software for their own use, we begin to see many of the challenges take shape. If for no other reason, then, we will quickly examine this scenario.

Still, there are many reasons that someone might build software for themselves. We might create a budgeting tool with automation that serves our personal purposes (perhaps using Excel and VBA, or perhaps with more sophisticated tooling), or like the example cited earlier, we may want to have a database with our favorite recipes in it.

In my case, one of the first pieces of software I wrote for myself was a Quadratic Equation solver. I wanted to avoid doing my homework, so I turned to programming a solver in C++.

Of course, the joke was on me. As I've learned and relearned over the years, to automate something requires mastery of its domain. So, this exercise turned out to be an effective way to thoroughly learn the subject matter. This was, of course, the purpose of the assignment in the first place.

Regardless the thing you might want to build for yourself, several challenges – several speed reducers – arise.

Lost in the code

The excitement of invention is a powerful driver. Many software developers are passionate about their craft because of how much of a thrill it is to create something useful. Even just assembling a few lines of code and watching the result can be a strong driver – an emotionally powerful experience.

Because of this, it can at times, even in this case where there are no other folks involved, be difficult to keep an eye on purpose. I may be building my recipe book for my own use, but the technical challenges involved in it may end up taking more of my energy, simply because they're a more exciting thing.

Lost the forest for the trees

Closely related to getting lost in the code is losing the forest for the trees. In fact, the former is often the cause of the latter.

The forest is often lost for the trees, also, not out of enjoyment, but because of how difficult the challenge is.

That is, sometimes the extended time dealing with low-level details leads to this dilemma. It can become difficult to step back and examine purpose. The vision for the working thing begins to dissipate due to the long intervals spent not thinking about it.

Lost interest

The thrill that comes with the initial idea and beginning to lay out the code for a project doesn't last. Emotional energy is like that. When a system begins to reach its peak usefulness, the excitement has often long since faded.

That's not to say there's not still thrill to be had in continuing the development, but the packets of excitement become smaller and take more effort to enjoy.

In addition to that, many times the earlier code is written so quickly and with so little care that in the later parts of the effort, it may become unmaintainable. This has a huge negative impact on the emotional incentive driving the developer forward.

My wife ran in a marathon in San Francisco several years back. They played loud exciting music at the start – ramping up the thrill of the runners as they left the gate. Of course, the runners that gave into this and ran hard didn't last very long.

The effect is similar at the beginning of a build. The thrill level might be high at the beginning, but success is more about stretching the enjoyment of the task over a longer period.

One person building for another

The second, slightly more sophisticated, scenario happens when the developer begins to build for another human being.

The general challenge that arises here is that we start to break out into two distinct but attached streams of thinking. The two streams are what to build and how to build it. Both are highly subjective, and both are subject to deep attachment by their respective thinkers.

Rigidity in either of the parties will result in a lack of clarity, bad feelings, and – through both of those – considerably less speed than would otherwise be possible. This general challenge is behind each of the specific ones presented when one person begins building for another.

Agreeing on need

On the surface, agreeing on the need may seem quite simple. All that we might expect to be involved is one person presenting the need to another – the latter taking that need and building out a solution to meet it.

The underlying problem here is that we view the abstract idea of a "need" as something static and well-understood by both parties. It is never either of these.

This is the reason that even discussing software development can be a challenge. Notions that we expect to be able to deal with abstractly automatically lose important detail.

When we discuss agreeing on a need, it should be understood that we will be defining that need and its solution in detail, as we go.

The reason for this is that with every new bit of behavior, and every new line of code, we create something that we couldn't have fully imagined before. Our guesses about the internal logic of the system and about how the behavior works are tested against a reality that we can't fully anticipate. Some of the details of that reality are completely hidden and some are masked by complexity.

As an example, let's say that we are building a new system to send out email notifications for some purpose. This notification is triggered by a specific action. Our initial assumption is that there is simply one class of users – the class that needs the email to do their work. When we create the first basic system – when we "bounce our idea against reality" – we might realize that there are actually two classes. The administrator that triggers the email, and the user for whom the email is central to their workflow. These imply differing sets of behavior. Further, if it's the first time we've decomposed user classes, it might even imply new behavior in the authentication and authorization aspects of the system.

Further complicating the matter is that this "bouncing against reality" happens not only in terms of behavior but also in terms of the specifics of the technical details embodied in code.

That is, "what" the system does is as un-anticipatable as "how" it will end up doing it.

Regarding the former, I've often said that a user doesn't know what they want until they have something in their hands.

As an engineer I used to think I was maybe being a little condescending toward users.

My mind changed, and my position on this solidified after a very specific incident.

It was 15 years ago. A working group at a previous employer came together to solve a problem we were facing. We needed to throttle the computing and communication resources that we were granting to clients based on their industry.

This seemed straightforward. We envisioned a page with several status indicators as well as a few controls to adjust things according to the operational context. No problem!

The thing that made this experience so poignant to me was that it amounted to a more-or-less controlled experiment on requirements gathering. Though we certainly didn't set out to do this.

The group consisted of a system administrator, an operator, a couple of developers, and our common boss, the director. All of us would potentially be users of the system. We all had a high degree of trust in one another. We couldn't have hoped for much more in terms of simplifying getting the requirements together.

So we had a well-arranged team and a pretty good idea of what we wanted to build.

We set out, then, to build the first cut of the system. We started with the user interface, to make sure we could quickly verify our vision.

We reviewed it and quickly realized that there were important things we got wrong. We made changes to right these wrongs and then went through the same cycle two or three more times. As we did this, we got closer and closer to what we all wanted.

After participating in this cycle and reflecting on it, I realized something important. My intuitive philosophy – that users don't know what they want until they have something they can use – was actually right on. It's not a knock against "those darn users." It's a counterintuitive reality that just became very clear having been simultaneously on both sides of the equation, in a fairly controlled – if unintentional – experiment.

This same rule applies to code. You don't really know the structure of the code that will best serve your purpose until you have working code in place.

We should note that making software work is only half the battle. Making it speak clearly to the next developer is the other, bigger half of that battle. This challenging target boils down to leveraging abstraction. Abstraction allows our limited human cognitive capabilities to grapple with something as broad and technically complex as computer software. It does this by letting us conceive of it in smaller, more manageable pieces.

To be clear, if we didn't need abstraction, we would simply write all of our software in machine language. Our need to communicate clearly with our fellow software developer necessitates abstraction. This need drives everything from high-level languages to the latest frameworks, to the way we structure the interactions between objects and functions within our system.

Because of this, writing software is largely about creating and leveraging abstraction.

Further, we can't abstract – we can't generalize – until we've seen more than one concrete example of our potential abstract idea. Abstraction is simply creating a group of things with a shared shape so that specifics can be disregarded. And so, we won't know what details are important, and what we can let go of, until we've seen examples.

For both behavior and actual code, we learn what works best as we build the system.

This makes agreeing on the need an ongoing, continuous activity.

Failure to accept this reality results in two primary dysfunctions:

- Inflexibility in the face of new information about the desired behavior.
    As a system is developed, new or alternative behaviors may begin to emerge as better approaches with which to meet the need.
- Inflexibility in the face of technical implications of behavior choices.
    You may be able to offer additional or alternative behavior when an understanding of technical capabilities is developed.

Inflexibility in either of these will result in not maximizing value created, and likely in hard feelings between the individual that will use the system and the individual building the system.

Agreeing need has been met

In the "one person building for another" arena, the second big challenge is agreeing that a need has been met.

The two players need to be able to do this so that they can stop working on one need and move on to the next. They also need to be able to pull together the lessons they've learned about behavior and about code structure as these lessons will likely apply to the next need that must be met.

It's possible to continue on without clarifying this learning, but it will simply result in less effective delivery. Less value will be created.

Further, if solid agreement isn't gathered, or isn't gathered in a timely fashion, it can also serve to damage trust between the two parties.

It's difficult to overstate the value of trust. Because of the complexity that is common to both behavior and technical detail, folks can easily become very invested in detailed specifics. Flexibility and openness to influence during the course of development work are indispensable characteristics of software teams, even in this very minimalist sense. And trust is the cornerstone of that flexibility and openness.

All that to say, in addition to meeting the practical need to collate learning and make informed decisions going forward, the ability to agree quickly when a need has been met supports trust and the ability for the pair to continue to work well as a team.

Agreeing on timing

The basic challenge with timing is that, as we've said earlier, software development is invention. It is pulling together countless details and not knowing ahead of time how those details will come out as they're all added together. It's an intuitive process where flashes of insight provide a big part of the progress that we make.

None of those things are particularly predictable. If we could explicitly call out every detail we were accounting for, and anticipate their effects on one another, we could make reasoned assertions about the related timing.

Arguably, this challenge – the lack of predictability – would have shown itself even in the simple case of an individual writing a program for themselves. Though since there is no other party to coordinate with, it doesn't present as much of a problem in that case. The only person disappointed in any lack of progress is the individual, who can quickly and continuously adjust in any of several ways – re-setting his own expectations, cutting out scope he was hoping to complete, or simply attempting to work faster.

In our current case, though, agreeing on timing becomes a central challenge.

The starting point is to recognize that the only concern when it comes to timing is that the sooner a thing is finished, the better.

A fundamental law of human action is that we value a thing today more than we value it next week. This is called time preference. Ludwig von Mises lays this out in his powerful work on the topic "Human Action," as follows:

> Time for man is not a homogeneous substance of which only length counts. It is not a more or a less in dimension. It is an irreversible flux the fractions of which appear in different perspective according to whether they are nearer to or remoter from the instant of valuation and decision. Satisfaction of a want in the nearer future is, other things being equal, preferred to that in the farther distant future. Present goods are more valuable than future goods [4].

So, whether it's software that we're delivering to our colleagues or software, we're delivering to an external customer – sooner is better.

Additionally, when developing software we get to more compelling solved problems and solutions the more we experiment in the real world. The more frequently we try our software on real humans who are of the kind that we are looking to satisfy, the better our solutions will be – and the more fit for the actual needs of real people.

Because of this, the more quickly we put the software together, the more quickly we can test and then repeat. Again, sooner is better.

Both individuals in our scenario here share the interest in getting software sooner. As we've laid out, software delivered sooner is more valuable, more valuable software means greater returns both for the creator and for the requester. Additionally, the creator – the developer – has the added interest that the sooner we deliver the software, the faster we can be on to the next, more interesting problem.

This brings us back to the problem of predictability.

Both parties want the software delivered as soon as possible. Neither party can do much more than guess about how soon that might be. This isn't hopeless, but it is clearly a key concern that will lay much of the foundation for the tools we will build out in later chapters.

In addition to this tricky – though somewhat natural – problem, there are two unnatural problems that arise from time to time.

The first is that timing is sometimes used by the individual requesting the software to create a sense of pressure.

The problem here is that it destroys trust and creates counter-productive anxiety.

The desire to apply pressure is based on a mistaken view that pressure will increase speed. In certain domains, this may be true. If we apply time pressure to predictable, repeatable, physical tasks like assembling a car or building a house, we may be able to extract greater throughput.

With software, as with any creative endeavor, applying pressure accomplishes the opposite. The fight or flight response that increases the speed of rote or memorized actions limits the creative impulse that is the core of software development – of invention in general.

The second problem that we can create for ourselves is different only in intention, but the result is the same. The individual requesting the software may have an external commitment or may have a personal need dependent on the software being developed.

To state this generally, in both cases, we've made tactical plans dependent on the result of invention.

This is always a problem.

Thomas Edison didn't tell everyone – "Hey, I'm inventing the lightbulb next Tuesday, so throw away your candles on Monday."

Some of the invention that we do is on such a small scale that we can sometimes forget that it is in fact invention. No matter how similar a thing is to something that's been written before – if it were truly identical, we wouldn't have to write software for it.

Just to recap, agreeing on timing between an individual who requests software and the one building it comes with three distinct problems:

- judging how soon we can possibly deliver the software (sooner always being better)
- using timing to create a sense of pressure
- creating tactical, time-sensitive needs dependent on the completion of software.

Agreeing on change

That we learn as we go is a challenging problem along several dimensions.

We may learn about technical capabilities. Or we may learn about the nature of the problem space – perhaps the need we were targeting is either different or not as real as first imagined.

In any case, the underlying challenge is that the learning – the new understanding – must be shared among both parties. Similarly, the implications of that new understanding – the new direction – must be shared as well.

This seems to be an ordinary problem, not much different from most business scenarios. That is, it's a matter of communicating clearly and exercising influence.

This is true, though there's some additional complexity. As we build software, communication and interpersonal influence happen very frequently and quite rapidly. It is, therefore, necessary to take greater care with working relationships. Further, this rapid communicating and relating will likely stretch an individual's ability to stay organized and clear about choices.

Agreeing on priority

The final agreement the two parties must share is regarding priority.

There are always a number of behaviors that both sides will be interested in creating. Sometimes the desired behaviors will be the same; many times they won't. It's important to remember that these two interests, even if it's really just two people, represent two radically different kinds of thinking, viz., what problem do we want to solve and how do we want to solve it? Those two different kinds of thinking lead to differing ideas about behavior.

Resources are always limited and desires are not, so there's always a choice to be made about what comes first. This makes getting agreement on the order in which things will be built an important understanding to be shared.

This is closely related to scheduling in that every aspect is similar in that it is more valuable sooner. This is the "time preference" that we learned about from Ludwig von Mises.

Combining the reality that we can't address everything at once with the facts that we want to maximize value and that each thing we deliver is more valuable the sooner it is delivered, we are left with a challenging problem.

The problem is to discover the order of the aspects of the need that when delivered – controlling for time – will result in the maximum overall value delivered.

One person building for an organization

The next level of complexity that we can add to our software development efforts is to replace the single requester with an organization.

In addition to the challenges in the previous scenario – just a single requester – there are two new challenges to recognize.

More people involved

Anytime people are added to a decision-making process, it slows down. Often, that slowdown is offset to a degree by the increased wisdom of the larger, more diverse set of views brought to bear on the problem. It's why most businesses have a board yet retain a single primary executive. In doing this, the organization seeks the wisdom of broader counsel and the execution speed of the single decision maker. The same can be seen in government – the common pattern is to have a legislature to create laws and a single executive to carry them into effect. This similarly represents broad counsel with a single real-time decision maker.

The speed and complexity of necessary decisions multiply the decelerating effect of adding people to the conversation. Adding every individual in an entire commercial enterprise can be crippling to the point of making software development impossible.

All of the required points of agreement laid out in the previous section are affected by this. That is, the more people we add as we attempt to come to agreement about need, priority, or timing, the slower we will be.

Coalescing the need

Agreeing on need is particularly challenging as the party requesting the feature expands beyond a single individual.

The need ideas must now coalesce across the group that is requesting. This group can often be as large as the business unit that owns and operates the software, or – in larger organizations – it can be large subsets of the entire enterprise. As the ideas are coalescing, the builder must maintain agreement with the continuously evolving, continuously tentative choices about direction.

This is an important note because – to be successful – the ideas must be informed by the related technical realities. These technical realities include everything from performance and throughput to the maintainability of the codebase. And importantly, they are discovered as the builder brings the system to life – in real-time.

This is a potent challenge. It is what separates software development from other creative endeavors. It's not insurmountable, but it shouldn't be ignored. Its solutions are far from intuitively obvious.

A team building for an organization

The final bit of complexity to add to this picture is to replace the individual builder with a team.

All of the previous challenges continue to exist.

As noticed in the previous section, replacing the individual requester with a group increases the number of people involved. Again, all other things being equal, this slows the process of arriving at the necessary agreement. The same thing happens when we move to a team of builders.

Technical agreement

The additional challenge that is faced when we move from one builder to many is that the technical agreement – that is agreement on "how" a feature might be implemented – is complicated in a new way.

There is a wide array of possible technical approaches for any given feature. Many of the approaches have no appreciable difference in how appropriate they are to solving a given problem. At the same time, as with any art, practitioners become (seemingly arbitrarily) attached to differing techniques.

Coming to technical agreement can, thus, be a particularly difficult exercise in interpersonal influence and teamwork.

WRAPPING UP ...

With all of this said, we've laid out the unique nature of software development, its general challenges, and how those challenges come into play tactically. We will continue in our effort to build up a comprehensive mental model by examining more closely the different ways that we can come to know things.

How we know things is a surprisingly important tool to have clarity on as we examine software development more closely. Further, it will be of utmost importance as we build up the concrete tools that we can use to be successful in our efforts to build software.

WORKS CITED

1. J. Collins, Good to Great, New York: HarperCollins, 2001.
2. P. McBreen, Software Craftsmanship: The New Imperative, Addison-Wesley, Boston, 2001.
3. C. M. Christensen, The Innovator's Dilemma, 1997.
4. L. v. Mises, Human Action, 1949.

Chapter 3

Ways of knowing

As leaders of people and builders of software, the world we live in is the unique one we've outlined in the last two chapters. While some of the unique problems in this domain are like those in other domains, they combine to create a tricky path to our goal – creating value for people. Because of this, we need to be well-versed in and ready to use the full array of our human cognitive abilities.

"Creating value" sounds generic and trite, but it is ultimately what we look for in our software. It's true that often software developers simply enjoy the challenge of creating – well – anything. The broader view, though, is that the ultimate purpose of software is to be useful to a human being. That might be the value of an entertaining video game or it might be the value of organizing a spreadsheet of expenses for an employee recently returned from a business trip.

For any kind of value, building that software is an act of invention. We are creating a new thing that must work with the reality of our problem space and result in some desired outcome. Both of these are highly subjective, highly fluid things that change both with the whim of the person for whom the value is being created and with the uncountable variables that make up the "reality" – the context – that they operate within.

We mentioned video game entertainment above. In the value that stems from this kind of software, we can see these dual subjective influences clearly. Being entertained is quite subjective – that's why there are so many genres of music and so many different types of movies and TV shows. We all have different tastes and those tastes are subject to change at a moment's notice. The details of the context change as readily – we have different computer capabilities offering different kinds of experiences – from varying monitor sizes and resolutions to VR hardware. The subject matter and how the game tells a story change as a function of culture.

So in the case of the video game, this is all very easy to see.

We see it clearly in the expense management case as well. The sense of "being organized" is as subjective as that of being entertained. There are different aspects of the information that can be highlighted or ordered – giving a different shade to the understanding extracted and/or communicated.

DOI: 10.1201/9781003382751-4

The context changes rapidly as well – when I started in the industry – much of expense management was still done fully with paper, even though we had computers and spreadsheets with which to manage them. We've since gotten real-time web applications and then mobile experiences with very aesthetically pleasing interfaces. We can update our expenses as we sip our Americano at Starbucks before the sales meeting. These are massive changes in context over the course of just a few years.

In the last chapter, we've outlined the challenges that arise when we start adding the people and interests necessary for broad software development efforts – highlighting repeatedly (and appropriately) that software is, at its core, invention – invention done with teams of people.

In all of this, we ultimately optimize for the "value" that we are putting into the world. But to optimize for this, we must create as fast as possible. Creating faster means more value based on human "time preference" (that things have a greater value the sooner we get them) and on the need to experiment to more rapidly zero-in on the most valuable need or part of the need.

That is to say, the ultimate path to value in software is speed.

Given the challenges we've laid out here, the subjective nature of the context and need, the complication that comes from different interests, and ultimately the need to optimize for speed, we must bring to bear the full complement of human cognitive capabilities.

There are three different pairs of cognitive capabilities that we will examine. For each of the pairs and each of the individual capabilities, we will develop a sense about when to use them and when not to use them. Further, we will examine how we can improve with each capability.

We will go through these in pairs because each pair represents two related capabilities – that are in all cases essentially opposites of one another.

Passion and Reason – One of the primary tensions we face as human beings is between our passion and our ability to think about – to reason about – our circumstances. As with all three pairs, neither is better than the other. Using them appropriately is about knowing what the particular tool is good for.

Implicit and Explicit – We have the capability to rapidly think through things while barely being consciously aware of that thought process. We also have the ability to think through things while clearly understanding that thinking process – even being able to adjust it, communicate it, or reason about it.

Deductive and Inductive – Our reasoning breaks down along another entirely separate dimension. So, while we might reason implicitly or explicitly, we engage in it either inductively or deductively. Inductive reasoning is observing patterns and developing general rules based on those patterns. Deductive reasoning uses patterns to either create new patterns or arrive at information about a specific circumstance that we didn't directly observe.

Software development is a layered activity and requires different thinking tools to be leveraged in different settings. Having a full understanding of the available tools, the extent of their usefulness, and what we can be doing to improve with them is our goal. Meeting this goal will provide a solid foundation on which to build up specific principles and tactics in coming chapters. It will further provide a starting point from which to gain general mastery in our ability to analyze problems in the software development space.

Stepping back again to our primary goal – we are looking to create as much value as possible for our customer – to do this we pursue creating software as fast as possible. Working from this approach, there are several examples we can quickly look at where we would apply different thinking tools.

For example, writing well-crafted code – down to the method (or function) level – powerfully drives faster delivery times. Doing this though is, more often than not, driven heavily by implicit thinking and passion. Explicit reasoning is often applied to structure the techniques applied or as a check to ensure that the system stays on the right track.

Designing a multi-team organizational structure is often a very explicit and deductive task, with well-defined principles that can be followed. Alternatively, the self-management of a single software development team, if done well, is much the opposite. It is very implicit – even during designated review times (which are often called "retrospectives" [1]). It is also very inductive – patterns of the team's own behavior and thus best choices for organization being analyzed empirically as they are performing.

Even more complicated, these solutions can overlap and connect. One of the most important ways that this happens is through Conway's Law [2]. We will get into Conway's Law in more detail in coming chapters, though the short explanation is that an organization and the software it creates tend toward matching structure. Because of this, the implicit, inductive work of structuring software often comes into tension with the explicit, deductive work of shaping your organization.

All of this to say – as we begin to really dig into solutions – the greater the understanding of and skill with these basic thinking tools, the faster and more appropriate the solutions will begin to be for your context.

The final thing we need to be clear on as we examine these thinking tools closely is that software development is not a physical science. One of the grave errors that many leaders and organizations run into when trying to set their software development into good order is that they take the kind of mechanicalistic, mathematical view that we might take toward a physical problem. In physics, if we want to find the position of a thing over time, we can use the following equation, and we can always be sure that we will get the right answer:

$$s = s_0 + v_0 t + \frac{1}{2} a t^2$$

That is to say, considering initial position (s_0), initial velocity (v_0), and acceleration (a), we will always know what the position (s) is after a given amount of time.

Reasoning about software development is similar to reasoning about economics. It falls into a category of study that Ludwig von Mises called Praxeology – the general theory of human action.

In trying to find all of the variables that will give us a function into which we can plug data and get the right concrete answer, we find ourselves looking at the black box of the reasoning of human beings. Because of this, until the point where our technology can give us direct access to these data – the thoughts, needs, and assumptions of individual humans – we must take human action as a given. Particularly, we must treat each individual acting and making a series of choices that improve their conditions based on their understanding of the world as a given [3].

This will put us in the best position to reason about our approaches to software development and help us to arrive at the best set of tactics to ensure that they become a reality.

PASSION AND REASON

The connection and distinction between passion and reason are at the core of what it means to be human. As humans, we have a long history of working – often not entirely successfully – to balance the energy and commitment that comes from passion with the understanding and accuracy that comes from reason.

A particularly powerful example of mastery in this balance is in the life of Abraham Lincoln. Even superficially, this can be seen through the circumstances of the American Civil War. Our founding philosophy was in internal conflict. The core precept of the natural equality of every individual was at odds with the carve outs (in the written constitution as well as in practice) for human slavery.

Abraham Lincoln, amidst the swirl of highly diverse, often quite spirited public opinion, charted a workable course through the bloody terrain of the Civil War to a new, better reality. This new reality reconciled and began the remediation of the conflicting philosophy and the conflicting action present at the founding.

He was able to do this because he was a man of uniquely powerful ability to reason and uniquely deep passion. Further, he knew when and how to use these capabilities.

During the course of the Civil War, Lincoln made many far-reaching decisions. One of the most important was making the "Emancipation Proclamation."

While Mr. Lincoln was known – sometimes frustratingly so – as being slow to come to a decision, the intricacy of the circumstances and the nuance of his action in this situation betray unequaled clarity. Mr. Lincoln was slow because he was thinking – he used his reason to guide his action.

As this major choice had its impact on the course of the conflict, Mr. Lincoln passionately carried it into practice. He did this by defending the choice and then supporting it with great energy.

When his emancipation paper was released, there was much celebration to be sure. But there was also dramatic criticism from many quarters. Lincoln's resolve in the face of this criticism demonstrated his deep passion for the purpose-rich proclamation. Lincoln's heart-felt desire to maintain the Union and his human sympathy for his enslaved fellow creatures echoed when asked to compromise on the proclamation in asserting that the proclamation was "a fixed thing."

He educated his colleagues in the cabinet and wrote letters to newspapers – educating the public about the impact of the action. "Through the worst days of discord and division, Lincoln never lost his confidence that he understood the will and desires of the people" [4].

With reason, he selected his path, and with passionate energy, he kept to that path under heavy fire.

Differences

The differences between passion and reason are stark in one sense, but they can blur together in another.

Passion is energy – it's the emotional thrill of doing something we love or that we're good at. It can be an almost uncontrolled drive toward a given target.

We can see passion in Lincoln's implementation of the Emancipation Proclamation in that even when there are external sources of pain as a result of his action, he continues forward. The internal sources of joy and even ecstasy that the act likely created for him counterbalanced the externally sourced pain and allowed him to move forward.

When I think of passion, I remember a number of years ago when I played baseball for my school. Now I was never particularly passionate about baseball but I had a classmate who was. After a game, he was intent on improving. He said, "I didn't hit as well as I could have, because I haven't taken enough cuts." That is, he hadn't taken enough batting practice. His passion to increase his skill as a batter made him hungry to spend his time on a repetitive, ostensibly mundane activity. He had an inner fire to develop his ability that pushed him through the boredom.

Or of course – as builders of software – passion often keeps us awake late at night, or long past our prime thinking and problem-solving time. Getting that solution to work that we've spent days or weeks hacking at can be a huge generator of passion.

Reason, however, is our capacity to understand our circumstances and to think through the actions that might achieve the results we want. It is our analysis of a situation and then our choice to go in a particular direction.

Imagine that you get very angry at your friend and then say unkind things to them. The passion of your anger drove you to a specific decision. Once our passions have cooled, it's common to look back on incidents like this and then reason through better courses of action. This is often done with a sense of regret.

This common scenario illustrates the difference between passion and reason. A better solution, of course, would have been to think things through before being driven to the unfortunate choice by our passion. Though in it, we can see clearly the difference between the two.

Importantly, the line between thinking and passion can blur. Often passion is thought of as a feeling and reason as a cold mechanical process. This simplifies things a bit too far and is likely the source of that blurring.

Reasoning can be implicit – it can be a feeling. We can think through things without having a conscious grasp on the steps we are taking to reason. We often say we have a "gut feel" or an "intuition" and jump quickly to an answer. This is reasoning even though it presents as a feeling. The right answer, or what we think is the right answer, simply feels better than the alternative.

So as we keep the line clear between passion and reason, it's important not to be reductive with our definition of either. Doing so can lead to mistaking implicit reasoning (or "intuition") for passion.

How do we use these tools

In general, as we've mentioned, passion is energy and drive. It helps us to get things done when specific circumstances might otherwise make a task unappealing.

Additionally, as an individual, passion serves as a useful indicator of our areas of interest. Having a natural energy in the face of a particular task gives a clue toward the things that we will be most successful and productive with.

I often tell aspiring software developers to simply try to write some programs if they are unsure about their fitness for the work. Going through the work of writing a list of instructions for a computer is typically either captivating or dull based on the predispositions of a particular person. That is to say, even nascent passion around the activity is often clearly observable [5]. At a minimum, it is always clear enough to add a datapoint to decisions about potential careers.

Reason, as we've said, is the ability to observe external reality and to then formulate and use generalized rules about it. By doing this, we can come to conclusions about how our circumstances might play out and what we can do to alter them to make them more amenable to our ends.

It is an important balance against our natural passion because while that passion energizes and takes us further in our chosen direction, reason allows us to choose the most profitable direction.

By choosing to reason about a set of circumstances, we are able to act more in alignment with the state of the underlying reality. This means the action will be more effective and whatever it is that we are attempting to accomplish will have a greater likelihood of being realized.

We've also mentioned that reasoning can be quite implicit. So, reasoning through a situation doesn't necessarily mean sitting down with pencil and paper and writing down every step of our thought process. It does, however, mean forestalling our passionate energy for the time it takes to choose a direction – rather than letting that energy drive is into whatever action we might be closest to.

If our action is akin to a sailboat, passion is wind and reason is rudder. We may go **somewhere** with a lot of wind, but if we carefully control the rudder, we will go somewhere we can be sure we want to go.

What problems do these tools have

Considering the sailboat metaphor, we can see the primary problem with passion. If we let it have its way with us, our efforts will be unfocused and ineffective. The great energy that we may apply to our situation will deteriorate our focus – blowing us in directions where we don't accomplish much or in directions that are potentially dangerous.

This problem is especially noticeable in young people. I remember when I was in my teenage years, I was full of energy. Though instead of being focused on thoughtful, productive ventures, it was often dissipated in random directions. Some random exploration is positive, of course. We discover our interests through experimentation in our younger years. Even still, there are many times when goofing around with friends might have been replaced with learning more about a particular area of interest.

The problem with overbalancing toward reason is more subtle. If we stop to consider everything and don't tap into our natural energy, or don't understand ourselves well enough to work in the areas that align with our natural passions, our activities can become emotionally dry. We may choose positive, effective direction, but we will have no way to get to where we are going. Our sails will have no wind.

One of the most powerful and common examples I see of this is in the center of our industry.

Many well-meaning people reason through their career choices and choose to pursue professional software development. It is ostensibly a great choice with its challenging nature and above-average compensation. Some, however, do this with a complete lack of passion for technology and for software development. They will never accomplish as much as they might have in a space that was more suited to their natural inclinations.

The same can happen in smaller circumstances. We might choose projects or teams, or even a single hour-long task that doesn't align with our passion. Because of this, we might dramatically increase the time it takes or decrease the quality with which it might otherwise be done.

How do we develop our ability to use these tools

Developing passion has really two angles.

First, we can remember Neo's first trip to The Oracle. Above the threshold to her kitchen, she had a sign that said, "Temet Nosce" – that is, "Know Thyself."

Knowing how we as individuals operate and the things that give us energy is an important indicator about the activities that we should be choosing to engage in [5].

So the first thing we can do is to make a mental note about the things that give us energy – and the degree to which they do.

The second thing that we can do is simply to try things. It's often surprising the degree to which we can develop passion for an activity simply by engaging in it. Every individual has certain predispositions for certain classes of activities. Though the boundaries represented by our predispositions are far broader than most people suspect.

I remember spending a lot of time flipping hamburgers and operating the drive through equipment at a certain fast-food restaurant when I was a young man. I also remember, after a while, having a really good time doing those things.

So – knowing thyself, and just trying things – these are how you develop passion. To boil it down to an algorithm, try stuff, see what works for you, discard what doesn't, and pursue what does.

Developing reason is similarly straightforward.

To restate once more, reason is choosing direction explicitly. It is using our intrinsic logical facilities to understand a situation, imagine a desired outcome, connect the two, and then act according to that connection.

When you feel very strongly about a particular set of circumstances and you immediately act, you are likely letting your passion lead, and not reasoning well. An additional test might be to ask yourself once a situation like this is over, "what was my reason for doing this?" If you have a hard time answering that other than by citing your strong emotion, it's likely a choice that could have had its reasoning enhanced.

To develop the ability to reason, just make a point of reacting less and making explicit choices more. That is, while a situation may stir up strong emotion or passionate energy, making a habit of setting that aside to think through the situation is what will grow the reason muscle.

Ultimately, the immediate desire to act shouldn't be entirely ignored. That would eliminate the advantage of instinct (or "implicit reasoning"). But for the purposes of developing a general reasoning capability, dialing it back a bit is a useful technique.

IMPLICIT AND EXPLICIT REASONING

Implicit and explicit reasoning offer the choice between thinking through things in a way that we are fully aware of or alternatively with little awareness of our own thought process.

At first glance, that extra awareness – like any additional information – seems as if it can only be positive. After all, the more information we have – even if it focuses on our own thought process – the greater the quality of our decisions and of our action.

Explicit reasoning (using logic you can express clearly in words) is in fact very powerful. It allows for a detailed analysis of decisions, communicating well to others, and real-time quality checking.

All of that capability comes at a cost though. That cost is the time and cognitive energy that it takes to be explicit about our reasoning.

This trade-off is why these tools and their strengths are so important to be aware of.

Frequently in software development and in leadership, there are times when it is advantageous to be explicit in reasoning – an example being when a team is agreeing on, well, just about anything. Concretely though, architectural decisions, process workflow, and tool choices can often benefit powerfully from thorough explicit reasoning.

Actual coding – writing a function or a class or a data structure – very often benefits from the speed that comes from implicit reasoning. Imagine for a moment if you took the time to thoroughly justify the logic of every single line of code you wrote as you wrote it. Your forward progress would grind to a halt.

Implicit reasoning is often called "intuition." As we mentioned earlier, it often seems like just a feeling about what choice to make. Do we name the variable "x" or "personCount." That 400-line method – do we leave it as is or break it down into smaller pieces.

Thousands of decisions are made by developers every day using implicit reasoning – they are made because one approach simply feels better than another. They are made by intuition.

Intuition is frequently romanticized – it seems magical mostly because we don't have access to the actual thought process, even when it's our own intuition.

It's not that mysterious though. It is really just reasoning that happens in such a way that we are unaware of the particular steps. Our observations are the premises of a set of general precepts being applied syllogistically. The output of this black box of reasoning is a feeling about what direction is likely the best one.

You can get a sense for this when you step back to analyze your own implicit reasoning. Pick a decision that you've made instinctively and pick it apart. Why did you make the particular choice? What were the factors in your decision? For one of those factors, why and how important was it to the decision? This reflection will bring to the surface the unstated reasoning you used to arrive at the decision.

To further demystify instinct, we should understand that it can be trained. We can learn to have instinct about particular things. We do this by exposing ourselves to the types of situations we want instinct in and then thinking through and analyzing those situations.

As an example, the game of pool can be a very instinctive one. You can step up to the table – see the ball that you want to go into the hole, the rail you want to bounce the cue ball against before striking the one you want to sink. After taking this data in, you simply make a quick decision about how hard and in what direction to hit the cue ball.

Or, as you're learning, you can think explicitly about all the angles involved, what other balls might be in the way, and all the other myriad of details that will be involved in the success of the shot. The more you take the latter approach, the more you will build the instinct necessary to just take the shot and eliminate the exhausting cognitive load of the analysis.

How do we use these tools

Once we decide to reason through a particular circumstance, the next choice becomes a question of which of these two tools we use – that is, should we reason about our circumstances explicitly or implicitly.

Choosing implicit reasoning means speed, but it also means decreased accuracy and decreased ability to communicate choices and their associated action.

Choosing explicit reasoning means the reverse. Our accuracy and ability to communicate our choices will increase, at the expense of how quickly we will be able to choose.

Further, this speed brings with it something else that is very important to software developers and software leaders – lower cognitive overhead. As we'll see in coming chapters, at times optimizing for an absolute minimum in cognitive overhead is an important part of our approach to software development.

One final consideration in choosing between these two modes of thought is that making implicit choices requires practice in the domain of the choice. Without practice – or what we might call a level of mastery – the chance of error increases dramatically. Explicit reasoning however – even without any degree of mastery – has a much higher probability of success.

So, a quick heuristic for making the choice might be the relative priority between speed and risk of mistake. Required cognitive load as well as level of mastery must also be factors.

For example, let's say that one of the five development teams that reports to you has grown to 12 people. For reasons we will discuss (and you may already know), this number of team members is excessive. As the leader, you will need to decide and then act to put the team into a better position.

You undoubtedly have a number of other high-priority, demanding, complex decisions in your personal backlog to be making. So the faster that this decision can be made – with the least cognitive overhead – the happier you will be, and more importantly, the more it will leave you equipped to deal with your other work.

So with this in mind – you might begin to lean toward making the decision using implicit reasoning.

Though as you start to deal with this situation, you recognize that your experience hasn't included dealing with many similar circumstances. Further, the results of this decision will lead to broadly impacting the life and work of a number of your colleagues. This brings the realization forward that you are a little less error tolerant than you might have assumed originally.

With all of these factors in mind, your final decision will probably be to think explicitly through the problem and its solution, possibly even writing your approach down and discussing with others (a powerful way to be very explicit in your decision making).

Once you decide the type of thinking to use, the only thing that remains is to do the thinking. With implicit reasoning, there isn't much to explain, for two reasons. First, we have all been doing this our entire life – we simply choose what "seems" to be right, the approach that feels more like the right approach. Second, by its nature, it boils down to subjective feeling – so beyond simply saying, "do what feels like it is the right choice," there is nothing more to be said.

With explicit reasoning however – there are any number of tools that can be used to really get a grip on the fusion of facts and logic that will yield the best outcome. They tend to fall into two groups though, writing and discussing.

While simply being able to articulate to yourself the thinking you are using is enough to get you into the explicit thinking zone, writing that thinking down on paper (or virtual paper) is even more powerful. This can be anything from a scribble to boxes and lines to poetry or prose. The closer, though, that you get it to a format that will communicate readily to another human being, the more explicit you will be.

This leads to the second broad category of tools – communicating your thinking to another human being. Again, this can be quite informal – a "watercooler" discussion in which you simply talk through the idea with someone with no expectation about understanding on the part of the other. Or it can be formal – with a group of people, a polished presentation, and even voting about the quality or appropriateness of the approach. As with writing, the greater degree of expected understanding on the part of the person or people to which you are talking about the approach (that is, the greater degree of formality), the more explicit you will become.

Albert Einstein said, "If you cannot explain it simply, you do not understand it well enough."

Whether you write or discuss – the more focused your communication, the more explicit your thinking will be.

What problems do these tools have

Implicit reasoning is probably the most prone to causing real problems. The biggest snag with this type of thinking is that it is readily mistaken for passion (and passion for it).

If mistaken for passion, intuition can be disregarded as being less valid as a decision-making tool. This is understandable but unfortunate. These are different phenomena – though they present very similarly – as feelings.

For an individual, it is important to be able to distinguish between the two, so that intuition can be used without guilt or hesitation.

When working with others, it's important to be able to either explain the intuition, remove the dependence on the unaccepting opinion, or – if necessary – fall back to explicit reasoning. When working with others, an important part of being able to use intuition effectively is to develop trust. Lacking a high degree of trust, explicit thinking is a viable alternative. Or at least it can be. Its lack of speed tends to be a motivating force toward developing trust.

A powerful problem that we briefly touched on in the section on passion is mistaking passion for intuition.

Since both passion and intuition present as feeling, this mistake is not uncommon. The result of it is almost exclusively negative. Remembering again that passion is energy and drive that can be directed, but without direction may go in any number of arbitrary directions. So if you are looking for a solid intuitive answer for a particular decision – and instead of intuition, you follow the feeling of your passion, the odds are that – simply because there are so many directions possible for a given choice – the direction you choose won't be a good one.

A common example of getting this wrong is when making an architectural or tooling choice. The shape of this choice is usually something like the following.

An individual engineer – during the regular course of development – might bump into a situation that is a bit broader in its implications than the average problem. Perhaps it is related to concurrency or maybe to moving data from one place to another. Whatever the problem is, its solution will likely affect the system in more of a macro sense.

Thinking is obviously needed here – though it is perfectly reasonable, particularly for a well-seasoned engineer, to approach even a larger-scale problem in a highly intuitive manner (that is, with implicit thought).

The problem though is that we engineers can become very passionate about specific techniques and tools. This passion can then be mistaken for intuition – either entirely or in part. This makes our decision less likely to result in a positive outcome.

This can similarly happen with leadership decisions. If we revisit our earlier example, and one of our five teams has grown too large, the same error can be made. It is possible that the leader gets excited about a new technique that he's read about our thought about and instead of querying his intuition about its application, he mistakes his excitement for intuition.

In both cases, the likelihood of success drops significantly the more thoroughly the energy of passion is mistaken for the reason of intuition.

There are two big keys to avoiding this particular problem. The first is to check your intuition occasionally – do this by being more explicit, from quickly writing out the thinking all the way to presenting it to multiple people.

Checking your intuition occasionally will give you a better feel for when you are dealing with instinct and when you are dealing with passion.

The second solution is to be aware of the level of mastery you've attained in the problem space that you believe you're being intuitive about. If your mastery is low, it's less likely that you have good intuition in that space, and so you should grant your "gut" less trust – checking yourself more frequently by being explicit.

How do we develop our ability to use these tools

Developing our balance between implicit and explicit thinking – and further developing our skill in each is straightforward to describe. The difficulty lies in just committing the time and energy to do it.

The first thing to do is to practice in the domain you're working in. This builds your ability to reason both implicitly and explicitly. It's particularly important for implicit thinking because unlike explicit thinking, you don't have a chance to review your logic in real-time.

This practice powerfully develops our thinking. The more concrete scenarios that you see and the more examples of the internal logic of the domain that you have a chance to absorb, the more you'll be able to do that reasoning yourself.

For engineers, this might come in the form of building as many different projects as possible – so that the array of problems that are common to software development are deeply absorbed. It may mean regularly practicing with kata – to get the small moves with IDE, keyboard, mouse, and tests thoroughly absorbed.

For the leader, this may mean shaking off organizational inertia and pressing on toward better structure and higher levels of throughput.

In both cases, it means finding the important, core problems inherent in software development and spending as much time as possible solving them.

The second thing we can be doing is to regularly practice turning implicit thinking into explicit thinking. This means writing, speaking about, and discussing your intuitions with others.

Doing this will increase the depth of your understanding in a way very similar to actual practice. This sharpens both implicit and explicit reasoning just like practice does.

INDUCTIVE AND DEDUCTIVE REASONING

We started by recognizing the need to either apply energy – "passion" – or engage in active reasoning. After that we made the choice between taking clear explicit steps in our reasoning and just jumping to the end by using intuition (or implicit reasoning, as we've been calling it). Our next thinking decision is whether we should use inductive or deductive reasoning.

As with the previous choices in approach we've made, understanding the trade-offs between the two options is just as important as building skill in both.

While the two ideas sound fancy, they are things that we've been doing since we were children. Simultaneously, they are things that as a society we've worked to hone. They form the foundation of both modern science and common sense.

They are tied together, complement one another, but are opposites.

Inductive reasoning – induction – is the act of turning multiple observations into principle. With it, we create an abstract idea from a set of concrete ones. This is an idea that is near and dear to the heart of the software engineer – creating abstraction.

This can be seen in the child that rapidly associates the cessation of many kinds of activity with the word "No." Recognizing this pattern, he then tries to stop activity he doesn't like by deploying the word himself.

It can be seen in the scientist that painstakingly records detailed results of large quantities of physical experiments. Whether it is measuring displacement of light around a large celestial body or the rate of acceleration of an object falling from the top of a building, the experimenter extracts the general principle by observing concrete instances.

The workings of induction, its ability to compel assent from us, along with its alignment to the structure of nature are deep mysteries that are outside of the scope of this book. Sufficient for our discussion is that induction is a tool that allows us to extract principles that we can use to solve the problems that we face.

Deductive reasoning – or deduction – is the method by which we take these principles and either solve particular problems or synthesize additional principles.

As children, one principle that parents work hard to communicate is the idea that stealing is not a desirable behavior.

There will come a time when a child goes to a store without his parents for the first time. Maybe this adventure will be with friends. Maybe a friend suggests that stealing a snack would be better than having to pay for it. If the general principle was absorbed, the child can use deduction to apply the general principle to the specific instance. That is, the decision to avoid stealing the snack will be a deduction from the general principle communicated by his parents.

In a much more sophisticated instance, Sir Arthur Eddington deduced from the principles of Einstein's General Relativity Theory that the deflection of light around the sun was double that of Newton's theory. Then, in 1919 during a solar eclipse (incidentally, demonstrating to the world the validity of the principles) made that observation [6].

In the process we use for software development, we accept a number of useful principles. One of them (as we will explore in coming chapters) is that software development done in small increments yields better results. For a given software development shop, then, building a workflow based on small increments is simply a deduction based on the broader principle.

Like induction, deduction is something that is not only built-in to human beings, but it is also something at which we can improve – to the point of carrying out highly sophisticated reasoning.

What problems do these tools have

The primary problem that we can get into with these tools is mistaking the timing that we use to apply them.

Induction is used exclusively to develop general rules. To be effective, a wide array of data must be gathered. If insufficient time or data is provided, the technique will be less effective – as we won't have the material in place from which to create general rules.

Deduction, however, depends on having a good set of principles in place in order to make judgments about our specific circumstances. Principles can be communicated to us by others, arise from our own inductive reasoning, or even from previous deductive reasoning. However, they make their way into our arsenal; if we don't have a set of principles from which to work, our deductions will be useless.

Additionally, induction is susceptible to its own success. This can often be seen throughout the course of software development. We will dive deeper into this situation in the next chapter, but certain parts of the work of creating software can be rapidly and powerfully enhanced through the use of inductive reasoning. This success can then lead to its overuse.

A common practice is for a team to evaluate its performance every couple of weeks. This is often called a "Sprint Retrospective" and was popularized by the Scrum framework [1].

As an example of the overuse of empiricism, through its regular evaluation, a team might recognize an estimation shortcoming. Part of their estimation discussion doesn't seem to be giving them the results they need. They brainstorm a better approach estimation and then try it. After a couple of sprints (to use Scrum's terminology), the bad results have dissipated.

They've generated enough data – probably dozens of estimates with actual delivered software – to define a pretty solid rule for the workflow on the particular team. The results bear it out, and so when doing future reasoning about their workflow, they now have a good rule to lean on.

Alternatively, an entire organization – containing multiple engineering teams – might be considering restructuring. This restructuring may result in a smaller piece of software for one team, ostensibly leading to faster delivery. After several sprints of this, it would be easy to believe that a useful rule-governing organizational restructuring might be extracted.

There are, however, any number of pathological organizational structures that can lead to the throughput of a single team increasing. Data that would produce a more reliable rule would involve observations from multiple teams, as well as from the organization as a whole. For example, did the "slowness" just move from one team to another, and even if it did, what happened to the throughput of the larger organization. It is possible that one or more team(s) being slower equates to better overall results from the larger organization.

After seeing the success of the method, it would be easy to be excited to use an empirical-only approach. It is important to remember though that we must use care in its application. We should always be diligent in our meta-rationality – choosing our thinking approaches with care.

Finally, deduction is not without its problems either. One is that we simply don't have a good grasp on the rules of logic. It's very easy to accept syllo-gisms in which the conclusion doesn't actually follow from the premise.

The other problem we might come across with deduction is that the rules that we are using are simply not of high enough quality or general enough applicability. Either way, our logic may be perfectly sound while the resulting outcomes will not be.

How do we use these tools

The strategy for best leveraging inductive and deductive reasoning follows from these two sets of problems.

The first step is to build up a collection of principles in the domain we happen to be working in. This can be done explicitly in that we make a point of clearly articulating in one form or another the principles as we learn them. Or it can be done implicitly – by spending time thinking and engaging in the domain we will naturally make observations that our cognitive equipment will turn into principles.

We should note again the several ways we might collect our principles. They can be communicated to us by others, they can be induced, or they can be deduced. And of course, a combination of these three techniques may be applied – for example, someone may communicate a principle after which we use deductive reasoning to ensure that it lines up with our previously existing principles.

So once we have a good set of principles at our fingertips, we simply need to go about the business of solving problems – applying deductive reasoning to connect our principles to the current concrete circumstances.

How do we develop our ability to use these tools

Developing our inductive and deductive reasoning is largely a matter of practice.

The first goal to consider is becoming as skilled as possible at rapidly deriv-ing clear, general principles. The key to really getting clarity and speed is by doing this as explicitly and as regularly as possible.

So, for example, after working through a particularly challenging software development problem, collect the lessons you've learned. Put those lessons on paper. Further, do the hard work to communicate those lessons to others. This will clarify the principles to the greatest extent possible.

Doing this regularly will ensure that you're collecting rules that are as clear as possible and that those rules can be quickly applied to new circumstances. As you practice, this induction will become faster and easier.

As we are collecting our rules, it's also important to take care with the data on which we base our rules. Two questions should be at the forefront of our minds as we proceed – do we have enough data to really make the rule compelling and are we sure that the data has the internal relationships that we think it does.

That is, often we generalize based on results that rest on an input parameter that we aren't aware of or don't realize is related.

For an exaggerated, contrived example, we might put a pot of water on 100 stovetop burners. Fifty are black and cold; 50 are blue and hot. The latter boil; the former do not. We may mistakenly generalize from this that water doesn't boil on black burners.

In the real world, this challenge is often far more subtle.

It is, therefore, important to remain vigilant in discovering and testing all variables that might affect the outcome of your experimentation and because of that affect any principles you might take on.

As for improving in deductive reasoning, we must practice recognizing and using those principles. This includes recognizing when they have been broken.

More basically, familiarity with the rules of logic can break down our ability to deduce accurately. This can be remedied in any number of texts on the topic. Though, as with inductive reasoning, practice is key.

Practicing effectively is a matter of making a point of thinking through problems while checking that you are continuing to apply basic logic rules appropriately. That is, you must first know the basic rules of logic, then use those basic rules to – repeatedly and very explicitly – reason about real problems.

WHAT TO CHOOSE AND WHEN

The key question then – when we look at the thinking tools at our disposal – is what we should use and when.

Interestingly, we should note that these thinking tools apply to the question of how we are going to think. In fact, that is the point of this discussion – to be intentional about our choice about how to think. So as we learn and practice with these tools, we will become more skilled in choosing which to use in particular situations.

Since practicing things explicitly improves both explicit and implicit execution, the coming chapters will provide an explicit deep dive into the specifics of building software, building a software team, and enhancing an existing software team.

I should also note that this extremely light coverage of human cognitive capability was meant to provide a basis for this deep dive. Undoubtedly, large libraries could be filled by the books on these topics written by folks smarter and better versed in these topics.

In each of the pairs of tools that we've discussed, the following pattern exists; one is more of an instinct than the other though both can be improved through practice.

Between passion and reason, passion is more like an instinct. Choosing between the two comes down to whether we need to chart our course or find the energy to execute on it.

Between implicit reasoning and explicit reasoning, implicit is more like an instinct. Choosing between the two comes down to whether we need speed in the former case, or the ability to communicate or evaluate our thinking as we are doing it in the latter.

Between inductive reasoning and deductive reasoning, inductive is more like an instinct. Choosing between the two comes down to whether we have a set of rules that would cover our current circumstances. If we do, we can deduce our response. If we don't, we have to try something, gather data, and induce a rule we can use in the future.

We will follow this chapter with one last piece of groundwork – separating the activities of tactically building software systems and of strategically building the people systems that build those software systems.

The way these thinking tools come into play in these two disparate systems is radically different because the systems have radically different natures. Once we understand those two systems in principle, we will discuss the approaches in both that will lead to the fastest creation of software, and ultimately to the most value in the hands of the customer.

WORKS CITED

1. K. Schwaber and J. Sutherland, "The Scrum Guide" [Online]. Available: https://scrumguides.org/scrum-guide.html# [Accessed 2024].
2. M. Conway, "Conway's Law" [Online]. Available: https://www.melconway.com/Home/Conways_Law.html [Accessed 2024].
3. L. v. Mises, Human Action, 1949.
4. D. Kearns, Team of Rivals, New York, NY: Simon & Schuster, 2005.
5. M. Buckingham, Go Put Your Strengths to Work, New York: Free Press, 2007.
6. E. Landau, "A Total Solar Eclipse 100 Years Ago Proved Einstein's General Relativity," *Smithsonian Magazine*, 24 May 2019.

Chapter 4

The two systems

In the preceding chapters, we've built out some important groundwork – groundwork that will guide analyses directed at the practice of developing software. This groundwork will also serve as a baseline for solving practical software development problems in the real world.

We've looked at the unique nature of software development – that it is not only invention, but that it is invention done with groups of people. We've realized that practically this leads to certain types of work that needs doing and to interesting coordination problems arising between those doing that work.

We've also looked at the set of thinking approaches available to us as human beings – how we might apply them in general, and how we can improve in our capabilities with them.

In this final piece of groundwork, we will make a couple of important observations that will ultimately result in a generalized strategy for applying our thinking tools to the unique problem of software development. It will also give focus to our effort to design practices that will ensure the success of a software development team.

SYSTEMS

"System" is an important notion in our analyses of how we develop software. The word itself, system, is somewhat overloaded in the technology world – so I want to be clear that we are using it in a general sense. Whether it's software, hardware, or people, the actors in our system create situations in which certain states or circumstances are causally related to one another.

One common system we come across when developing software is the engineering team – it's processes and relationships result in specific outcomes and aggregate behaviors. For example, a team might define roles and processes such that after someone in the developer role codes a feature, it must be manually tested by a person in the tester role. This creates interesting aggregate behaviors – features that appear to take double the time to release relative

DOI: 10.1201/9781003382751-5

to the time they took to code and a team where individuals swing wildly between underloaded and overloaded with work.

The discipline involved in elucidating and leveraging systems is known, not so surprisingly, as systems thinking. Peter Senge describes it poetically in his fantastic work on the topic:

> Business and other human endeavors are also systems. They, too, are bound by invisible fabrics of interrelated actions, which often take years to fully play out their effects on each other ... Systems thinking is a conceptual framework, a body of knowledge and tools that has been developed over the past fifty years, to make the full patterns clearer, and to help us see how to change them effectively [1].

In our mission to create value, the simplest, most abstract system might be one that contains two circumstances.

1. We do something.
2. Because of this, value is created for our customer.

Ultimately, this is the procedure we are after, though because it is so abstract, it is not of much use. What is that something? What other somethings have to happen before we can do this "something"? etc.

We might make our system a bit more complex by choosing exactly what we want to do to create value:

1. We build a house.
2. We sell the house to customer, thereby creating value.

To further complicate things, we might have additional circumstances that deepen the causal relationship:

1. We acquire nails.
2. We acquire lumber.
3. Since we have lumber and nails, we build a house.
4. We sell house to customer, thereby creating value.

Step 3 is a result of Steps 1 and 2 as well as the effort to build the house. Step 4 is a result of Step 3.

Without any additional explanation, "Systems Thinking" is a shockingly powerful exercise. It makes explicit the causal relationships that we take for granted in many cases. In my experience, simply making these relationships explicit leads to finding problems, inefficiencies, and other challenges that were hidden and would have otherwise remained hidden.

DIVISION OF LABOR

An important pattern arises in systems related to business – division of labor.

As Adam Smith points out in his immortal, "The Wealth of Nations," when the market is large enough, we begin to be more and more specific about the products or services that we offer [2].

Whether this separation is broad, across multiple large-scale businesses, think of the division of labor between the tire company and the motor vehicle company – or whether it is small in scale – such as might be seen in a working group, with two employees focusing on particular types of work – the principle is the same.

That principle is that at certain points in a given system, there may be full, independent systems about which we know nothing beyond the input and the output.

Consider the idea of interacting with an interface in a programming language. This principle is based on the same fundamental human capability – that of dealing with things in the abstract. Due to this capability, we can often carry out our valuable activities, with only the knowledge of a very small part of the contributing work. Our human systems can be modular in the same way that our software systems can be.

So we can have a system that we operate that is dependent on other systems – though so long as we know what the "interface" with that system is (and we comply with it), we need no other information about it.

In our example above, "acquiring nails" is really an interface to a large (unknown to us as house builders) system – a system that includes things like mining ore, heating a furnace, and shaping steel.

This is a powerful – and essential – advantage we have in dealing with our systems. It's powerful in that it allows us to focus on our mental energies – allowing the creation of more value. It's essential because as humans our mental energies are in fact limited and need to be focused – otherwise, we wouldn't be able to do anything.

Some systems also tend to be concerned with radically different types of work – as with the nail production and house building systems. The latter requires the former, but the tools and the techniques involved in each are very different. Thinking about them separately (even having different people or different organizations performing them) is thus supremely advantageous.

SOFTWARE DEVELOPMENT CONTEXT

In software development, there are a number of systems that we use as the "nails" of our craft – there are also however systems that use software development – that are client systems.

Our business or organization is a larger system that tends to view the software development system as an abstract interface with which it interacts. Our society as a whole – or at least the subset that represents our business' market – in turn, views the business as an abstract interface with which to interact (they pay us money, we give them a product or service – input/output).

The key in each of these relationships is the clarity of the separation and of the interface with the client system.

The definition and clarity around this relationship allow either side to be more ignorant of its "implementation details" – its additional causal relationships. This is useful in human systems for the same reason it is in software systems – it reduces the complexity of both sides of the relationship. In human systems, that means that costs go down and thus the satisfaction of needs goes up.

THE TWO SYSTEMS

There are two distinct systems in play when we build software. They are often conflated. This conflation leads to unnecessary cost and to using the wrong thinking and problem-solving tools at the wrong times.

The first system is the computer system. This is the actual code, computers, networks, and peripherals that make up the running system – the system that is directly serving the needs of your customer. It includes everything from the cloud provider to the software written by your team, to the browser running on the customer's computer.

This automation that this system provides – the service that it provides – is the immediate value that you as an organization, as a business, are providing to your customer. This is true whether you are a unit within another business creating value for your peer business units – or whether you are offering value to customers that are outside of your organization.

Often in conversations with software professionals and even software leaders, this system, the one directly adding value to your customers, is the only one that comes up.

This is likely due to the fact that the computer system is not only the most obvious, but it's also the most directly attached to both the mission of the organization and its revenue.

The second system is the people and technology system that builds the computer system.

This includes the process used to build the computer system, the skills, and relationships. It further includes the arrangement of the people involved in the building of the computer system, and even the existing technology itself. The architecture, testing, and the cleanliness of the code become parts of the people and technology system that creates the computer system, going forward.

There's a temporal aspect to this that can make it a little confusing if we're not careful.

To restate, the current existing people and technology system collaborates to build a computer system that creates real value for customers. That computer system then becomes a part of the people and technology system that will collaborate in the future to create yet more sophisticated computer systems.

The way these systems are connected over time is another reason that it's so easy to think of them as a single system.

It is important though to think of them separately. At a high level, the easiest way to see this is to realize the rate at which the two systems change.

The computer system itself is under constant evolution. Computer systems that mean to actively add value never stop moving. Features are constantly being added and bugs removed. The value that was created yesterday inspires new value that can be added tomorrow.

The people and technology system that builds that computer system changes at a much slower rate. People may be added and removed – though since both adding and removing people is an invasive, painful thing, it is (and in fact it must be) something that is done slowly and deliberately.

Didn't we just get finished saying that the architecture and cleanliness of the codebase that we create today are part of the people and technology system tomorrow? Yes – but changes in those are what matter. The shape of the architecture will not change at the rate that changes are made to the computer system. Thousands of lines (or more) of code and configuration may change before there's a material change to architecture. The cleanliness of a particular codebase is a property that emerges over the course of many, many concrete changes to actual code.

So while we may be making changes to the computer system, the elements of the system that become a part of the people and technology system that build the computer system going forward change slowly as a function of concrete code or configuration change.

If we look again at the basic position equation, we see a similarity:

$$s = s_0 + v_0 t + \frac{1}{2} a t^2$$

If we're accelerating, position will change rapidly over time, while velocity – though changing – will change slowly.

The actual state of the computer system is akin to position – it changes rapidly. The people and technology system will change more slowly, while ultimately having a dramatic effect on the state of the computer system.

I don't want to imply an actual mathematical relationship here – but one way to look at the relationship is as if the state of the computer system is the first derivative of the state of the people and technology system that builds it.

In addition to this "rate of change" difference – the most apparent difference – is that the required skillsets, tasks, and participants are all generally very different. All of this undoubtedly justifies carving out separate systems and dividing labor.

However, the difference that makes the division absolutely unavoidable is the thinking tools that apply in either of the two situations.

We'll make a couple of general observations about the differences, then we'll look closely at the two sets of activities so that we can dig deeper.

Building a computer system is often though not always very detailed – many, many decisions need to be made very rapidly. This lends itself to implicit thinking based on many years of learning, recognizing, and leveraging implementation patterns – that is to say, induction. Further, a high degree of passion is needed to keep momentum as the pile of details is worked through.

Building a people and technology system takes foresight and an understanding of patterns that have been discovered in a broader arena of solutions. Further, there is less actual invention at this level. This means explicit thinking with a healthy dose of deductive reasoning comes to the forefront among thinking tools.

In both cases, the thinking tools may overlap at times, but the focus of each is basically opposite of the other. This means that for a large portion of the effort, even the most effective approach to reasoning about the problem space will be at odds between the two systems.

To get a better handle on this, let's look closely at each of the systems, the variety of work that goes into building them, and the type of thinking important to these specific pieces of work.

The computer system

Building a computer system involves several important pieces of work. We'll take a close look at that and then briefly discuss the common roles that are designed to accomplish this work.

While I am outlining the work here in an order that roughly matches the sequence with which you might first run into these activities in a brand-new system, it is by no means a "lifecycle." These activities happen repeatedly, continuously, and frequently in tandem as long as the system lives.

Working with others

Building useful software requires working with others.

We did cover the trivial case in Chapter 2, where a software developer might develop software for their own use, by themselves. We included this description to draw the distinction in workflow that are observable when particular types of actors are added to the workflow, though the case itself is almost nothing more than a thought experiment.

In order to work with others, there are an array of tools that must be brought to bear – communicating, influencing, working on a team, leading, and adjusting to the needs of others.

Countless volumes have been written on this topic – Stephen Covey's 7 Habits of Highly Effective People, and John Maxwell's 21 Irrefutable Laws of Leadership come to mind.

As might be guessed from these book titles, there are principles that can be put into play. But those principles are always fairly abstract. Working with others boils down to accommodating and leveraging human behavior. The specifics of that are based on the individuals involved, differing world views, and even moods.

Working with others means learning principles and skills, and then adapting to specific situations. The primary thinking tools involved are implicit thinking and inductive thinking.

Value prediction

The purpose of the computer system is to create value for a human being. Creating value with software means making an educated guess about a process whose automation would be useful in the future – and then doing the work to automate that process.

Prediction is the heart of this process. It's driven by implicit reasoning – by flashes of insight into the potential needs of our fellow humans. Once that insight is achieved, sketches or working software can be used to further uncover the potential need.

This experimentation (or inductive reasoning, as we called it earlier) will make ongoing value prediction possible.

Validating this work can be a very explicit task performed with deductive reasoning. Primarily though, predicting usefulness is done with intuition and experimentation.

Readable code

A big part of building a useful computer system is writing the code that creates specific behavior.

When writing code, though, it's important to remember that there are really two "audiences" to target.

First, though not necessarily most importantly, we target the machine that executes the instructions that the code represents. At the risk of stating the blindingly obvious, this is how we create specific behavior – by having the machine execute specific sequences of concrete instructions.

Second, we target those that must read code after it's written [3]. The more quickly someone can understand the code they read, the more quickly they will be able to change it. This, in turn, means more rapid change to the overall system. And this, of course, leads directly to our primary goal – more value in the hands of our customer.

This is why we have high-level programming languages (or really any programming languages at all). If we were interested only in creating behavior, we could just as readily enter machine code instructions.

There will always, however, be people interested in changing – and thus reading – code. Even if these are the same folks that wrote the code in the first place, making it understandable becomes quite valuable.

Frequently, the act of writing code is looked at as an entirely explicit, deductive act – analytical or even "scientific" we might say. This is true for some of the specific tools we use to write code such as choosing data structures or measuring the performance characteristics of certain algorithms.

However, let's remember our two targets – creating behavior by communicating with the machine and supporting delivery speed by communicating well with the next developer. Both of these are often best dealt with implicitly and with experimentation (that is to say, with induction).

With regard to behavior, we use induction because we can't predict with any degree of specificity the behavior we want to create ahead of time. The behavior that will best meet the needs of our customer is deeply embedded in their attitudes, assumptions, and thought processes. We can therefore only approximate it and then adjust the approximation based on feedback.

This isn't unique to software development. It is a feature of the entrepreneurial process, of which software development is a subset. In writing software – as in understanding and attempting to meet human need, generally – the mind of our customer is an impenetrable black-box – even to the customer themselves.

The only information we have access to is the response received to a particular product or service – in our case, to a particular piece of software.

This means we can ask questions, intuit or guess about the need and the best way to meet it. We can then put that attempt to understand in front of the customer and gauge the response.

To restate in terms of our thinking tools, this activity is driven by implicit thinking and inductive reasoning.

Similarly, when targeting readability for the next developer, we are targeting the response of human cognitive machinery. That is to say, readability is subjective and based on the response of the reader.

There are patterns that have been noted that if followed have the tendency to make things more readable. But the only real way to discover if code is readable is to put it in front of a developer and have them read it.

So which of our thinking tools will we leverage when attempting to write readable code? Our primary tool will be implicit thinking – we're using our own intuition about behavior and about readability to make many rapid choices. We will also be using inductive reasoning. Like behavior, readability is validated against the target audience.

As we mentioned earlier, there are patterns and tools that we might use during the course of writing code. These tools are more explicit and can be reasoned about deductively. Since they only put us in the ballpark in terms of addressing the needs of our two audiences, they are subordinate to implicit and inductive approaches.

Validating

Validating the thing we put in front of our two audiences – the behavior and structure of the code we've created – comes with some important advantages.

Validation is often called "Quality Assurance" (QA) or "Testing" – the prevailing mental model is that we test to make sure that we aren't creating bugs. It's sometimes framed as "we QA in order to ensure that we are meeting requirements with high quality code."

This sounds positive but it represents a limited view that is based on a faulty mental model. The faulty mental model is that there is some objectively "correct" behavior and structure – and that we have any way of knowing what that is.

Both of these assumptions are always false.

Software development, building a computer system, is a subset entrepreneurialism. We take a guess at what might meet a need in the future. This future state is not something we can predict, concretely. With our prediction in hand, we then build something, offer it to people, and see how well it meets the need. We keep what works.

With that as the basis, the power of validation becomes clear. We want to:

1. Ensure that we've performed the experiment that we set out to.
2. Ensure that we haven't changed the resulting software from previously successful experiments.

Validation – ensuring that we're performing the experiments that we set out to – results in minimizing time between initial experiment and a met customer need. It does this through two primary mechanisms.

1. We create momentum through self-trust. Confidence that we are experimenting in the way that we set out to and that we're not damaging any of our previous success is crucial. It gives us an emotional push forward as well as the fearlessness that comes from knowing we can focus on the experiment at hand. This is true whether we're a single developer or a team of developers.
2. We create adaptability through shared understanding. The more that our entire team has clarity – shared clarity – about the nature of the experimentation that is being accomplished, the more flexible it can be. We can painlessly choose to work on different features than we set out to initially because minimal discussion and absorption will be needed by the broader team. Alternatively, problems arise when the team is unclear on the current direction and there are a number of different opinions about what's actually being pursued. Changing direction – working on a different feature or feature set – will require difficult conversation. We will not be as adaptable as we could have otherwise been.

Looking back at our basis, we validate to ensure that we're actually performing the experiments that we set out to and that we aren't invalidating previously successful experiments.

Both of these should follow a priori from the growing list of feature definitions that have risen out of the value prediction (and confirmation) accomplished throughout the course of delivering your software.

Or at least it would seem this way. The real challenge in validation, however, is in the explosion of specific, unforeseen circumstances that result from building out a real software system. In practice, these are often called "edge-cases."

We mentioned earlier that building software is a highly inductive process because the mind of the customer is a black-box that we can't understand without seeing how they interact with real software.

The reason for this is that any inquiries we as providers of systems might make to uncover the inner working of the mind of the customer must be abstract compared to the step-by-step instructions needed by the computer to provide the behavior.

This is because if we provided those step-by-step instructions, we would have – for all intents and purposes – built the actual software. Laying out the step-by-step instructions is the time-consuming aspect of building software. Writing the actual code is all but trivial once we understand exactly what steps to take.

Dealing in abstractions saves all of this time and makes more realistic the idea of at least communicating a kernel of what might be a helpful computer system.

So – to be concrete – we might discover that a user wants to be able to log into their system so that some control can be had about who can perform certain actions. A detail that would be lost in that particular formulation is the password restrictions, or the need for two-factor authentication, or that the password shouldn't be displayed on the screen. These are things that are assumed in many cases today but can be lost in the abstract language used to uncover what will be useful to the (potential) customer.

Many of these details are uncovered throughout the course of development. As they work, a software developer might reasonably run across the password field and assume that it needs to be obfuscated so that it doesn't display on the screen.

Many details are not uncovered like this, though.

This makes validation, for the same reason as actual coding, an intuitive, implicit activity.

So – while, in the abstract, validation may appear to be an explicit, deductive exercise – in reality, it is not.

Deploying and releasing

Deploying and releasing are two intimately related activities carried out during the course of creating a computer system. They might appear at times to be the same thing, but they represent an important distinction.

Releasing is the act of actually putting the system into the hands of the people that will use it.

Deploying is the act of updating software and computing resource such that if a person was to have access to it, they would be able to put it to use.

Looked at simply, the actions represented by these ideas are entirely concrete – they can be specified clearly and specifically, and performed in a repeatable, predictable manner. This means that the thinking tools to reach for are explicit thinking and deductive reasoning. Things can be boiled down to checklists, if so desired. No experimentation is necessary.

There is an important caveat to this. Initially discovering the concrete deployment steps is as much invention as writing code. As such, it rests on experimentation – on inductive reasoning. So when we are initially deploying the system or when we change its shape sufficiently to require new deployment, we use inductive reasoning.

We should note that with a naïve approach, coding, deploying, and releasing are completed serially. That is, in order to technically and conceptually put a feature in front of a user, developers must stop building features and do the work to put the feature out.

In this section, we will dive briefly into a more sophisticated deployment and release approach. Though we will leave for later sections deeper discussions about how and why we would put them into use.

The first discovery that we've made as an industry and that is highlighted in Jez Humble's memorable volume, "Continuous Delivery," is that we can and should automate anything related to deployment and release that can be spelled out explicitly. If we can be explicit about the steps we take to deploy and release a system, we can have a computer do it for us.

This workflow automation begins to decouple software development from deployment and release. That is, it allows us to continue building, even as we put features in front of a user.

The second powerful discovery that we've made is that we can decouple deployment from release, so that development, deployment, and release can all run independently.

The way we do that is through the use of feature flags. A feature flag can "release" a feature that has previously been deployed, so that we can make the choice to release the feature independently (though after) the code for the feature has been deployed.

This decoupling means that when a development team finishes a feature, it can move on completely without having to maintain context about the feature, since it would have been deployed.

The third important technique that assists in both of these decouplings is automated validation. By automating the validating work that we do, we further eliminate any need to maintain context. This is due to the fact that the development team will not have to worry about unexpected changes to behavior after deployment.

When we add these three techniques into our deployment and release work-flow, we improve throughput considerably. We also, however, change the nature of the activity.

In the simple case, it's a single activity with a checklist-style set of work to move from development to software in the hands of customers.

In the sophisticated case, we are always building our meta-software suite – tests, workflow automation, and feature flags.

This suite is identical in nature to the software we are building for our actual customer – the features that are useful are hidden behind the black-box of human understanding. Teasing them out is a matter of experimentation. That experimentation will bump up against the array of unanticipated details that are wrapped up and forgotten about within the abstract packaging we use to communicate about them.

The only difference is that in this case, the development team tends to be its own customer.

More importantly though, we're back to reaching for implicit, inductive thinking tools.

Operating and monitoring

Software can many times resemble a traditional, physical product. At other times, it can more closely resemble a service one human might perform for another.

Even when it's "shrink-wrapped" – targeted at being a self-contained system that a single person uses – telemetry and other operational details are often sent to back-end services for analysis.

Occasionally, systems are completely isolated and are essentially identical to a physical product – often even being embedded in a physical product.

When a piece of software is on the other end of that spectrum, the software can seem to be imitating a human being and performing some service for the end customer. That might be giving stock quotes, providing banking services, or getting directions to a physical location.

So if, prior to generalized computing, we had a binary way to add value to our fellow human beings – either by providing a product or a service, we now have much more of a continuum between those two extremes, most real-life systems falling somewhere in the middle.

No matter where we are on that continuum, we have two general problems to solve: making the product-service available to the customer and being able to remediate any problems that might occur as the customer uses it. The location on the product-service continuum will, though, dictate some of the specifics involved in doing those two things.

Generally, making the service available means that we have to couple the software to a computer system that offers all necessary capabilities. In the case of packaged software delivered to the end-user, the computer system will likely be the customer's personal computing device. In the case of software more on the service side, the computer system may be a server owned by the organization that developed it. Or, more likely, the computer system will be a combination of resources owned by the customer and resources owned by the organization that is provisioning the service.

Remediation means troubleshooting the computer system, using data collected at runtime to reproduce the problem, and then either providing a work-around or modifying that system to change the behavior. The more that the system tends toward the product side of the continuum – or more importantly – the more the actual mechanics of the system rest on the computing hardware belonging to the customer, the more indirect this becomes. The general approach, though, is always the same.

There are two sides to handling these two sets of problems. We have to "operate" the system. That is, we have to provide sufficient instruction to the humans and machines involved in making the system go. We must also "monitor" the system. That is, we must build the system such that we can quickly gather information about any problem that might occur. That information should allow us to solve any specific problem that arises.

As we consider the thinking tools we might employ here, we recognize that these two tasks will be handled differently.

Operating a system will consist of a set of concrete, explicit steps. This means explicit thinking and deductive reasoning. Among the work we do to build a computer system, this is a bit of a standout in how concrete and clear it can be.

Monitoring the system, as we mentioned, involves capturing the right data, interpreting the captured data, and then providing solutions to any problems that arise.

All of these rest on intuition and experimentation. When building a system, only the actual use of the system will prove out what data will be useful, though a software developer's intuition will help to determine that. Any interpretation is highly dependent on the specifics of the system. This interpretation may border on the explicit at times, though due to the quantity of information, practically it tends to remain intuitive.

Overall approach

The work of building a computer system – because of the richness of detail and the subjective nature of adding value to people – implies a certain set of thinking tools.

This can be seen in almost every bit of work necessary to use software to create value for people.

With the exceptions of the naive approach to deployment and the operation of a computer system, every necessary activity rests on experimentation and intuition.

So as we set out to build our computer systems, we face three hard realities:

1. We need team members that have highly refined intuition. The more seasoned our team members are, the more they will be able to make good decisions in the moment as they build out systems.
2. This can't be compensated for by controls external to the individuals. The more we try to "manage" people into good decisions, the more things must be explicit. The more things are explicit, the less we are working within the reality of software development. The richness of the detail in this work means that the more we try to force things to be explicit, the slower we will go.
3. The core of our computer system building workflow must enable regular, rapid experimentation.

We will look next at the second of the two systems that we are involved in building – the people and technology system that does the work of building the computer system.

As we do this, we need to be sure to take notice of a key difficulty – the thinking tools necessary to build the computer system and those necessary to build the surrounding people and technology system are entirely different.

This wouldn't be such a bad thing, except for the fact that the two systems are so often conflated in the minds of their members and stakeholders.

The people and technology system

As we discussed earlier, the workflows and systems that we interact with and are part of in life and in business are often very complex and even connect with each other. In fact, as economists from Adam Smith to Ludwig von Mises have recognized, many systems can be connected to each other through a very simple interface – the exchange of goods or services.

In this way, people around the world contribute to collective activities without sharing any information other than the good or service we choose to exchange.

Milton Friedman gave a famous lecture on the creation of a pencil – demonstrating, as he said, that "there's not a single person in the world who could make this pencil." The lead, the wood, the paint on the outside of the pencil, the rubber eraser – they're all provided by people that do nothing but agree on a simple exchange of goods [4].

The people and technology system that builds our computer system works similarly – since we know the interface between the two systems, we can work on one system and ignore the details of working on the other.

In the case of the computer system – if we are interested in constructing a people and technology system that will result in the computer system that we want, we can forget about the details of actually building the computer system.

This is convenient, because both activities are complicated, so the more we can choose to not think about, the better off we will be. It is also convenient because building each of these systems requires opposite sets of thinking tools. Building the computer system is intuitive and experimental – building the people and technology system that constructs a computer system, as we will see, is explicit and deductive.

To get into this, we need to look closely at the activities involved in building a people and technology system. We will use "people and technology system" as shorthand for "the people and technology system that constructs software." I do want to be clear though that the interface here is handy because a well-built people and technology system will result in good software generally – it's not specific to any industry, set of features, technology, or type of work.

Understanding shape

The most important factor in building the people and technology system is understanding shape.

There are three areas that we work in when we are building a people and technology system, and each of these systems is related to the others by their shape.

We must shape our team, shape our software, and shape our workflow.

The optimal shape in each of these arenas is similar and connected. Mel Conway made a powerful observation about the nature of invention – an observation that certainly holds true for software development. He found that, "any organization that designs a system (defined broadly) will produce a design whose structure is a copy of the organization's communication structure" [5].

There is some consternation about calling this a law that "law" has certain connotations that don't hold true for this particular observation. We should reiterate at this point that like economics, all of software development is more or less based on human desire – that is, as we've phrased it earlier, software development is not a physical science. The rules that we reason from need not be as predictive as those we might come across in physics in order to be useful.

Conway's "Law" is one of these. It's incredibly important, very valuable, and its truth is borne out by the experience of many, many software organizations.

The practical importance of Conway's Law is that if we alter the shape of our organization without altering the shape of our software, everyone with an interest in the system will feel uncomfortable. This discomfort may not be explicitly understood – its origin may be looked at with varying degrees of sophistication.

It will be felt, though.

It will inspire action. However, the better the understanding of this law, the better the handling of this discomfort will be.

So how does this apply to the three shapes we mentioned earlier – the shape of our team, of our software, and of our workflow?

From Conway's perspective, the shape of our team (the people involved and their understanding of their roles) and the shape of our workflow are both aspects of "the organization's communication structure." So they, together, will be a reflection (or reflected by) the structure of the software.

We separate these when we discuss building a people and technology system because they can vary independently and the tools and techniques for dealing with them differ.

Shaping the team

Shaping the team is of primary importance. Both the shape of the software and the shape of the workflow provide supporting roles. Their ultimate value is in the impact they have on the shape of the team.

The reason for this is that, at least for now, people are the ones that do the work of building computer systems. The communication networks among the people involved can radically hinder or powerfully support rapid creation of software.

This boils down to how dependent one team – and even one person – is on another. To the extent that teams and the people on them can make choices about how to implement and operate their software independently, they will move quickly. To the extent they can't make those choices independently, they will move slowly.

Dependency comes in two general forms – activity and authority.

Having an activity dependency means that in order to do something, someone else must first do something. So, for example, in order to build my user interface, I may require data storage from a database that must be implemented by another developer. I have activity dependency on that developer.

Having an authority dependency means that in order to do something, someone else must give me approval. So, for example, in order to change a database table structure, I need approval from a particular VP. I have an authority dependency on that VP.

Arguably, authority dependency is a subset of activity dependency. In practice, though, they look very different and are often handled in different ways.

There is some dependency that is unavoidable. Since the faster a software development organization is, the more value it delivers, optimizing a software organization means removing all but the absolutely essential dependency.

Dependency reduces speed in that the individual or team depended on will never have the same buy-in or emotional connection to the ultimate value that the dependent seeks to deliver. The need will also have to go in a queue to be balanced against other needs from dependent individuals or teams – which means that there's a whole universe of conversations and work immediately created around judging relative importance.

Idea to production

Some obvious questions follow from this, such as:

- What is the minimal set of dependencies?
- How do we eliminate those that are not in this set?

With a software team, this can't be boiled down any further than to Werner Vogels' immortal formulation, "You Build It, You Run It."

Software should be written by a small team that not only does the work to design and code it, but also to operate it when it's put into use. All technical activities involved in the delivery of value to a customer through a piece of software should be done by a single self-contained team.

"This is impossible! Some software is just too complex for a small team to handle," you may object.

We will deal with this in the next section on "Shaping the Software." The short answer to this objection is that all software if it sufficiently complex such that it requires more than one team to handle its development is sufficiently complex that it can be decomposed into pieces that individual teams can handle.

So, any dependency that relates to the building and operating of the software should be eliminated. There are practical challenges to this in certain contexts. The existing structure of the organization might make removing the dependency more damaging than it otherwise might be. Fixing the structure that causes this problem then becomes the first priority.

Aren't all the dependencies that might exist – those related to building and operating software (that is, to use the vocabulary we laid out earlier, the computer system)?

No.

Now remember there are two different systems in play here – the computer system, and the people and technology system that builds the computer system.

The dependencies that we should eliminate, for the reasons listed above, are those specifically related to building the computer system.

The responsibility to build the people and technology system usually doesn't fall on the team building the software. They're radically different responsibilities, and both complex in their own way. Further, the state of the people and technology system powerfully affects how the build of the computer system proceeds, though they are not bound closely in time. The feature the team is building won't block on some change to the people and technology system, and while the approach to building the computer system will affect the people and technology system, a single change in the former will not immediately imply change in the latter.

So practically speaking, there isn't a short-term causal relationship in either direction.

We can thus think of them separately – and activity in one system doesn't represent a dependency in the other.

The final responsibility for shaping the people and technology system rightly and typically falls to the software engineering leadership team.

However, a collection of changes to the computer system can represent a change to the people and technology system. This change may represent an authority dependency on the leadership team. This dependency wouldn't block a particular feature – but the team would look to the people and technology system steward (the software engineering leadership team) for authority to make the move.

This dependency is useful since having the development team take on management of the people and technology system is impractical and at the same time it doesn't actually block any of the value that the team is working to create.

The reverse of this situation is also true – if the engineering leadership team looks to make a change to the people and technology system – they will be dependent on the team or teams whose people, software and computing resources represent that system.

So dependencies related to actually building computer systems (software, etc.) should be eliminated. Dependencies between the two systems, however, are often necessary and should in many cases remain.

Shaping the software

The overall shape of the software is important to the structure of the people and technology system in three ways; in clarity, in supporting independent teams, and in supporting rapid scaling.

Clarity

The codebase should be clear and easy to understand. The ability to be quickly read and understood by a fluent developer means that a team will be able to rapidly change the computer system. As we've repeated a number of times – speed is at the core of value creation in software development.

Supporting independent teams

By leveraging "Conway's Law," we can support the team shape described in the previous section by structuring our codebase accordingly.

Our target is a small team able to manage all the activities involved in building and operating a piece of software. The common objection that we highlighted earlier was that some computer systems are just too complex.

This doesn't need to be so.

Any large computer system can be broken out into subsystems by feature – while serving the user in the same way, it would have when it was consolidated into a single system.

These subsystems must be fully independent, independently releasable, communicating with one another only when necessary and only through channels that are explicitly defined and required by an actual feature of the system.

To repeat, it's quite possible a collection of subsystems is presented to a user as if it were a single system. The illusion of that presentation does not preclude the breakdown we are discussing here – which, again, is possible for any computer system.

So, for example, I may have an ecommerce website – on which users login, shop, and purchase. Each of those use-cases, logging in, shopping, and purchasing, can all be separate systems even while together they provide a unified experience – as if the ecommerce website were a single computer system.

Thanks to Conway's Law, when our software is shaped this way, it promotes teams that are small and independent. That is, when we make sure our computer system is small enough for a single team to fully manage, it provides teams with the opportunity to manage the computer system without dependency.

Supporting rapid scaling

To take this a step further, our computer systems should be shaped such that the teams that are building them can scale rapidly.

As a computer system becomes more complex – even after we break it down in to smaller subsystems – the overall size of the organization may need to increase in order to be able to continue delivering changes to them.

Splitting the system down into smaller pieces so that individual teams can manage them is important, though as features are added the number of subsystems will increase. The number of teams needed will thus increase.

To scale rapidly, it's important that the organization is pro-active in ensuring there are at least two subsystems per team. This means that when a team is added, there's already a system broken out for it.

Deciding on the scope and breaking out a system as a team is added – that is to say, when the organization is under pressure – is far more difficult. More troublesome, it creates a drag on the organization's ability to scale.

Shaping the workflow

The final shape that needs to be considered as we're structuring our people and technology system is the shape of our software development workflow.

This includes everything from how we type in our code, where we store the code, as well as all of the activity involved in moving the code along the stability continuum out to production.

As with the connection between team shape and software shape, Conway's Law applies to the workflow we use to deliver our software. That is to say, there will be a pressure toward workflow being shaped much like the software and the other aspects of the team.

That being said, the primary concern is to ensure that there are no dependencies between the team's workflow and that of any other team. The workflow should be self-contained and managed fully by the team that uses it.

As mentioned earlier in the shape of the software, the system(s) that the team manages should be independently releasable. That is they should work through the workflow that the team sets up for itself without requiring or being required by other workflows or release processes.

Finally, to fully eliminate unnecessary dependencies (even within a team), everything that can be automated should be automated.

For example, in the past, a common practice was to do a lot of manual system administration work to take program code and install it on a production server. There should be almost no manual activity, unless some explicit approval is needed during the course of the development workflow (to meet a regulatory or other external requirement).

People and technology system thinking tools

As you can see, with the people and technology system, there are a number of well-defined premises from which we can reason without having to resort to experimentation.

This is another reason why – as we mentioned earlier – the team delivering the actual computer system should be separate from the team delivering the people and technology system. The thinking tools that are applied are almost entirely opposite.

While building the computer system is a highly implicit, very experimental enterprise, building the people and technology system is explicit and avails itself to deductive reasoning.

TAKE-AWAYS

There are three important take-aways here. First, that there are two separate systems, second, that we can save energy by only working in one system at a time. Third, that the required thinking tools are – for the most part – opposite between the two systems.

The next two major sections will be broken out along these lines. "Leading in Software Development" will dig deeply into building out the best possible people and technology system, including explaining the tools and techniques necessary to do that. "Areas of Competence" will similarly dig into the details of building out the best possible computer system, including explaining the tools and techniques necessary to best do that.

WORKS CITED

1. P. M. Senge, The Fifth Discipline, New York: Currency Doubleday, 1990.
2. A. Smith, Wealth of Nations, London: W. Strahan and T. Cadell, 1776.
3. R. C. Martin, Clean Code, Boston: Addison-Wesley, 2009.
4. M. Friedman, "YouTube," Free To Choose, 2013. [Online]. Available: https://www.youtube.com/watch?v=67tHtpac5ws
5. M. Conway, "Mel Conway's Home Page | Conway's Law" [Online]. Available: https://www.melconway.com/Home/Conways_Law.html

Leading software development

Chapter 5

Leadership

Exercising skillful leadership is of primary importance in creating real value for customers with software development.

Due to the unique challenges we laid out in preceding chapters, this is not quite as straightforward as it might be in other business settings. Most recently, we discussed the "two-systems" – the idea that there are two unique actions in play as we seek to build out software. There is the work to build the people and technology system – the system that surrounds and builds the computer system. There is then the work of building the computer system itself.

These are based on opposite sets of thinking tools – the former being explicit and deductive, the latter being implicit and inductive. This alone is enough to suggest that leading each would be somewhat different in practice.

The situation is further complicated by an important underlying truth that building a people and technology system is accomplished with a set of fairly well-defined, infrequently changing principles, while building a concrete computer system is not. The nature of a computer system is discovered as it is built – its principles being learned and evolved as the system is realized. This underlying truth results in the differing types of thinking we must apply between the two systems. It also, though, brings with it specific practical leadership challenges.

Countless gallons of ink have been spilt in an effort to elucidate the nature of leadership in its most general form. We won't attempt to retread much of that ground here. What we will do is try to get at the heart of what it means to lead so that we can marry that with the additional complexities introduced by software development's unique nature.

We will spend our time in this overlap for two reasons. First, it's relatively untouched ground. Most leadership literature devotes little specific advice even to the general arena of creative endeavors, and none to the singularly unique space that is leading in software.

Second, the skill with which a software development organization is led is the point of greatest leverage toward producing maximum value.

DOI: 10.1201/9781003382751-7

WHAT IS LEADERSHIP

"Leadership is influence, nothing more, nothing less" – John Maxwell.

Also Maxwell: "If you think you're leading and no one is following, you are only taking a walk."

When you boil away all the corporate doublespeak, inspirational poster fodder, and hype – what you're left with is that leading is simply doing something and having someone else do something that goes along with it.

An interesting question, though, that never really gets asked in the literature is why is leadership important? Why do we care about leadership? Why do we spend our time reading about it, thinking about it, and going to conferences at which it is the central theme?

We probably don't ask this much because most of us seem to intuit the value with little effort.

Just to be thorough though, let's think about this intuitively obvious value for a second.

Why? Reflecting on our motives can often clarify our action. More importantly, though, it will give us some useful vocabulary to use as we begin to marry leadership with software development.

The real driver, leaving things general for the time being, is accomplishment.

And just to be totally thorough, we should unwind accomplishment before we proceed. As human beings, we have broad imaginations and a world that offers limitless opportunity for improvement. No matter what the specifics of our current situation happen to be, we can always imagine a world in which they are incrementally better.

As soon as we envision such an improvement, we are almost compelled to make it happen – a sense of primal discomfort drives us to this.

Which is likely why we have such a deep understanding of the value of accomplishment – since accomplishment is simply moving the state of the world from what it was, to what we imagined that it could be.

Often, our imagination – our vision, to use leadership parlance – about what the world could be is beyond what our greatest lone exertions might be able to produce. So we work with others.

When we work with another human being, we work with someone with a unique view of the world and a unique imagination about its potential future state.

As does mine, that view of the world and that imagination combine to create a discomfort – a drive toward the realization of that image. Ultimately, that will result in action to that end.

If there are differences in our picture – our vision – of the potential world, that will obviously result in actions that will be geared toward differing ends. There may be certain pictures that have complementary actions, but more likely, differing vision will result in incompatible action.

We will be "paddling in different directions" – and as such we'll likely accomplish very little.

To accomplish something together, to move the world to a better state, the people involved must choose to paddle in the same direction – to take complementary action. This, of course, boils down to the fact that they must share their envisioned destination.

In order for two people to share their envisioned destination, one or both of them must regularly alter their picture based on that of the other. This is because our mental images are constantly shifting based on the plethora of inputs that we are constantly processing.

So to restate all of this, we are constantly picturing improvements that we can make to our world. Because we are, we are driven to take action to make changes to realize those pictures. Because our imagination often exceeds our own capacity, we need others to help us. Because others are driven by their own picture of future possibilities, working together requires bringing the individual pictures into alignment. Because our pictures are constantly evolving, this alignment must be done regularly.

This is influence. This is leadership.

LEADING THE BUILDING OF THE COMPUTER SYSTEM

Applying leadership to software development seems straightforward on the surface. It appears to be like any other kind of human endeavor – we want to accomplish something that we can't do alone. This necessitates working with others which in turn necessitates the alignment of our work with the work of others.

This really isn't a terrible place to start honestly.

As a small startup or even as a large enterprise, when we begin to build a new system, the decision points are limited and often the number of people needing alignment is limited. So the need for leadership – the need for influence – is itself, limited.

As the system and the team grow, though, the need increases.

To look closely at this, there are three areas of decision that we deal with from the time the system is small through to maturity.

Features

The specifics of the functionality of the system represent many, many decisions. Some examples might be:

- When should the "withdrawal" feature check for availability of funds?
- What type of characters are required in a password?
- Should the social media user be able to post photos or videos?

In every domain, on every system, there will be thousands of decisions to be made about exactly how things will work.

On a small team of one or two people, gaining alignment on the nature of the feature-work may be quick and easy.

As that team grows, the alignment becomes more difficult. Maintaining alignment – that is, influencing – begins to take considerably more energy than it did at the outset.

Technology

The technological approach to providing capability to the customer is the second area of decision.

This can include everything from programming language choices, to hosting providers, to MVC frameworks and dependency injection. As with feature choices, alignment and decision-making are straightforward when the team is small, and rapidly increases in required energy and time as the team grows.

Metawork

Deciding how to work together is an ongoing effort, even for a small team. For a small team, though, it often takes so little effort that it isn't even thought of as work in itself.

This can include things like when deployments are done, how they're decided upon, how help is sought if a team member gets stuck, or how features are broken down into smaller chunks.

The Scrum framework [1] famously focuses this into a "retrospective" at the end of its "Sprint." This focus is helpful in reminding us that metawork is work – though there are other ways that it can be handled.

The problem

Growth is the problem.

This may sound strange, since growth is often the very thing we are seeking in business – to be able to serve more people by building a larger team and a larger system.

In each of the three decision areas we call out here though, the energy and time required to influence dramatically increase with every person added. The more people there are to be influenced, the more effort the addition of a single person brings. That is to say, this cost is exponential as a function of number of people involved.

Imagine a software team of 15 developers, 2 product managers, and perhaps 4–5 business analysts and/or dedicated software testers. For every feature that one individual may bring to the table, there are 21 other people that need to be brought along to shared thinking – 21 people to be influenced. In order to participate, each of those people will have input that, if we really intend to influence them, will need to be assimilated.

That is to say, each of those 21 people will need to influence each of the other 21. If they aren't able to, they won't have buy-in to decisions that are made and won't be as open to being influenced in general.

If this situation seems impossible, you're analyzing it correctly.

In practice, what teams do when they get to this size is that they simply begin to neglect individual influence. This is why teams this size tend to be slow, cynical, and not particularly engaged.

It's important to note that the team is the full group of people that it takes to build and operate a piece of software. It's common to break people out into "teams" of reasonable size while not actually making them independent of other "teams." If you have 4 teams of 4–5 people that are all required to talk in order to make a change or deploy to production – you don't really have 4 teams – you have one team of 16–20 people.

No matter the specific scenario, one of the early warning indicators that a team is too large is "status meeting stand-up." The daily standup is a (rightly) popular part of the software development organization. Ideally, it is a time for software artists to energetically engage with one another and find solutions and inspiration to take to the specific part of the software that they are currently building. When the individuals don't have a chance to influence the decisions that affect them, the standup becomes a simple status reporting meeting.

This is an indicator that the team is too large because, as we covered above, the too-large-team almost immediately results in the inability for people to influence direction. Further, letting the team grow too large is a very common, very subtle problem that can only be avoided with intentional thought aimed at the structure of the organization.

This leads to the ultimate solution to the problem – stepping back from simply thinking about the building of the computer system to thinking about building the people and technology system that surround and build the computer system.

LEADING THE CREATION OF THE PEOPLE AND TECHNOLOGY SYSTEM

The outcome of leading in the naïve fashion outlined above and focusing only on the building of the computer system is that the team will grow without bound. This means that the leadership required will grow without bound. Since this requirement is exponential with respect to the size of the team, the required influence will quickly become impossible to provide, no matter how skilled the individuals or the organizational managers.

The solution, then, is to step back and make the people and technology system – as we've been calling it – a first-class citizen in terms of work.

The people and technology system, as we've discussed, is the "system" that builds the computer system. It includes everything from the process that folks use, to the run-time environment, to the quality of the architecture and code the computer system is built with.

Much of the content of the people and technology system is really stylistic – that is to say, it doesn't matter much precisely how you do it. There are a handful of things, though, that done a particular way will result in avoiding the constantly expanding team, and thus result in a faster, more productive organization.

The art in leading the people and technology system is knowing what these principles are and holding the line on them. When the business pressure is high – maintaining the people and technology system won't appear as urgent. It won't be the proverbial squeaky wheel. Continuing in the most effective direction in the face of short-term pressures is the real key here.

Prior to that, though, is knowing what the principles are. This is a topic we will cover in-depth in coming chapters.

SUMMARY

It is easy – and quite common – when thinking about software leadership to think only about the very obvious issues of features, technical solutions, and basic metawork. Thinking – in this manner – only about leading in building the computer system will certainly be productive to a point. That point, though, is the point where the team really begins to scale and to multiply its impact.

If, particularly on the executive leadership team, a concerted effort isn't taken to step back and look at the people and technology system as the organization begins its scaling journey, the software and the team are really at the beginning of their end.

WORK CITED

1. J. Sutherland and K. Schwaber, "Scrum Guides," 2023. [Online]. Available: https://scrumguides.org/

Building the people and technology system

My good friend Jeff and I were looking for something to do on a warm summer morning in Poulsbo, Washington. We were both in our teenage years. Neither of us were known for our ability to plan well for the future.

Both of our afternoons and evenings were spoken for by our employers, two of Poulsbo's high-quality fast-food establishments.

So, we figured we had a good chunk of the day to burn in one way or another. We decided to take a small rowboat out around Liberty Bay – a small inlet that was in the center of town. Its shores weren't far from our respective employers.

We rowed out quite a way before we started to tire out. About the same time, we started to think about how much time it might take us to get back to dry ground.

When we did turn around, we found ourselves on a bit of a clock due to our impending work shifts. We also found that rowing back was taking a bit more effort than rowing out had. We had used a lot of our energy on that initial trip.

If I'm remembering right – and it's been a few years at this point – we both made it to work on time. Though I do remember that return trip being far less enjoyable than the trip out to the half-way mark.

STEPPING BACK

Building software that really makes a difference means stepping back and intentionally building out a high-quality "People and Technology System."

As we might remember from earlier chapters, there are two systems that come into play in our work building software. There's the computer system that we are building – and there is the People and Technology System that builds that computer system.

Taking this step back can be challenging though. It is always very easy to focus on the concrete outcome that is currently in front of us. It is easy to focus on the specific software that our organization is building – and to put all of our effort, all of our influence and leadership, into those specific concrete things.

The problem with this is that the People and Technology System builds our software – if it is not intentionally maintained it can fall into disrepair – a lot like the software itself. Analogous to the "Technical Debt" that software developers frequently worry about, there is a People and Technology System Debt that can cause the system to break down.

How do we take that step back though? Isn't it irresponsible not to spend as much time and energy as possible to create the best possible product?

The adventure Jeff and I had on Liberty Bay is instructive here.

We were concerning ourselves with the specific movement of our small vessel. Our energy, our action was going directly to moving it – we moved the oars, and that good old "equal and opposite reaction" combined with the sweat of our brow propelled us.

Had we prepared sufficiently, we could have built a system that propelled the vessel for us. We could have spent the effort that we put into the rowing into piecing together engine parts and we could let the energy of some gasoline in the system we prepared propel us. Not only that, but over time, we could have had many more journeys of similar length and enjoyment, at the expense of far less energy.

We could have moved back from producing the specific output we wanted, to investing our energy in a system that would give us as an effect, the outcomes that we want, for which we'd only need to provide a little bit of direction.

This same thing is true in software. If we step back and build an effective "People and Technology System," the action of actually building software takes far less energy. That system can then be used over and over again, to produce software with less energy. It does degrade, so an eye needs to be kept on it to keep it running properly – but that's the small investment in guidance that it takes going forward.

CREATING SYSTEMS

Building an effective system can be a real challenge though.

Often, we set our minds to turning a particular goal into reality. There is likely an obvious action that we can take that connects intuitively to whatever the goal is. If we're late driving to an event, for example, the most obvious, most intuitive solution might be to simply drive faster.

The obvious, intuitively related answer can cause new problems that work against your purpose in subtle (or not so subtle) ways. In the case of hitting the gas to make it to your appointment on time, you increase the probability that you will be pulled over by law enforcement, making you later than you were to begin with.

The general solution to this is to learn to see the systems involved in the work that you are interested in doing. Find the components of the system and their causal relationships. Understand how changes imposed on the system impact and cascade through them.

A great resource for learning about this discipline – System's Thinking – is a work that we've mentioned in previous chapters; Peter Senge's "Fifth Discipline" [1].

This is where the foundation that we've laid in preceding chapters begins to connect.

In Chapter 1, we illustrated how software development is entrepreneurial. We observed that when we build software, we are discovering and creating the business that we're in. So, as we look at the work we do – as we analyze software development itself – it's important to remember that primary goal. That goal is to build something useful for a human being – to create value – with software.

Value

In pursuing "value," it is important that we're looking at our activities at the right level of abstraction.

That is, our goal is never to "build banking software" or to "write a social media app." While one of these may be our current task, a goal stated this specifically can only be temporary in software.

It is more useful to think about how we're solving a problem for an actual person. This might seem general enough to be totally vacuous, but it's not.

As software practitioners, we are always in the business of uncovering needs and meeting them. The form of this may change over the course of time even within a single organization. But the point remains the same.

So as we step back and look at the shape and constitution of the machine that makes our programs, it's important to remember that the output of that machine is value – real, tangible, human-need-meeting value.

Speed

As a recap from Chapter 2, creating value in software rests on the ability to delivery quickly.

If we are able to put our software into the hands of our customers faster, it means that we will be able to better determine the existence of the need we expected and how well we've provided for that need.

If we are able to put our software into the hands of our customers faster, it is also as a result that much more valuable. This is due to the law of time preference. Something today is worth more than something a week from now.

As we look to our software to meet needs, to create value, we recognize that delivering it faster means that it does both of those to a greater degree.

So a properly functioning People and Technology System builds software and it delivers it as fast as possible.

The systems

The target is to focus less on the Computer System and more on building out the People and Technology System. We want to keep the ultimate goal in mind (value through rapid delivery) while carefully narrowing focus. To do this, it's important to first be able to see the People and Technology System. Once we can do that, we will be best positioned to make the changes to it that will result in the outcomes we are interested in.

This then is the fundamental model that we will use to think about and enhance the software development organization. With this model in our hands we will examine the specifics of a well-constructed People and Technology System.

THE SHAPE OF THE PEOPLE AND TECHNOLOGY SYSTEM

In terms of the thinking tools we outlined earlier, building a People and Technology System is a much more explicit, much more deductive activity compared to building a Computer System.

We will find that as we solve problems in this space, as long as we don't forget about them, we won't have to solve them again in the future. That is to say, while building software itself is an experimental activity, building the People and Technology System is fairly static, based on principles that aren't subject to much change.

Disciplined target elaboration

Software development is invention. It is the act of uncovering a reality – of finding a need and meeting it. As all human needs (and their solutions) are, this reality is subjective. It is also in constant motion. Our needs as individuals and as societies change and evolve for many different reasons. Because of this, software development – building the Computer System – is always empirical.

I recently found myself upgrading the mobile capability for a website that I operate. Initially, I wanted to add a drop-down menu specifically for controlling the blog article capability. When I began to try out the new changes to the website, I realized that it made the mobile page feel particularly busy. Rather than enhancing the sense of control and value, it detracted from it.

This is a very simple example, but it has within it a common characteristic of software development. No matter who you are, developer or high-level strategist, you can't really know what best meets a need until you have something to try using.

From moment to moment in our effort to build a Computer System, it will be important to regularly re-evaluate the direction that we're heading. And we need to do this in a controlled, disciplined manner.

Adjustment with learning

That software development – building the Computer System – is empirical in approach means that the organization, the team, and the individual must all learn quickly and accurately. They must, further, be able to put the things learned into immediate action.

Further, even though it lends itself more to a priori reasoning, building the People and Technology System requires the ability to learn and adjust quickly as well.

It's a very rare organization that fully understands the work of building software. In fact, it's not just rare – it doesn't exist. While the principles in play don't change, the understanding in a particular organization will evolve over time – the understanding both of the meaning of the principles and of the application of those principles.

Even assuming constant forward motion in the ability to understand and apply software development's core principles, there's no real end to the scale of improvement. There's no arriving at a place where improvement is no longer necessary.

This is the case with principle more generally – there will always be new, concrete applications of the principle that will extend our own understanding.

All of that to say, improvement can go on indefinitely, bringing with it indefinite and ongoing levels of reward.

Slack

Thinking creatively requires time that isn't fully spoken for by specific tasks. Those that are building the software must know how to create this slack for themselves and be supported by those around them that understand this necessity. To ignore this will be to dramatically decrease the output of the People and Technology System.

Even as I write this book – an activity that is on par with writing software – I've gone through periods where I've tried to fill up every possible bit of energy with writing. When I've done that, I've found myself ultimately less creative, and have even had to step away from the writing process for extended periods to recover.

I've experienced the same effect in writing software; it tends to present as an uncomfortable feeling, which is really a warning light from our biological equipment telling us that we're degrading our own effectiveness.

It goes against a certain instinct to use the energy and time that we have when we have it. Though, following this instinct blindly ignores the discretion we have to trade future results for immediate ones. We don't want to try to kill the Golden Goose to immediately get all of the golden eggs – Covey well-illustrated the folly of that [2].

Adam Smith said it well in Wealth of Nations [3], "It will be found, I believe, in every sort of trade, that the man who works so moderately, as to be able to work constantly, not only preserves his health the longest but in the course of the year, executes the greatest quantity of work."

This, of course, was written in a time with very few commodities – when even things like making shoes or baking bread required a certain degree of creativity.

Independence of action

How quickly an organization can think and how quickly it can learn – what we might call "cognitive throughput" – is the primary bottleneck for the overall pace it takes delivering software.

This necessitates independence of action.

That is, the individual or group that chooses to work on a particular thing must be free to make choices about that thing (within appropriate, principled constraints) on their own. That is to say, colleagues that have chosen not to work on a thing should refrain from inserting opinions, or influence once the work – and their choice not to participate – has started.

The thinking and learning that represent the limiting factor in software development become obvious, immediately. The context, the discarded avenues of investigation, the state of the actual software, as well as a number of other details all represent applied cognitive effort. It must be re-applied any time someone steps in from the outside to attempt to add value to the build.

This means either the person or people doing the work must stop to teach, or the learner must invest a similar level of effort to come up to speed.

Not only is this wasteful, in the latter case, it also creates a race condition. The context that is being learned is quickly deprecated as new learning is accomplished by the original doer(s).

All of this to say, once a piece of software is selected to be built by a person or a group – and this includes everything from small, incremental maintenance, to greenfield systems – that person or group should exercise autonomy within the guiding principles of the organization.

So concretely, a person might choose a feature or bug to code by themselves and expect this autonomy. A pair or group – a "mob" as it is commonly called – might do the same and expect the same autonomy.

A common violation of this important idea at this level is the out-of-band code review. In this exercise, colleagues that haven't been involved in development will review and even block the integration of code once it's been written.

This applies as we get to higher levels of granularity as well. A team might select a set of features or a subsystem to build out. External reviews or approvals that would prevent independent action come with all the same problems listed above.

An example of this nature is the idea of the blocking architectural review – again, feature-focused teams lose their autonomy in the name of external review.

So, whatever the level of granularity, if a person or group chooses to build a piece of software – they should be left to do that within predetermined principles, and not subject to their work being stopped by outsiders.

No shared technology

Almost a corollary to the idea of independent action is that of refraining from sharing technology.

In the software development world, we often look to share resources. This can come in the form of creating libraries to share or of sharing runtime platforms like web-services or databases. This often stems from the perception that time, energy, and most importantly, money, can be saved because we can write something once and then repeatedly reuse it.

Sharing technology though necessitates third-party involvement in the particular piece of software being developed. Preceding the initial share, the shared software must be adapted to the new need – this means infringing on the autonomy of the team doing the sharing. A common trap in this is the belief that a piece of shared technology can be sufficiently generalized to meet any reasonable need. In the most basic sense, this is impossible because technology is only ever driven by concrete need. Often, the team that is building the software will attempt to imagine all of those concrete needs in order to generalize. This is radically expensive. Further, all of that expense is waste since much of the generalization will never be needed.

As we know, building out a piece of technology is not a point-in-time event. It continues on as needs evolve. So the same problems that arise with the initial share will continue for the lifetime of the shared resource.

These consequences eliminate any economy of scale advantage that might have otherwise been present. Worse still, the impact on the autonomy of the sharing team will dramatically decrease its throughput – while this is difficult to measure its cost would be difficult to overestimate.

There is one exception to the "no sharing" rule. That exception is that if the shared technology is productized, autonomy can be protected, and the costs controlled and offset.

There are two ways that this can happen. The first is to buy the shared piece of technology from an outside vendor – off the proverbial shelf. The second is that product infrastructure can be built around the resource.

The first case is common enough that it likely doesn't require any further elaboration.

To build product infrastructure around a resource that we are interested in sharing, though, is slightly more involved. The primary concern here is that, for the team it belongs to, workflow plumbing exists such that its priorities are balanced alongside the other products that the team owns. It's important to note that balanced priorities are those in which each of the changes in a list has a distinct relative level of importance. That is to say, there's only one first priority, only one second priority, all the way down to the nth priority – of which there is only one.

There are a lot of practical pieces that must be in place to ensure this – which we will get into in upcoming chapters.

The one big caveat in all of this is that practically, unless there is revenue tied to it, the organization simply won't spring for the process plumbing necessary to make your resource shareable.

Low resistance workflow

Naïve development workflow is a frequent culprit for deficient throughput on many teams.

An example might be a hypothetical production server needing to be configured in a specific way.

The obvious, and seemingly quick, solution to this is simply to perform the configuration manually. When we begin to look at the situation somewhat more broadly though, we can see that what might appear to be a quick solution actually slows delivery down considerably.

Frequently, configurations can change based on the specific needs of the system that is being built. Further, it is often required that additional servers be added and removed for activities such as functional testing or performance testing.

The manual work that looked quick at the beginning begins to multiply. Worse still, when changing configuration manually, errors can become more frequent. It also often happens that the knowledge of such manual work comes to exist only in the minds of the small handful of team members that actually carry it out regularly.

So, an approach that seemed like fast and efficient ends up being a powerful drain on throughput.

Another example of a naïve workflow causing a delivery slowdown is when a team chooses to forgo source control management. Fortunately, the tooling is so cheap and easy these days that this particular error is less frequently committed (pun intended).

But when this was a problem, it was often done because the software initially appeared to be small and easy to handle. Deploying by copying it directly to a server or transferring it using shared storage often appeared to save time. As the software or team expanded a little bit, it became clear that this quick fix would end up being another lamentable drain on throughput.

There are countless examples of this. This represents the primary pattern to handle, with workflow – it is hampered by the cumulative impact of a number of small choices. That is to say, making one of these poor choices may not sink your entire development practice. But a modestly long train of them will.

More importantly, every little bit of throughput you seek out of your system results in increased value even over time. It's similar to investing, you don't just get an immediate return – you get a "passive income" into the future.

A key part of building a People and Technology System, then, is to be intentional about the state of workflow – ensuring the resistance is as low as possible.

Code clarity

When we discuss code, we almost immediately think that we're talking about how we're going about building the Computer System. This is not quite accurate. It is, though, an important categorization to get right, and it turns on a vital truth.

For any code written, there are always two audiences. There is the computer that has to execute the code, creating a particular behavior. There is also the next developer – the person that must read, understand, and ultimately modify the code that is being written.

For the next developer – the person that tomorrow will be modifying the code that we're writing today – it is as important that we target them as that we target the particular behavior that we're creating. This may seem almost counter-productive. The whole point of building software systems is to make a computer do a particular thing. Isn't it?

Yes, it is. Though we have to mix into that another piece of the ultimate reality – that we can't solve a problem in one sitting – we always have to change our software.

Said with more snark, there are two kinds of software, the kind that never changes and the real kind.

In fact, that we have high-level programming languages at all is tacit support for this fact. If we didn't care about the next human understanding our code, and only worried about the functionality we create – we could write it all by hand in machine code.

So, aside from the features we release to our users, it's important that we are writing our code with the utmost level of clarity. That clarity is an investment in the speed of future changes – an improvement in the People and Technology System.

The two systems do get very close to each other in this specific case.

In reality, writing code is two separate activities. It's core to creating the features of the Computer System. It is also the creation of clarity (if done well) for the People and Technology System. How well these distinct but attached activities are performed can (and should) be judged and remediated separately.

For the purposes of building a People and Technology System, the task at hand with respect to our code is to ensure that it is written with as much clarity as possible.

Good people

The raw material of a great organization is great people. There are decades of platitudes that speak to this very real concern. Those platitudes arise because we generally understand this truth though have a very difficult time being and making the judgment calls necessary to really find and leverage great people.

We don't have much chance if we don't get down to the very basic building blocks. So let's ask the first question – what is a "good person." For the purposes of our discussion here, we won't ask that in the cosmic or absolute sense, we're not looking for perfect, but fitness for productivity, especially in the world of technology.

Jim Collins lays a fantastic foundation for all of this in Chapters 2 and 3 of his fantastic "Good To Great" [4]. In Chapter 3, Collins tells us to think first about who is on our team, and after we have that right, we are to think about what business we will do.

It is important to consider the work of finding the "right people for the bus" (to use Collins' phrase) first-class work, because having lower quality people radically hinders the organization's ability to build software.

So more specifically – what are the traits of "good people" – how do we know when we have the right people on the bus?

Collins notes in Chapter 3 that his research indicates that character is more important than technical capability. Similarly, he found that "No, those who turn good into great are motivated by a deep creative urge and an inner compulsion for sheer unadulterated excellence for its own sake."

Even more interesting, though, is his model of the "Level 5 Leader" in Chapter 2. The Level 5 Leader according to Collins has a combination of professional will and personal humility.

That is, this type of person aggressively pursues accomplishment not out of personal ambition or out of lust for position or recognition, but because accomplishment, adding value to others, is a worthwhile endeavor of its own. This type of person recognizes the intrinsic worth involved in serving his fellow man and pursues it vigorously. He calls it the Level 5 Leader – but really there's nothing that makes this exclusive to those that lead – I've always thought this should be called the Level 5 Person.

At any rate, all of this boils down to what we will, from now on, simply refer to as character – the ability to choose the best long-term course in the face of short-term passions.

Why does character make a difference in our ability to deliver software systems?

In fact, it not only makes a difference – it underpins every activity that leads to maximizing speed and thus to maximizing the value created by the software that we build. Each of the preceding parts of building a great People and Technology System, as we will see, rests entirely on character. This is because they each represent a tradeoff between short-term gratification and long-term success.

Disciplined Target Elaboration – the short-term pressure here is that development might seem to go faster if we spent the target elaboration time just building. The long-term reality is that we will quickly find ourselves off track if we don't regularly spend time clarifying our direction.

Adjustment with Learning – learning is uncomfortable as is changing our habits or direction. The short-term pressure here is avoiding that discomfort. The long-term reality is that there is no way that we will be able to grasp the all-but-infinite complexities of software development at first glance – without the ability to learn and adjust we will fail quickly, and completely.

Slack – the short-term pressure in creating or providing slack – is the emotional gratification that comes with the feeling of productivity. This is somewhat ironic – since that feeling can in this regard send us in the opposite direction of actual effectiveness. That actual effectiveness is the long-term reality – when we allow our creative mechanisms the space to breath, we ultimately bring more impact to our work.

Independence of Action – both as the director of dependent action and as the one receiving the direction, surrendered autonomy can seem appealing in the face of pressing business concerns. Decisions are simplified as less communication and learning are necessary – leading to potential reduced discomfort in either case. The long-term reality is that motivation and ability to adapt will be injured, which both negatively impact throughput.

No Shared Technology – this one is simple enough to understand; the short-term pressure is that it, on the surface, appears to eliminate the work of building the needed thing. The long-term reality is that sharing requires either building out the organizational plumbing to make the shared item a legitimate product, or, lacking that, an unfortunate and dramatic reduction in the autonomy (independence of action) of the share-er and the share-ee. This, of course, means slower delivery and less valuable software.

Low Resistance Workflow – the short-term pressure is simply the additional time recovered by not bothering with automation in the face of delivering a particular feature or system. The long-term reality is that neglecting automation will make a system increasingly difficult to manage as it grows. This will slow delivery and reduce the value of the software being created.

Code Clarity – the short-term pressure comes in the form of the discomfort that accompanies seeking the additional understanding that it takes to write code clearly. The long-term reality is that, like the unautomated workflow, as the system grows, if clarity is not maintained, the system will become increasingly expensive to change. This will slow delivery and reduce the value of the software being created.

Good People – not to be recursive here but having high-quality people is necessary to find and retain high-quality people. The short-term pressure is often to hire quickly in order to get someone in the door – since there's always so much to be doing. The long-term reality is that if we are selective particularly with the character of potential hires, every single area that's important to the ultimate goal of delivering high levels of value to our customer will suffer.

So, not only are high-character, high-quality people necessary in the general sense, as Collins demonstrates in his timeless classic, it is also non-negotiable in the specifics of software development. An organization will not be able to construct a successful People and Technology System with anything other than this prized raw material.

PUTTING IT ALL TOGETHER

Building a People and Technology System – one that, almost as a side-effect, regularly and with increasing speed, produces increasingly valuable software – requires several important pieces. It requires first and foremost leaders who can take the step back and see the components and causal relationships in the system. That is, they need to know that a system exists, and have the capacity and desire to reason about it.

More practically, that leader must understand that People and Technology Systems have a common set of these components and relationships. They must become experts not just in the general case of analyzing a system but specifically in analyzing this very specific type of system.

We laid these out in broad terms, highlighting the fact that the one underpinning piece of the People and Technology System is an organization made up of high-quality – that is to say, high-character – people. Without this, every single other necessary piece that would make a People and Technology System work will be compromised.

In the coming chapters, we will get increasingly tactical in how we put all of these pieces into place and in how we continuously mature in them once they are in place.

WORKS CITED

1. P. M. Senge, The Fifth Discipline, New York: Currency Doubleday, 1990.
2. S. Covey, The 7 Habits of Highly Effective People, 1989.
3. A. Smith, Wealth of Nations, London: W. Strahan and T. Cadell, 1776.
4. J. Collins, Good to Great, New York, NY: HarperCollins, 2001.

Chapter 7

Principles

The central question to answer as we examine how to build our software development organization is "What does it mean to be successful?" That is, how do we know that we've accomplished what we set out to do.

As you might have guessed from discussion in previous chapters, this question can be troublesome for a number of reasons. Is success measured by my happiness? Is it my manager's happiness? The CEO's? Surely, there is someone we can look to as a reference to determine our own success.

We posit that the ultimate win is creating value for a human being. Solving a problem with software and receiving a reasonable return for our efforts is the "success" we're looking for. However, the nature of developing software with groups can make this success difficult to see, let alone achieve.

Of course, a big part of this challenge proceeds directly from how we conceptualize the things that software development brings to the business.

To start, we often view problem discovery as distinctly part of the entrepreneurial work that a business engages in. Someone, probably one or more of the top leaders, finds a problem and the rest of the organization then spend their days solving it.

Even if there is a statement from the top of the organization attempting to define the "problem" that the organization is solving – streamlining banking, connecting friends and family, or bringing people together – actual problems will be far more concrete, discrete, and detailed.

This kind of statement – the ubiquitous mission statement – is important. But it doesn't really represent the practical, concrete problems that the business will be solving. Instead, it's more like a definition of the field that the organization will be playing on – an important limitation that keeps energy from being overly diluted.

This mission statement "problem" is distinct from the minute, discrete problems whose solutions will improve the lives of people. Finding and solving those – that's the practical entrepreneurialism that, now more than ever, is a continuous part of the thriving business.

The old view of business was that we created an offering and then we managed it operationally, for decades. We enjoyed our return for taking that idea and offering it over and over and over to consumers.

DOI: 10.1201/9781003382751-9

Technology – and software in particular – has catalyzed the transition to a more continuous search for and evolution of value being provided. Clayton Christensen, in "The Innovator's Dilemma" [1], shows, even in businesses built around physical products, that any company that hopes to find one product and provide that product repeatedly will not last long.

Since the publishing of this powerful work in 1997, software has revolutionized the economy.

Software now costs almost nothing to replicate [2]. Repeatedly offering the same value with software costs very little relative to repeatedly rebuilding a particular physical "widget." The effort an organization might have spent re-provisioning the same solution has evaporated. Because of this, organizational resources are free to be allocated far more heavily to problem discovery and solution creation – that is, to entrepreneurialism – or more specifically, to software development.

The key insight for us is that the actual development of software is core to the practical entrepreneurialism that many of today's organizations are regularly involved in carrying out. This is in contrast to the common, though mistaken, perception that software development is simply another business-operational competency akin to accounting or a production line.

As we discussed in Chapter 2, this challenge combined with the exploding communication networks that arise when trying to discover and create with a group of people creates a unique set of problems.

Getting our heads around this set of problems is the first, most important hurdle to begin to be intentional about the software we develop. To unpack this and gain an understanding of the interactions between these challenges and to figure out how to leverage them for our benefit leads us to the powerful idea of systems thinking.

As we discussed in Chapter 4 and then again in Chapter 6, there are complex causal relationships, and many varied components involved in an organization that builds software. In fact, we laid out the two systems that we build. We build a computer system to provide value to the user, and we build a people and technology system that builds the computer system.

Knowing this, you could analyze your software-developing system, find the leverage points, and derive the best shape of the people and technology system – a shape that will give you the results that you're looking for.

Fortunately, we've already done this and we laid out this shape in Chapter 6.

This shape is based on another key insight that the speed of delivery is the ultimate lever in creating value for your customer. The faster you move, the more experiments you can conduct. More experiments per unit time mean that the knowledge of the problem and the shape of the solution come into closer alignment with each other and with reality. Further, as a matter of human nature, we value something now more than something later.

The shape of the people and technology system that we put forward in Chapter 6 will result in speed and thus the value that represents the success we are hungry for.

How do we create that system though?

Chapter 5 discusses the importance of leadership. There are, after all, people involved in this people and technology system – which means that if we want to get things shaped in the right way, we have to influence people. "Leadership is influence, nothing more nothing less" [2].

What actions, specifically, do we need to take to ensure success – to be really about the business of creating value and reaping return.

Every context that we find ourselves in, when it comes to building software, is unique. The shape of the people and technology systems is in varying degree of fitness for our ultimate outcomes – and the individuals have varying mixes of the competencies that result in great software.

Because of this, what we will first lay out in this chapter will be a framework of principles. These principles will give you the best starting point from which to act within the context of your software development organization. They will provide a basis for strategy – while at the same time being a firm foundation for tactical decision-making.

Building and growing a software development organization is an art, though – one that will take a lifetime to master. So simply reading about these principles is the beginning. Absorbing, thinking about, and applying them to a specific context is the path to mastery.

Once we have this framework in place, we will – in the following chapter – discuss the specific competencies of software development, how to leverage them for the best outcome, and how to ensure you and your team are always growing in your ability to apply them.

The four principles are as follows.

PRINCIPLE #1: SEEK SUSTAINABLE SPEED

Delivery speed itself, as we've said repeatedly, is our primary interest in software development. It is almost identical to the value we provide to our customer.

So it should come as no surprise that speed would be a part of the primary principle that we apply as we're building and growing our software practice.

It should be noted though that we're looking for sustainable speed. There are many approaches and techniques in software development that, in the short term, appear to lead to fast delivery, yet ultimately lead to slower delivery.

The principle then is two-fold. Aggressively pursue speed, though temper that pursuit with the consideration that choices that appear to provide it often do not.

Another consideration in the use of this principle is that, after time, leaders develop an intuition for the choices that result in speed. As we mentioned when we discussed thinking tools, developing this intuition is in fact a powerful improvement in speed itself. This is due to the fact that less deliberation will likely be needed before taking a particular approach.

That must be balanced against the known shortcomings with intuition. An intuited answer may be arrived at faster, but it is also likely to be less accurate.

As an example, imagine that a team is working on a large system. The system is in production; the company uses it operationally and is, generally, structured around how the system works.

There are ongoing changes to be made and the development team basically makes changes as they come in. Once a week, they strategize about the best use of their time.

Imagine, now, that a bug report comes in.

Seemingly, the fastest thing to do would be for someone to simply fix the bug and move on.

This is a common scenario and this seemingly correct course of action is a common reaction. We might further complicate our scenario by considering the political clout or noisemaking ability of the bug requester. The more painful or the louder the request, the more speed that simply granting it appears to bring.

If we step back and apply some thought to this question, we will notice something unexpected. This is a scenario where a solution that might look fast on the surface is actually likely to slow down overall delivery.

Some questions we might ask to get at the deeper context:

- What is the developer working on that the bug will pre-empt?
- What context will they lose?
- What is the trade-off in value between those things?

These questions seem simple on the surface. They get at the challenges with this common scenario though. In fact, if we are asking these questions in real-time, we are taking the first steps toward real, sustainable speed.

There is a challenge though. Even if you do ask these very appropriate questions, two additional problems arise. One of these is that the analysis itself is actually quite cost-intensive. The other is that the analysis usually involves the developer in question. This means that you're adding a non-optional, non-trivial expense in the best case. In the worst case, you're destroying the context, and pre-empting the very work you intended to make the decision about.

We should note that altering developer work by directly requesting a change of direction is almost always a losing proposition. While this is certainly a counterintuitive reality, we must recognize the need to stop and think when things that seem like choices for speed present themselves. In fact, in my experience, the more forcefully a situation presents itself, the more likely making the obvious or low resistance choice will not be a choice for speed.

So the first step is to recognize this particular pattern. That is, don't take decisions about delivery rate for granted. Make a habit of – at least in your mind – stepping back and thinking about the effects of the decision that might reach further into time and further into your system.

To recap, in this scenario, we were first confronted with the need for the bug fix. That was decision number one – should we just interrupt development work for the given fix. The second decision was how much trouble should we make out of whether or not we allow the fix request to go through. The third decision was how to deal with a loud stakeholder. At each of these decision points, we can fairly dramatically impact delivery speed either positively or negatively. I'm sure you can imagine several of either possibility. It's important to note though that, in very common scenarios like this one, there are often manifold ways to improve your impact or to damage it.

To use the thinking tools we developed in earlier chapters, you may come upon a situation like this and initially have to be pretty explicit in your thinking. You might trace out in your mind, or on a whiteboard, the impacts and the causal relationships that come into play. You might deduce the impacts that we have outlined as flowing naturally from the way the people and technology system functions. You might even opt to verify that deduction with an experiment – carefully letting change come into the group in the manner that you believe will cause problems.

Assuming you're noting your learnings and internalizing the operation of the system, this explicit thinking will become an increasingly intuitive action. You'll simply know by seeing a situation when it is fraught with danger to your people and technology system.

More importantly, of course, you'll know how to deal with it quickly.

The general solution to our scenario is simply to create regular checkpoints where change can enter the team, and to hold those checkpoints to be sacrosanct. Those checkpoints may be based on a unit of time or completion of the preceding work, but whatever the barrier is, it should be held up without fail. This follows directly from the problem we laid out above – as soon as we stop to validate if the return warrants the investment, we've already made the bulk of the investment – so it's always a de facto choice to proceed with whatever the change is.

To discover a solution like this for yourself means following the same thinking patterns that seeing the problem takes. At first, it will be explicit as you and your team learn the techniques for dealing with a particular problem. You may arrive at those techniques deductively by thinking through the details of the people and technology system, or you might try some different approaches experimentally, or you might apply a combination of the two.

In both circumstances, finding and solving the problem, using thinking from those outside your organization, can be helpful. In terms of thinking tools, this is like adding premises to your deductive reasoning, or starting points for experiments for your inductive thought. However aggressively or tentatively you use outside resources, though, it is important to know that there has been thinking done in this space and that it's available for your use. Though ultimately, you are responsible for the choices you make – so don't take outside advice carelessly.

PRINCIPLE #2: ADVOCATE AUDACIOUS AUTONOMY

Autonomy is powerful because it results in speed.

Its appeal is doubled because it's something that human beings enjoy and were made for. No matter the time, cultural context, or location – human beings more thoroughly enjoy their lot and reach higher levels of performance when they enjoy a high degree of personal liberty.

So the great software leader recognizes the direct connection between autonomy and the speed that equates to value in the hands of our customers as well as the powerful impact this has on the lives of the people carrying out this work.

What is autonomy though – if we get down to it, what does personal liberty – personal freedom – look like in the software world?

Autonomy exists when those performing the work never come to a point where the continuation of their work depends on the involvement of anyone not involved in performing that same work.

This is particularly easy for me to recognize if I am the one doing the work. Again, personal liberty is such a hardwired part of being human that it takes quite a bit of conditioning to accept the idea that it's ok to not have personal liberty. This is true whether you're a software engineer working on code every single day, or a leader at any level in an organization. If the work you're conducting is blocked (to use a popular software term) on the work of someone who isn't actively involved in that work, your sense of autonomy will drop.

If you're an engineer, this work may be on the computer system itself. Your boss, or a colleague from a different part of the organization, or even a team member not involved in the specific work may stop your work from proceeding, dropping your sense of autonomy. Many times, diminution of autonomy is put solely at the feet of the legitimate authority – a person's manager. This casts too small of a net for autonomy violators.

Similarly, if you're a leader, you may find yourself working on the people and technology system. Your work can be halted by subordinates, your own manager, or folks from across the organization.

A prime example from the former case is a variation on the problem we discussed in the earlier section on speed. Imagine that you are an engineer building a particular computer system. You are in the middle of a particular feature, moving toward a goal that you and your team thoroughly discussed. Three days into the work on that feature – with about three days of work left – a strong personality from outside the team demands you stop and work on another feature. You cannot continue the work you were involved in, and you can't even start the new work until you understand the demand – a double anti-autonomy hit.

If you're a leader working on your people and technology system, you can find yourself in a similar situation. An important part of making sure your people and technology system is positioned to deliver is to ensure that they are automating their workflow in alignment with the architecture of their system and the shape of the team.

A common "blocker" in this situation can be an external "dev-ops" team – a team built around the idea of building engineering automation for others. Your assignment to your team might be something like – "your development process isn't automatic enough, please continue to move us into a place where our automation is as thorough as it can be." The external dev-ops team might insert itself in the work with varying degrees of forcefulness, but the bottom line is that to one degree or another, your sense of autonomy as an engineering leader is dramatically impacted.

So wherever you find yourself in an organization that builds software – autonomy will always be at risk of being reduced or eliminated.

As a leader, you need to recognize this as you are building your people and technology system. Creating autonomy for yourself and for your team will allow you to deliver (sustainably) faster. That will result in more value.

The real question, though, is how do you create autonomy?

Strictly speaking, you don't.

Human beings – unless they've been subject to dramatic conditioning to the contrary – expect to be autonomous. We expect to be able to learn about and then manipulate our environment without much interference.

In an organization, then, the lesson to take is that promoting autonomy is about not preventing it. To the greatest extent possible, you shouldn't step in on others' work, and similarly – to the greatest extent possible – you should prevent people from stepping in on the work that's not theirs.

Of course, this last bit is where it gets tricky, because are we not reducing autonomy in hopes of allowing more of it?

This is a very key part of the equation – and why we need to be so clear about this principle.

It is not legitimate autonomy to use it to take autonomy from someone else or to give up your own.

So in the case of one party looking to remove the autonomy of another by injecting themselves into the workflow of the latter, we have to be comfortable stepping in to stop that in whatever way that we can. The same is true in the case where one person or even a group seeks to reduce their own autonomy. This, surprisingly, happens more than one might think. The latter case is usually simply a misunderstanding of the impact that making a particular choice has on the degree of their own autonomy.

With all of this, there's an important caveat.

What if people are doing the wrong things – counterproductive things – things that work against the goals and intent of the organization?

The solution to this is to embed guiding principles into individuals and teams and to shape the people and technology system in such a way as to make the intent of the organization the path of least resistance. The more that you lead in terms of guiding principles and through the structure of the system, the more you can be sure of a positive outcome while not doing damage to the autonomy of your people.

There still is the potential that a decision made by an individual is so bad that it needs to be dealt with immediately. In this case, the most important thing to do is to know ahead of time how to recognize a decision of this caliber – making sure that the guideline is as loose as possible. Will the decision cause loss of life or perhaps cause a certain amount of financial loss or...? Whatever your criteria are – the more latitude you can provide prior to intervention, the faster your team will be.

To reprise our example from the previous principles, let's imagine again that an outside player brings a change to a developer while they are in the middle of working through another, unrelated piece of development.

There are a couple of things to consider as we do this.

First, there is legitimate concern that the requested feature could represent something so important to the business and its customers that it is worth stepping on the autonomy of the team members that could potentially be charged with its building. It's a legitimate concern – but in my experience – a highly unlikely one. Though unlike the effort evaluation, uncovering the value of the feature can be done by the requestor, so simply asking the question doesn't eliminate autonomy.

Second, the obvious solution is simply to tell the requestor to put the feature in the queue and wait until the team has a chance to pull it and work on it.

As we mentioned, viewed simply, this can be seen as impacting the autonomy of the requestor. Though, as we said, autonomy that is used to reduce the autonomy of someone else isn't legitimate, so putting a stop to this is justified.

However, the way to eliminate the need to even have to step in with this kind of situation is to shape the system and habits of interaction such that the expectation by anyone asking for a feature is that they are asking the development team for help and that it involves conversation and collaboration to move toward execution.

Done well, this means no one has to step in even on the illegitimate autonomy of the requestor and the requestor doesn't accidentally step on the autonomy of the development team.

PRINCIPLE #3: REITERATE RESONANT RATIONALE

In the previous section, we glossed over how we might go about creating direction in terms of principles. In order to be guided by principles though, it's important to first understand them. That is, after all, why we are starting with principles in this chapter as we begin our journey to create and operate software development organizations.

This approach though makes up our third principle.

It's a principle that's been articulated in a number of different ways over many years.

John Maxwell has called it "Vision Casting."

Simon Sinek has called it "Starting with The Why."

We will call it Reiterating Resonant Rationale.

The idea is that when an organization has a shared, high-level, not too specific set of beliefs about the direction it is going, people can make concrete tactical decisions that are both pushing in the same direction as the rest of the organization and simultaneously autonomous.

This magical formula is the key that resolves the seeming tension between every individual exercising liberty while not diluting the focus that working together as a team creates.

It's not as easy, though, as it sounds on the surface.

There are three points that we baked into our formulation of this timeless principle.

Reiterate

It's not as simple as putting a vision statement up on the wall, or in your email signature. It's not as easy as "rolling out" the vision at a one-time meeting.

To really share the direction of the organization, that idea must be repeated ... a lot. It must be repeated within the context of relationship. It must be repeated in real-time communication where questions can be asked, body-language can be read, and it must be communicated by people that believe in it.

Resonant

Not only must the idea be repeated it must be something that a given individual can believe in and feel that they own. This feeling of originating or owning the direction is almost more difficult to achieve then the repetition necessary for people to comprehend the idea in the first place.

One of the most powerful ways to build a resonant idea is to involve everyone in its formulation, from the earliest possible stages. There is art to this – and many times it's impractical to put an entire organization in front of a blank whiteboard.

The more intentionally we can put the unfinished idea in front of the entire organization, the more thorough the buy-in will be. Again, this doesn't mean everyone is in front of the blank whiteboard as we start. Selecting from a set of options, allowing feedback on a result, or even providing – if no other possibility is available – a clear choice whether to continue with the organization under the new direction or not, if explicitly made, can generate the necessary buy-in.

As with any other individual to individual influence – the more the directional principles are open to change, the more the organization as an entity is influence-able by its members – the more that the individual members will be influence-able by the organization. This means deeper internalization of a vision that proceeds from the latter.

Rationale

The substance of the direction needs to follow logically from the context the organization is in externally and in its relationship to its members.

That is to say, if a person is to internalize the formulated direction, they must believe that it connects directly to the reasons for their partnering with the organization – the impact they expect to make on the world around them as well as the return the expect to reap for that impact.

That is to say, it's important to understand the environment the organization is working in. Formulating a direction may seem like an entirely open-ended exercise, but it's not. It won't resonate if it doesn't fit logically into its environment.

This is why we place so much value on and have spilt so much ink in an effort to really describe the nature of software development. Not only is it very different from many other areas of human endeavor – if it isn't understood well by its practitioners, formulating a good, principled direction will be impossible. This short-circuits autonomy, which short-circuits the ability to deliver rapidly and means that we will just produce far less value.

PRINCIPLE #4: SUFFICIENTLY SEPARATE SYSTEMS

Also reaching the level of principle is the idea that systems – computer systems – should be sufficiently separated.

This is another principle whose primary value lies in its support of autonomy.

When a system or systems that belong to one team begin to become connected with other systems such that deployment or even development begin to necessitate conversations and interaction between members on the separate teams, we've created systemic dependencies. These are dependencies that individuals (even leaders) are powerless to avoid.

Looked at from the point of view of autonomy, this means we've put an almost immovable obstacle in front of the autonomy of the two teams involved.

And as we've repeated a few times already, less autonomy means less speed, less speed means less value delivered to the customer.

Organizations that find themselves in a situation in which they are violating this principle often feel as if there's no other option than to simply accept the state of the system along with its negative impact on autonomy. Those that haven't gotten to the point yet often treat the problem as easily avoidable.

Neither of these senses are true.

The way that organizations get into this situation is by making short-sighted decisions as they begin to scale.

Initially, a software development organization will only have a single team, so there is no opportunity for one team to have any interest in another team's system. So, almost no thought is given to this problem because it presents absolutely no pain. The initial challenges begin as the team outgrows itself.

Once the team is 10 or 12 people strong, it will begin to lament their situation – looking back at the speed and collaboration of days gone by. As the teams grow, the necessity of breaking into smaller groups will become unavoidable. At 20 people, any coordination becomes almost untenable, to say nothing of the daily standup and the common expectation that it stays shorter than 15 minutes.

Having waited this long to split was the first mistake. The pain will now be such that the most intuitive, most direct solution will become very appealing. This is unfortunate because the most effective solution here is quite sophisticated and counterintuitive. In almost every case, since the pain has reached such a height, the organization will choose the suboptimal relief in favor of the more sustainable long-term solution.

The obvious and wrong solution is to split by skillset – which is what most organizations choose. That is to say, we'll make a team of our "backend" developers, "frontend" developers, "DevOps" developers, "database" developers – we'll shape teams around shared skillsets.

At this point, you're probably asking – what does this have to do with sufficiently separated systems?

This requires a quick explanation about an interesting effect in software development – "Conway's Law" [3].

Conway's Law – while perhaps not a law in any strict sense – is uncanny in how predictive it actually is. It basically says that an organization will create software that matches its shape. Practically, this means that when the shape of the organization and the shape of the software get out of alignment, there will be discomfort that is only sated by making the two match.

Applying that to the story we were telling, our frontend/backend/database teams will, over time, result in "systems" that align with those teams.

What's the problem with that you might ask.

Value to the customer – requests from outside the team – that is, what we are really building – is never a database table, a JavaScript function, or a Jenkins job. Real value is in features. Features cut across each of the areas that we've broken our teams down into.

That is to say, we have created systemic dependencies between our teams. We have structured our organization to reduce the autonomy of teams and individuals.

The solution to this challenge is to maintain as a principle that every system should belong to and only require the work of one team. Concretely, this can imply a number of different tactical approaches – which we will get into in later chapters. For our purposes now, though, if you find yourself with sufficiently separated systems, make sure you're doing nothing to compromise that. If you find yourself with blurring lines between systems, you should remediate that as quickly as possible.

WORKS CITED

1. C. M. Christensen, The Innovator's Dilemma, 1997.
2. P. McBreen, Software Craftsmanship, Boston: Addison-Wesley, 2002.
3. J. Maxwell, 21 Irrefutable Laws of Leadership, Nashville, TN: Thomas Nelson, 1998.
4. M. Conway, "Mel Conway's Home Page | Conway's Law" [Online]. Available: https://www.melconway.com/Home/Conways_Law.html

Chapter 8

Tactical competence

In unpacking how to lead a software development organization, we've looked first at basic leadership skill – how well are we able to influence people. Then, we looked more specifically at what it really takes to build up the people and technology system at a high level – following that up with general principles that can be leveraged to this end.

In this chapter, we will look at the tactical competencies that will make these principles a reality. They are competencies over which the leader should have an increasing level of mastery. They are competencies that the entire organization should be pursuing as their primary avenue of growth.

These competencies – when applied with skill and thoughtfulness – will realize the principles we spent the last chapter discussing – and ultimately will result in the speed of delivery and value to the customer that has been our singular focus.

It is key though to recognize that these competencies are the area where the software development leader really does lead. He should be ahead of the pack in terms of mastery but also in terms of acting in alignment with them. Now that we've laid all our background, it is at this point where software development begins to look like a typical human endeavor.

That is to say, leading in each of these means several things. It means, first and foremost, understanding them deeply – how they work within the framework of the principles that we laid out earlier. This understanding should connect the specific actions and targets in each of these competencies to the ultimately reality that we are working with. It's a common thing to see that engineering organizations will take the tools and specific techniques that have been successful in one organization and attempt to apply them thoughtless in an entirely different context. Sometimes there are some positive results; many times there aren't. The reason for this is that if an approach like that is taken, we're leaving it up to a high degree of chance that the solution fits the local needs.

One example of this that was fairly widespread was the reaction to the so-called "Spotify Model." In 2014, a series of videos explained how Spotify, as an organization, chose to structure its software engineering efforts. The different components of their habits and process were named in quirky ways.

DOI: 10.1201/9781003382751-10

Their explanations did however reveal a fairly thorough understanding of some of the principle for which their quirky-named components were the concrete realization.

Throughout the industry, rather than working to really understand the principles, many organizations simply copied the quirky names and more-or-less kept their same way of working – with their same, not quite connected to reality, mental models. After some time, there was some grumbling that "The Spotify Model" didn't work – or didn't work that well.

This, of course, is not at all surprising – while those adopting "the model" were using the nomenclature and some of the concrete techniques that Spotify was displaying – they still weren't doing the work to actually understand the dynamics at play in people and technology systems, and in particular, in the people and technology system in their organization.

The next thing that you need to do, as you use these competencies to lead is to pro-actively work to put the structure in place that enables them. As we get into each of these areas, we will see that much of their efficacy comes not from individual choices that are made during execution but from the interplay between individuals and different parts of the system.

This leads to the final, and certainly not the least important, issue to consider as you are leading your organization. You must keep your view up and on the broader interactions, not letting it become entangled in the delivery of specific features. This isn't as easy as it sounds. There are a number of ways where the distinction between looking at the people and technology system and looking at the computer system itself can become blurred. For example, one of the competencies is software craftsmanship – making sure code is clear and easy to read. The distinction between the broader concern of overall clarity and the creation of the specific capability that's currently being delivered can be tricky to see since the actual typing of the code affects both. The broader clarity of the codebase, though, emerges from more than just the one code change that's currently being entered. Similar complexities exist in the other competencies as well.

The real take-away is that to lead, you should start by placing your view on the people and technology system, and then be careful not to be drawn into the work on the computer system. Do not start by thinking about a specific concrete piece of work, or you've already basically lost this battle.

So – to jump right in, there are four competencies – people and process, software craftsmanship, architecture, and workflow automation. In this chapter, we will look at their impact in terms of the leadership principles we laid out in the last chapter, and then discuss what a leader needs to be able to recognize how it supports speed and value, and when it might be off track and need some correcting.

We will get deep into the details of each of these competencies in Section III – the intent in this chapter is to provide a basic look at this, particularly from the leadership perspective.

PEOPLE AND PROCESS

People and process is a wide-ranging competency. An organization that works well should have people that have mastery in each of these competencies (or the potential for it) and should be arranged such that they work well together.

There are several considerations to have well in mind when considering the level of mastery of the organization.

First, the overall level of mastery in an organization will determine the level of value that is being delivered.

Second, the ability to judge level of mastery is limited by the level that an individual has attained. This important reality has some important implications. In hiring, the people used to evaluate potential hires will represent a cap on the mastery that might be selected. The leader, ultimately, acts as a cap on mastery as well. So, not only should the leader be pursuing and pushing mastery with an extreme sense of urgency, but he should also only use his best folks in the interview process.

Finally, and probably least obviously, if there is too little mastery in the organization, it can create a stagnant, weak culture that will neither promote growth nor attract folks with higher degrees of mastery. So, if you will be including folks on the lower end of the mastery spectrum, it's important that in the overall balance, they don't make up too large a segment of the organization.

In terms of the structure of the workflow and the way that team members work with each other, there are a number of useful practical tools available. There are a lot of intricate problems, many of which we outlined in Section I when we looked at the unique problems of creating software with a group of people. The Scrum Framework [1] is one of my favorite tools – it can frequently be taken right off of the shelf and applied to almost any software development context. Built into its seemingly arbitrary habits and structures are years of wisdom in dealing with the uniqueness of software development.

Ultimately, you can't stop there – really mastering this competency means doing the systems thinking for yourself. It means understanding all of the competing and complementary forces – all of the components and causal relationships – and being able to leverage them in a dynamic context with different people and differing sets of skills.

As we've said, getting people and process right will lead directly to speed and thus to value delivered to the customer. Having people and process dialed in also leads to autonomy. This is true because people with mastery will understand and know how to support autonomy in others. A well-structured workflow also supports autonomy in that it keeps working groups small and decisions as local as possible.

SOFTWARE CRAFTSMANSHIP

Building a computer system involves creating art for two distinct audiences. The first is the user of that computer system – the intuition that can be leveraged when engaging with the actual functionality represented by the system, and the potency with which the system meets the need of the user are primary measures of this.

No less important than the user of the functionality is the next engineer that will need to change and thus to understand the system. This "next" engineer may be the one building the system currently or it may be a different person in the future. In both cases, the need to comprehend the system rapidly and thoroughly is both important and hinges as much or more on the attention that the original author brings to the system than it does on the ability of the future engineer to understand it.

If comprehension weren't something we were concerned about, programming would better be done with machine code instructions rather than high-level languages. Those high-level languages provide all sorts of advantages in terms of viewing things in the abstract, constructing our instructions in the abstract, and giving those abstractions clear names that communicate intent without providing unnecessary detail.

The purpose of all this, again, is to create behavior that the computer will provide with code that a human being can understand and modify.

One objection to our example about writing code in machine code rather than a high-level language might be to point out that we're not using the language not to provide readable code to some future developer, but because it is simply easier to write code in that high-level language. The question we have to ask ourselves with regard to this objection is – why is it easier? It's easier because as we're writing, refreshing ourselves on what already exists takes far less energy in the high-level language. We are the next engineer in this case, even though the comprehension and creation are happening simultaneously.

Consider a simple example – writing a string of characters to the screen. Even leveraging operating system calls – which are in themselves a form of higher-level programming – there are a number of things to do.

- Define the string to write.
- Load 3–4 different registers with command values (numbers) and memory locations.
- Make the system call to write.
- Make the system call to return the control to the operating system.

Making one more simplifying assumption – that we're using assembler rather than actually keying in the machine instructions – we still have 15–20 lines of code to write. Almost none of this code directly reflects what we're looking to do – viz. writing a string to the screen.

In a high-level languages Python or JavaScript, this can be reduced to a single line of code that concisely expresses our intent. The effort to re-integrate the activity being performed is far lower. Further, this reality is multiplied over the many specific actions that are taken throughout the course of real-world systems.

The activity that's expressed in the CPU-specific instructions is necessary. When we're printing out a line, we have to make that system call, and we have to get the registers set up correctly, or nothing is going to be printed to the screen. So, to meet the needs of the first audience, the user, we need to make sure these things happen. Our user is expecting "Hello World" to be put to their monitor, and in order for that to happen, certain things must be presented to the CPU.

So for the first audience, there really is no difference between the 20 lines of CPU instructions (whether that's assembler or the actual keyed-in machine code). For our second audience though – for the next engineer, the person who has to comprehend the code in order to change it – for them, the two are not equivalent.

The sheer quantity of code creates additional comprehension work. The fact that in the machine/assembler code the instructions are conceptually unrelated to the goal adds yet more to the comprehension work. With the difficulty in comprehension comes an increase in time to make a particular change.

Software craftsmanship is reducing the effort needed to comprehend code.

It's balancing the needs of the audience that's expecting behavior with the needs of the audience that's expecting to be able to change the behavior with a reasonable amount of effort.

Ultimately, it maximizes the value that the software-developing organizations provide to its customers. It does this by directly supporting the four principles that underpin productive software engineering – sustainable speed, autonomy, resonant rationale, and separate systems.

Sustainable speed is a direct result of a well-crafted system. This is due to the fact that ease of comprehension is the fundamental focus and ability to change a system rapidly is directly related to how quickly it can be understood.

Further, autonomy is enhanced with well-crafted code. This may seem counterintuitive, but it is true for two reasons.

Creating a system that is quick to understand and thus to change creates the impression of competence with outside observers. Stakeholders – people with an interest in the creation or modification of the system – that don't otherwise have visibility into or understand how the system changes – have a more favorable impression of the skill of the team building it if they are quick to respond to requests.

As we mentioned, crafting a system well means having intention revealing abstractions that allow rapid comprehension. A side effect of building things in this manner is that the system can be viewed as being made up of building blocks that can be rearranged readily. The common term for this is modularity.

This modularity means that your systems have clear lines across which different people and teams may work, without having to create request and response queues. For example, if we go back to our Python example of writing a string of text to the screen, we call the "print" command with the string as a parameter. Details of the required system call may change – for example, as we move from Linux to Windows. As a caller – or rather as a user of this abstraction – I don't have to get involved in the implementation details of the print statement.

Very similarly, well-crafted systems – or rather the modularity that is implied by their high level of craft – allow straightforward separation of systems at higher levels.

Finally, well-crafted systems support the idea of "resonant rationale" in that it doesn't hinder changing or refining direction regularly. A more poorly crafted system – because of the difficulty involved in change – would make engineers less eager to change it. It would be more difficult to bring it into alignment with a healthy and thus constantly evolving rationale. Simply put, well-crafted systems multiply the ease with which buy-in is obtained to a flexible vision.

ARCHITECTURE

Architecture can be a rather fuzzy, poorly defined idea. As with many popular ideas that are put to use within the world of software development, they can take on different meanings in different contexts and can offer more confusion than clarity.

Architecture can often be boiled down to something along the lines of, "the high-level structure of a computer system." Though there are two distinct ways to think of the high-level structure of a computer system and indeed, the idea of architecture can be used across both of them.

These two areas are the feature set – the actual behaviors of the system – and the set of technical building blocks used to provide them.

In the latter case, when we use the word architecture, we are almost always viewing things above the level of actual code. We are often discussing database servers, queue providers, container abstractions and orchestration, and any number of off-the-shelf or in-house-built components that don't themselves represent the features that our customers are interested in but provide the capabilities our technical teams need in order to provide those features.

The former view – that the features of a system define its "structure" or architecture – is a bit of an abuse of the term. We will get into why this is in later chapters as we clarify the tactical specifics of delivering great architecture, and as we discuss the people and process components necessary and sufficient for managing and controlling the direction that development of a particular system takes.

For our purposes now, the structure of a computer system above the level of code is what we are addressing and the meaning that the term will hold. Arguably, it makes sense to talk about structure and architecture even at the level of code. Drawing a distinction between micro and macro architectures can be helpful here, though we will tend to refer to code-level structural choices more as software craftsmanship since viewing things through that lens at that level is more helpful.

Now that we have dialed in the meaning of architecture a little bit, the one question we want to ask is how does this support the principles we laid out in the last chapter? More accurately, the question should be – how does *good* architecture support the principles laid out in the last chapter?

So there's one more distinction to be made before we proceed – viz. what makes architecture good?

This is an important question, because there are all sorts of architectures that can be chosen. In fact, even if no one makes a conscious choice, architecture will emerge. This is due to the reality that the computer will need instructions to accomplish any non-trivial tasks that we build for, and choices will have to be made about how to arrange those instructions. Even if minimal energy is spent on this, our need to be able to understand will lead us to some kind of arrangement.

All of that to say – you will have an architecture. How do you decide if you've got a good one? Further, is that question even useful?

To start with, let's take one more step back – what impacts can an architecture have on our ability to put value in the hands of our customers?

Often when the question of the quality of architecture is brought forward, discussion centers around so-called "non-functional requirements" or NFRs. NFRs are things like up-time, throughput, or security. They are feature sets that tend to take a bit of extra work to uncover, because they are broad sets of things that users tend to assume are part of any system – even though the levels of the different NFRs can vary widely.

With all that said, NFRs are features and while large component selection and usage can impact their delivery, they should be handled in the same way and with the same process every other feature should be. Strictly speaking, they are not a thing that we should pull into the question of architecture, because their specifics and priority should be decided on in an appropriate context. And while many of the specific decisions and details concerning the big blocks that do make up the architecture of the system make a big impact on some of these features, those specifics need to be driven clearly by the user.

So clarifying our definition of architecture a bit more, the structure of the computer system above the level of the code without regard for any feature it delivers is architecture. The features we build may drive certain specifics about the architecture, but its arrangement as such is the only thing we are concerned with when we discuss architecture.

Back to our question then – what impacts can an architecture have on our ability to put value in the hands of our customers?

The real impact is through two of our four principles – architecture can be arranged such that we have separate systems through which multiple teams can work in harmony while maintaining autonomy. That autonomy means we deliver more rapidly – which gets us to our goal, more value for our customers.

All of that to say – good architecture is architecture that maintains autonomy across all of our delivery teams by keeping their systems separate. This may be a bit of a counterintuitive result, but it also radically simplifies the idea of architecture next to the confused tangle that it normally represents.

WORKFLOW AUTOMATION

There are a number of activities that take place throughout the course of taking an idea from the back of the proverbial napkin out to the production system and into the hands of the user.

We write code, collaborate with others, test, deploy, and observe running systems. Much of this can be automated by just applying a little bit of intentionality throughout the course of building the system.

That automation means that a computer will be doing many of the tasks that we would have otherwise been doing. This means it will be faster and more accurate – where more accurate really boils down to still faster execution.

As with software craftsmanship, the additional speed that is inherent with automating workflow also results in additional credibility and thus autonomy.

Autonomy is also enhanced because, when easily automated processes are left manual, the team working on the features begin to be distracted by the manual work they create for themselves. Leadership often solves this problem by pulling one of the more obvious, but ultimately counterproductive levers – creating an additional team primarily responsible for taking care of the manual work – historically known as "operations" or ops, more recently styled, "DevOps." This creates a dependency on the newly created team autonomy has incrementally decreased.

PRINCIPLES AND PRACTICE

Chapter 7's principles include sustainable speed, autonomy, resonant rationale, and separate systems; these are the guardrails that make for an effective software-developing organization. Remembering that the ultimate target is that first principle – sustainable speed – is what leads to real value and that the remaining three principles really serve to support that principle and that natural outcome. In this chapter, we introduced the practical mechanisms that bring these principles to life.

The more the leader understands these powerful principles and masters the competencies that embody them, the more value a given team will produce.

Not only because the team will be structured such that value will be almost unavoidable but because the leader will be able to select team members that have attained high degrees of their own mastery in these important areas, further freeing the leader to refine the people and technology system.

WORK CITED

1. K. Schwaber, "Scrum.org," 2023. [Online]. Available: https://scrum.org

Section III

Areas of competence

Chapter 9

Areas of competence

Overview

In this section, we will be diving deeply into the practical, tactical competencies that make for a great software development organization. We viewed these briefly in the last section – in the last chapter. The perspective we were taking there was looking at the competencies as a set of things that will have to be led through.

In the coming chapters, we will discuss specifically how to execute on each of these competencies. We will examine the practical steps to take to make them work, the ways we can grow in them, and the pitfalls we might come across in each of these arenas.

In the chapters and sections leading up to this, we've laid the groundwork so that these competencies not only make sense, but in many ways begin to appear obvious.

In the first section, we went over the unique shape and unique qualities of software development. It is invention – it's creative, instinctive, and unlike many familiar domains of work, it doesn't really lend itself to concrete, repeatable planning. We can depend on the reality that we will never know what we're building until we've built something that our potential user can try out.

We also noticed that, unlike many creative or inventive acts, we tend to build software along with others. This adds a complexity that we demonstrated as we examined the different scenarios implied by group software development.

To support and understand all of this, we took view of the way that we think and act. We built out some thinking tools and we demonstrated how they might be used. We noted that there are three axes along which we have to make a choice about how to think in a given context – reason-passion, implicit-explicit, and deductive-inductive.

Leadership underpins all of this. In Section II, we walked through how the basic principles of leadership apply to software development. We then formulated a new set of principles that connected the leadership work we do directly to that primary driver, delivery speed dependent customer value.

As mentioned above, all of this groundwork puts us in the place where we can dive deeply into the areas of competency that lead to great software

DOI: 10.1201/9781003382751-12

development. Further, as we get into them, we will see how the groundwork we've laid really points to the unavoidable necessity of each of these.

We've already looked quickly at them in a leadership context. But as a reminder, the four competency areas are as follows:

Software Craftsmanship – The way in which we put together the details of the actual software.

People and Process – The way in which we structure ourselves and our colleagues in order to deliver software.

Workflow Automation – The way in which we automate the development process.

Architecture – The way in which we structure our software at a high level.

Whether we recognize it or not, if we've attempted professional software development in any capacity in the past, we've engaged in these four areas of competence. We may not have had an explicit understanding of any of their principles or practices – we may not have even been able to articulate that we were engaging in them. Undoubtedly though, we were engaging in them.

These competency areas are a fundamental reality. The skill with which an organization handles each of them defines how well it will be able to deliver value to a customer.

That skill needn't be explicit – there are a lot of good software development shops that couldn't tell you why they're successful or how the practices they have stumbled across are supporting their performance but nonetheless perform far above average.

To use our "thinking tools" vocabulary, our ability in these four areas of competence may be implicitly understood and leveraged. The point and the power to be seen is that leveraging them, whether explicitly understood or not, is what leads to positive results.

Why should we even talk about these principles then – if they can be discovered and used implicitly?

Accidentally stumbling across these important principles can take a lot of time and luck. This means that, for an organization that isn't performing, improving their lot could potentially take a great deal of experimentation, and chance. Intentionally improving is difficult, if not impossible.

Further, even for those that have discovered enough to improve their performance, moving forward further falls prey to the same challenge. It will be almost impossible to do intentionally. Particularly when you factor in the short-term delivery pressure that often exists in software organizations.

Understanding these principles explicitly allows us to do several things.

First, it allows us to communicate them with others. If we don't have an explicit understanding of the areas of competence, and we look to just "feel" our way into a better mode of delivery, those we work with must be open to frequent, arbitrary experimentation. Some people may be open to this – many aren't.

Second, it makes it possible to know the progress that we are (or aren't) making.

Because we know concretely how the act of building software works, and the skills that we must develop in order to improve at it, we are able to understand where we are in our progression and what we need to do next.

At the time that I'm writing this, I've recently begun to use calisthenics in my fitness routines. Knowing my progress with this type of exercise is much more about how the exercise evolves rather than simply adding more weight as I might do when weightlifting. For example, one of my goals is to be able to do pull-ups as a regular part of my routine. To get there though, the first step is to start with rows – which is a less intense exercise for some of the same muscles that will be involved in the pull-ups. Next, I will be doing chin-ups – I can already do one or two at a time – which I was never able to do before. By the time you're reading this, hopefully I will be doing pull-ups every day.

I was never able to make real progress toward this goal until I understood explicitly the progression I needed to follow. Or perhaps, I wasn't able to recognize any progress I did make – and because of that, I didn't leverage what advantage I did have.

Either way, the explicit understanding has made a world of difference.

The same is true of software – having an explicit understanding of the principles at play, and the progression that can be made with them will allow the individuals, the leaders, and the organization to more quickly, and more effectively leverage the advantages that they do have.

The other question that might be asked about these four areas of competence is – how and why does the nature of software development give rise to these?

To summarize again from earlier chapters, what we're doing when we build software is using the computer to provide some behavior that meets a need for a concrete human being. We're inventing. As much as if we were trying to figure out electricity, the light bulb, or the automobile. The individual we're building it for will not know what they need, much less will the inventor who is looking to meet that need. There will be vague ideas and a lot of trial and error. This is how invention works.

There are two complicating factors in software development. First, this invention is done with groups of people. Second, "physical" realization is trivial – inventing a new feature on a social media site can be as simple as writing some code and then deploying to a server. Millions of people can instantly use it. For millions of people to use a new physical invention, you still have to build millions of replicas of it – even after its "invention."

Because of this, we've had to figure out how to enable groups of people to experiment rapidly.

It turns out that this means crafting software well, shaping architecture in a way that's conducive to rapid, independent change, structuring our groups of people such that they can work together well, and automating everything they do. This is why these areas are central to the delivery of software.

One last thing to mention before we dive into the specific areas – there is a bit of overlap and interconnection between the four areas of competency. So, for example, we will see that the optimal architectural approach is influenced heavily by principles in the people and process area.

I mention this because understanding precisely, tactically what your organization needs to do in order to deliver better is only one half of what we are going for here. The other take-away should be that you deeply understand the nature of software development and can readily see the systems involved – and think skillfully about how to address even those specific problems that arise in your context.

Ultimately, the concrete tools, the more abstract principles, and the discussion about the two different systems should be sufficient to think through and solve any problem that might arise in this domain. This is done with the "systems thinking" approach discussed in Chapter 4.

The remainder of this section will be devoted to diving deeply into each of these four areas. Once we accomplish that, in the following section, we will apply all of our learning to common concrete scenarios. That will place those specifics in our toolbelt for when we come across them ourselves. Further, it will illustrate how everything we've been discussing in the abstract makes for a powerfully impactful software development organization.

Chapter 10

Areas of competence

Craftsmanship

Craftsmanship is a powerful idea and it brings with it rich meaning.

For many years, we've understood the craftsmanship that goes into what we now call custom furniture, or custom clothing, or custom shoes. We have to spell out the fact that it's the "custom" work – the one-off creations – that reflects a craftsman's touch.

This is because most of our needs can be met by items that are designed once and then duplicated over and over again by a machine – whether this is furniture, clothing, shoes, or any number of other items that we use on a daily basis.

Years ago – before the machines took over with the industrial revolution – our regular needs, if they were met, were met with "custom" human labor. Our shoes were put together by hand, by an expert in making shoes. Our clothes were sewn – maybe even by our own hand. However whether the creator was the wearer or was someone else, they brought skill and taste to every stitch.

When things are reproduced by machine, the details in which the gift of the craftsman is expressed are compromised for the running of the machine, or even simply just not paid the same attention to in the original design. One way or another, the specificity, the trained control that draws every detail into the impression of the final product, is simply not handled with as much skill in the concrete realizations of the ideas. The clothes, while more available, are ultimately made with less taste. Same for the books, the food, and the shoes.

Fortunately, having the ability to use a machine to increase availability doesn't eliminate our ability to carry out custom creations, but the relative expense means that to the person purchasing, all the extra cost – the difference between the many hours of high-cost human labor and the low-cost machine execution – must be justified by the satisfaction brought on by the craftsmanship.

Practically speaking, this means that the demand for crafted physical items is simply very low.

This almost sounds like a sad state of affairs. There's something so human, and so powerful about bringing our full faculties to the creation of the items

DOI: 10.1201/9781003382751-13

people use in their lives from day to day. And in many ways, the automation of the industrial revolution seems to all but eliminates the use of that capability.

The reality though is that this craftsmanship has moved from the physical creation back to the design of the thing. We can get very specific about the design of the shoe or clothing item – we can bring the same level of craftsmanship that we brought to the actual physical realization, but we do it in a way that then is made available to many more people than if we were creating one-by-one.

Side-by-side, the art of making a shoe that will be produced at large scale vs. the one-off shoe will be different. As mentioned, the former will consider the very fact of working at scale, and so part of that art is not only designing what will work on the foot, but what will do that while being able to be created rapidly and in automated fashion. That we've added some complexity – or maybe difficulty is a better word – simply means that we have a margin of effort that we must divert from the actual state of the end product.

That is to say, we have to figure out what the machines will look like and how they will work. There are dozens of new possibilities for optimization – many of which will have tradeoffs not only with other aspects of the automation but with the end product itself.

All of this invention, all of this craftsmanship, was simply a step back from crafting the actual item.

Similarly, with the computer revolution, we've created generalized machines. These machines do things that can be altered with simple reconfiguration of electrons – by programming.

With the same machines, we can create all kinds of new automation – new invention – simply by entering some text into them with a keyboard.

As it was with the shoes when machines came on the scene, so it is with the machines as the computers come on the scene. Physical reproduction is no longer necessary to realize the same kind of invention.

We've stepped a second degree away from the production of the end product.

The invention is now in the programming – as is the craftsmanship.

Boiling this all down though – what is craftsmanship? It's several things – it's paying close attention to details, getting those details right, and realizing that right is an entirely fluid, subjective thing. It's art.

We know when we get a hand-crafted, custom item from a skilled craftsman. It's beautiful, it works well, and it exudes a sense of quality.

A really potent question is – generally – how do we become a craftsman?

There are three aspects to this:

1. The First Creation [1] – In his landmark book on personal effectiveness, Stephen Covey explains the concept of the first creation. This act always precedes any actual creation – it's the internal picturing of the final state. This can be done with intention, or it can be done quickly and haphazardly.

The craftsman does it with intention – getting as clear a personal grasp on the final state that he can so that when he begins creating, decisions are quick, and direction is clear.

This isn't to say that the craftsman knows ahead of time exactly the direction his work will take. Again, this is creation, so the target will evolve as discoveries are made. This means that the "first creation" will be done more than once, adjusting for changes as the final outcome emerges.

2. Experimentation – Craftsmanship is done experimentally – empirically – to use the thinking tools terminology from earlier chapters.

Whether it's the shoe we're crafting, the machine, or the software – we're balancing an underlying reality and underlying state of the universe against the needs of a human being. This means that much of getting the details right means trying out a few things to see which balance of nature and human need strikes the right chord.

A critical part of experimentation is knowing what the target is.

Because the ultimate target is the appreciation and use of a human being, when we're creating, we may not know who the actual person will be that will put our wares to use. Fortunately there are many human beings to be found around us. In fact, most of you reading this are likely human.

A time-honored technique for gauging the probable acceptance of a final product is to test it with several kinds of audiences, from most casual to least:

- Yourself – The first and most available test audience for the craftsman is himself. In fact, really getting to the forefront of a given craft largely depends on the quality of audience the craftsman represents. This is usually referred to as taste – but is maybe more usefully thought of as how well successful self-tests correlate to successful adoption by the real target.
- A trusted evaluator – The second test audience a craftsman can leverage is an individual or group whose taste he trusts. As an individual, the craftsman has his own very specific set of tests. While they may be broad and well-educated, they are limited. Addressing a trusted advisor broadens the base of opinion – increasing the likelihood that anything that isn't working might be spotted.
- The public – The final test is against the actual target. This kind of test is the most accurate, but also brings with it significant risk as it could result in reputational damage if care isn't taken with it.

  The musician is one of my favorite examples of this technique. Whether it's the DJs of today – or the jazz artists of decades past – they'll try out their composition or musical idea first on their own ears, then maybe with a band or a producer, and then out "in the club" – playing it in front of people who are paying to hear their music. The reaction at each level informs the next and allows the musician to dial in their details until they get the most positive reaction from their tests.

3. Wisdom – Perhaps a word that is less commonly used today is one of the other major factors of craftsmanship. This is the idea that we have extensive implicit knowledge about how the problem arena that we work in. It means that we know how to think and act with respect to that arena quickly and accurately, particularly as it relates to getting the kinds of results we are interested in – as we discussed when we were talking about experimentation.

Imagine the old-world shoemaker. They've made hundreds of pairs of shoes – every time they cut a piece of leather and attach it to the shoe – their work is so practiced that it almost looks like they're not even thinking about it. They know how to adapt if anything goes wrong – or if there are any irregularities with any of the supplies. This is all wisdom.

The way we get this is through evaluated practice. We repeatedly go through creating and experimenting – as we do, the actions we take, we connect with success or failure. We may not realize that we're doing this – which is what makes the knowledge so implicit. Nonetheless, with each cycle, we're more adept at creating.

A note here about practice – it doesn't need to go all the way to the third audience – to the public consumer of our creation – but it does need to be thoughtfully evaluated. Singing in the shower won't prepare you for singing in front of an arena audience of 20,000. You may be able to evaluate yourself to a certain extent, but likely your focus is on showering rather than on critically examining your craft.

So that's the three-step path to generalized craftsmanship, but we're here to dig into the craft of software development.

As we've mentioned, software craft can be seen as an evolution of our ability to create and provide value to one another. First, we crafted the shoe, then we crafted the machine that created the shoe, now we craft the behavior of the machine that creates the shoe.

CRAFTING BEHAVIOR

The craft of software is the craft of behavior.

So behavior is the object of our "first creation" – and it is what we experiment with to find the right thing. It is behavior that is the focus of the wisdom we look to develop through practice.

This is where we get into the very specific, concrete actions that we can take to engage in this craft.

Crafting behavior with the first creation

The first creation, as we mentioned earlier, is a concept that Stephen Covey brought forward in his book *The 7 Habits of Highly Effective People*. It is the idea that there is a very human connection between being able to make good, quick choices about a thing that follows from first picturing that thing in the imagination.

Covey applies this concept to an individual's entire life. A fantastic exercise that he promotes in that book is to write your own obituary. The point of this is to think about what you want your life to have looked like, particularly when you look at it in retrospect. If you start with that picture in your imagination – of the way you want to intentionally make your life go – you can aim your choices more intentionally at your target.

This exercise is powerful – it makes you think through relative importance in a way that is directly attached to what you want to happen. If you want to have had rich relationships throughout your life – sitting alone watching hours of TV might become less of a priority.

It doesn't just operate on a conscious level either. Once you have this picture in your mind, and you believe in it and are hungry to pursue it, those decisions that work toward your goal – they feel like the things you want to be doing. So the choices not only make more explicit sense; they make an intuitive sense as well. Which means that you can make decisions more quickly and with more conviction. Both of these mean that the ultimate outcome will be better.

So as we craft behavior, how do we apply a very intentional first creation?

Well, first of all, much of this is complicated again, as we said in earlier chapters, by the fact that we're doing this with groups of people.

The first creation, then, must include everyone that will be a part of crafting the behavior. This will vary from organization to organization, but there are generally several classes of folks that are connected in one way or another with crafting behavior.

Executive Leadership – These leaders have a strategic interest in the particular behavior. They will be looking at the broad direction of the organization with respect to how it meets peoples' needs, and even who those people are that the organization is targeting.

Behavior Experts – The common names for folks that fall into this bucket are "Product Managers" or "Systems Analysts." Regardless, the nomenclature – this group of folks, while taking a slightly less strategic view than the executive leadership – tends to have the deepest understanding of and vision for the behavior that is being created.

Engineers – Engineers have the technical capabilities to turn ideas into fully realized behavior. Because their interests are so technical, at times, they tend to view behavior as secondary. This will likely be an ongoing challenge simply because of the way our human cognitive machinery works – the things we focus on are the things we come to believe are the most important.

These classes of people are conceptual. As we discussed in earlier chapters, one person might represent all three or there might be dozens in each class.

However, these classes are populated; every individual must develop that first creation – the clear picture in their mind. It must have the level of detail necessary for the role (or roles) that they fulfill. Further, that picture must remain synchronized with everyone on the team.

This is where the primary challenge exists.

The solution is to create habits that can be done without thinking or planning that regularly resynchronize every member of the team from the executive to the engineer with regard to the "first creation," to the shared picture of the end-state.

This is a primary purpose of the "People & Process" competency – so we will leave the how-to specifics for that coming chapter. The take-away here though is the understanding that getting this clarity and intentionality around the collective first creation takes real work but is a necessary component of delivering valuable software.

Crafting behavior by experimenting

Experimentation requires a target – a goal that determines whether or not the experiment has been successful.

In general, that goal of the behavior we are crafting is to meet a need for real, concrete human beings. As we discussed earlier, this may mean using three different classes of people to conduct our experiments such that they have the best possible chance of reflecting reality: ourselves, our trusted evaluators, and – eventually – the actual, targeted individuals.

Specifically, the goal is to realize what we conceptualized in our first creation – to the extent that it is possible and useful.

It is conceivable – in fact, it's likely – that our first creation will need to evolve as we learn. We will learn about what is possible with the aspects of the domain we are working in and we will learn what behaviors will actually help people. We uncover both of these things with experiments.

Really, there's a loop between experimentation and conceiving our end-state. They feed into each other as we work through crafting behavior. Our experiments inform our vision and our vision directs our experimentation.

With that reality understood, it becomes apparent that the more rapidly we can move through this cycle, the more appropriate our solution will be, since we will execute more experiments more accurately.

The real leverage to be sought in crafting software is that of rapid experimentation. The remaining competencies – architecture, people and process, and workflow automation – all center around that reality. They each provide a piece of the experimentation puzzle that when fully assembled results in the fastest possible turn around on that experimentation. This then results in the best possible software that most capably balances the underlying reality of the domain and the needs of the human being.

Turning experiments around as rapidly as possible also reveals another important dimension of the craftsmanship we apply to our software – the craft we apply to the code itself.

Just as the behavior that we craft is targeted at a human being – so is the code we write to create that behavior. If we were only concerned with the behavior itself, we would write everything in machine code and forgo things like high-level languages, object-oriented programming, and descriptive variable names.

The reason these things are valuable is because, whether it's by the same individual that originally wrote it or by someone new, all code we write will have to be changed in the future. To be changed, code must be read and understood. To be changed quickly – as is necessary for our rapid experimentation – code must be conducive to being read and understood quickly.

This is yet one degree further removed from the actual user, but it is a separate arena of craftsmanship coequal with the craftsmanship that we apply to behavior.

That is, historically, craft was used on the individual shoe, then it moved back a degree and was applied to the machine that created the shoe. It moved back yet another degree and is applied to the behavior of the machine that creates the shoe. And while the behavior still requires that craft be applied to it – in order to do that well, we must also apply it one degree back from that – on the code that creates the behavior of the machine that creates the shoe.

With every degree, we move back from the shoe, the craft that we apply generalizes further. Which is why we can be writing about software craftsmanship in general – knowing that it applies similarly, whether the actual end domain is actually shoes – or if it's finance – or if it's logistics.

We will discuss this additional application of craft shortly.

Crafting behavior with wisdom

Developing wisdom with regard to crafting behavior is a matter of evaluated practice.

We've carried out our first creation, and we've experimented against that first creation – against our collective shared vision of what the end-state of the behavior should look like. And we've adapted that vision as we've learned.

Absorbing the lessons we've learned throughout this path of experimentation and adaptation happens almost automatically.

Even if you do nothing else as you are delivering software – as you are creating behavior for a real person, the practice and exercise you get in this craft will be absorbed. That is, you will gain wisdom.

To multiply and enhance this effect requires one additional action – reflection.

There are two opportunities for reflection – for yourself, and with the other folks you delivered the software with. This should include as much of the three-part team as possible, executive leaders, behavior experts and engineers. The more inclusive the group is, the more it will make an impact in terms of increasing the wisdom with which the team produces its behavior – its software.

It should be noted that these conversations may require some care – and executing them can represent a skillset of its own (which we will discuss further next chapter as we dive into People and Process). For each of the three groups, uncovering areas to improve means being emotionally vulnerable – and thus requires a certain degree of strength and maturity – both on the part of the facilitator and each of the individuals.

Don't rush into these conversations. Plan them out. Think through the relationships between participants, and make sure that the facilitator has the emotional awareness to carry them out in a constructive fashion. It would be an easy thing to charge through creating the opportunities to talk while at the same time doing damage to relationships and to the team's ability to learn from its experience.

CRAFTING SOFTWARE

In discussing our ability to craft behavior, we highlighted the centrality of experimentation. As we begin building out a behavior, we will have a target in our mind that we've come to with our first creation. We will then try to turn it into a reality. We will then experiment on ourselves and on others realizing that it has come short of its potential. We will then visualize the changes we need to make, and then repeat the cycle.

Moving through this cycle as rapidly as possible means zeroing in on that potential as fast as possible – which means more value in the hands of the user, and more return in ours.

We can be quick to visualize and experiment, but without one remaining piece, we won't move as rapidly as we might.

That remaining piece is found in the structure of the actual code that we are building.

In order to make a change and attempt a new experiment, code must be quick to be changed. This means that it must be quick to be understood.

We can think of this as really crafting our systems for two different audiences simultaneously – its behavior we target the user with, its codebase we target any developer that needs to make change in the future.

If this latter audience were unimportant, we would write everything in machine code. It's easy to see though that even if I happen to be the next developer to make a change within seconds of initially authoring it, making it easy to understand enables rapid experimentation. It's why we use high-level languages and frameworks – to make understanding easier for the engineer.

In my first professional software engineering role, one of the most interesting pieces of development work that I engaged in was a reporting engine. It was built into the existing web application and exposed all of the raw data for building custom reports that could then be saved and executed later.

By the time it was working, every change I made to it I all but crossed my fingers and hoped for the best. The system was very generalized – at the time, it was a bit beyond my ability to build while keeping the codebase clear. The resulting tangle got to production and worked well, but upgrading it was not something I would have relished – though I never had to.

So what are we to do?

How do we build systems such that they are always clear and communicative and that they enable rather than hinder the comprehension of the next developer to read them.

The first thing to do is to realize that this is indeed a craft coequal with the earlier addressed craft of building behavior. This means that there is a real audience – and that the response that we're after is a subjective one.

This all means that we have to rely on the same set of tools for software craft that we did for behavior craft. Viz. first creation, experimentation, and wisdom.

All of this is complicated somewhat by the fact that we're carrying out two different crafts in tandem – with the results of each being roughly connected. You can't change behavior without changing the software, but you can change the software without changing behavior. So there's a little bit of decoupling, but there's not a huge gap between the two.

Where the magic is: Abstraction

Let's repeat this again, human understanding – particularly by a developer interested in changing the system – leads to faster experiments, which leads to a more valuable system.

Human understanding is a subjective target – though to get there, we basically need to do one thing well. We need to create high-quality abstractions.

When we said that high-level languages and frameworks are for the comprehension of the developer – it is because they offer sets of well-crafted abstraction. That abstraction is what makes text that is ultimately destined to be executed by a computer to be at the same time comprehensible – rapidly comprehensible – to a person. This really is a bit of a wonder if you think about it.

Why does abstraction do this?

For the reason abstraction helps human beings in the physical world. It allows us to think about only the details of a situation that matter – discarding ones that can be safely ignored.

If we had to think about all the details of the table we were sitting at each time we prepared to eat, we'd have little cognitive energy for anything else.

We are able to think of the abstraction of the table, forgetting the size, shape and composition of the legs and of the table-top.

So it is with programming. Though in programming, we are regularly building our own abstractions on the fly. This differs from the physical version of the problem in that we're dealing with creating the abstraction and then leveraging it. But it offers the same basic function (so to speak) – it allows us to discard irrelevant details and think only in terms of the details that are important to the task at hand.

To go back to my AppleSoft BASIC days, one of my favorite abstractions was the PRINT function. It took a single string parameter as an input and wrote that string to the screen. Under the hood of that simple function was memory accesses and copies, moving text into the video memory area so that the hardware might pick it up and display it.

Another potent example for me was back in 1995 about the time Java started to pick up real popularity. I had been writing multithreaded programs in early Windows versions, which was complicated. In fact, most of the multi-threaded programming I had been doing was on MS-DOS, which didn't even have the concept of a thread and was for most purposes a single-threaded operating system. To do something "in the background" or in what we might consider a "thread," one had to set up a handler to respond to the hardware clock interrupt, so that it could wake up, do something, and then go back to sleep. It was often like building a new threading system each time you needed to do something like this.

When Java came out, I remember being ecstatic because creating a thread and starting it safely was only 4 or 5 lines of code. You simply created a "Thread" class with a "run()" method that had the code in it you wanted to execute in the background, and then you "start()"ed it. By comparison, this new mechanism was exceedingly intuitive and obvious.

These abstractions are easy to take for granted. In fact, that's probably the mark of a great abstraction – its penchant for being taken for granted. Which is unsurprising, because the goal is to create something that is obvious and inspires as little thought as possible.

When you collect abstraction after abstraction built in this fashion, clarity emerges from the system because line after line, you are minimizing the thought it takes to comprehend, and maximizing the meaning that is coming across to the reader.

To repeat, this is the stock and trade of high-level programming languages and frameworks. Whenever we reach for a particular language or framework we do so because it offers leverage for understanding the code we write better. For example, we might reach for React for web code or Spring Boot for API writing – in the former, we could just write plain JavaScript, and in the latter, we could write the web request/response code to provide the API. It is in the hopes of getting thoroughly vetted abstraction that will enhance comprehensibility that we pursue these tools.

As we've hinted, good abstraction has two qualities:

- What it does is intuitively obvious.
- What it does is useful.

The PRINT statement in AppleSoft BASIC is intuitively obvious and eminently useful. The Java Threading API (c. 1995) was as well, particularly by the standards of the day.

The reason for this should be clear. The more quickly that a line of code is intuitively meaningful, the less work will go into understanding it.

The question, then, is – how do we create good abstraction?

We should keep it at the front of our mind, that our target is to write code that inspires rapid comprehension in a reader. This is inherently subjective and is the reason that this is a craft.

The starting point though is two-fold:

- It should be well-named.
- It should do precisely what that name would indicate to the reader.

Creating SOLID abstraction

One of the best sets of tools that will immediately put your abstraction authoring on to solid ground is the SOLID Principles as cataloged by Robert Martin.

SOLID is an acronym that includes five principles – one for each of the five letters of the word SOLID. Each of the principles rests on those that follow it – the earlier ones being more fundamentally important and the following principles falling into increasingly supportive roles.

Single Responsibility Principle – This is the "single" most important principle – a unit should have one and only one reason to change. This is to say, whether it is a function or a class or a method on a class, our abstract concept should include only one behavior. That behavior may involve multiple actions at lower levels of abstraction, but there should be one responsibility that a particular unit owns. Looking at PRINT again – it has a single, simple thing to do – put a string to the screen. Though as a part of that, as previously mentioned, it will move things around in memory.

Having this clarity leads directly to the second of our two-fold definition of high-quality abstraction – that it does precisely what its name says it does. If we have clarity on this, picking a name to describe the action will be straightforward. If we don't have clarity, or if we're doing a number of things – picking a clear name will be difficult.

So even with no other principles in hand, understanding this one puts us on very good footing.

Open-Closed Principle – Using the tools inherent in the language, the more that a unit makes the path of least resistance adding code rather than modifying the existing implementation details, the clearer the code will be.

If implementation details are more readily changed than added to, the less defined the responsibility will seem. So, as we noted above, the Open-Closed Principle supports the Single Responsibility Principle by adding credibility to the responsibility and thus to the overall abstraction.

So, for example, if we have a class that encrypts text, as we're building it, we might note that we're using a specific algorithm to encrypt the text. We might subclass based on the encryption algorithm, so that in the likely case that we want to use another algorithm, we can simply add another subclass rather modifying the existing one. This would add credibility to the interface in the eyes of client code.

Liskov Substitution Principle – This principle probably has the least intuitive name. The point though is that client code using a subclass (or interface implementation) should be able to do so with complete ignorance of the replacement's existence. This is possible when, while the behavior might be different, it is fully compatible with the behavior implied by that original interface.

So even as we add new subclasses, the one restriction we need to accept is that we'll behave according to the expectations that its construction put forward.

If we need to do something wildly different, we should not use the same type. This adds credibility to the interface and to all of its implementations directly because every time a developer comes across one of them, the sense of consistent behavior will be reinforced.

It supports the Open-Closed Principle in that being strictly obedient to the interface makes for less temptation to modify the details of any of the implementations.

Ultimately, this supports the Single Responsibility Principle, both indirectly through the previous two principles and directly. Obedience to the original interface puts very clear, effortless definition around the responsibility the additional subclass assumes – and guides the ultimate shape of it by limiting options. This makes finding and defining the single responsibility simpler, and that means an abstraction that can best reflect its name.

Interface Segregation Principle – This principle really centers around a single revelation that the interface of a unit serves the client code, not the unit itself. So, whether that's a function, a class, or a method on a class, the "interface" of that unit should be viewed in the context of the client code. We use "interface" in a generalized sense here. A function or a method, they both have contracts that determine the number and the types of the parameters that they take, and the result they return, so this principle applies across any kind of programming unit – and thus across different programming paradigms.

It is true that when these principles were first expressed it was within the context of Object-Oriented Programming – and so, the "interface" in this principle was the interface of a class. This same historical context is true for all of the SOLID principles – they were uncovered in that context – though that doesn't mean to say that the underlying truth that they represent is pegged to that context. This principle, for example, as mentioned, applies to functions as much as classes, which means that it even crosses the programming paradigm line from Object Oriented to the Functional Programming paradigm.

I call this out specifically, here, because interface is (historically) such a specifically Object-Oriented concept – and that concept is in the name of the principle.

That we "segregate interfaces" is, in a way, only a concrete realization of the actual principle. In Object-Oriented design, particularly with languages that use multiple inheritance or multiple interface implementation, a concrete class might expose more than one interface through which client code may interact. The point of this principle as it is typically expressed is that the particular interfaces should be specific to the needs of particular clients. In this way, we segregate the potentially larger interface of the overall class into a set of more purpose-specific interfaces.

What does this do for clarity?

It puts further limits around the responsibility visible to the client code. If in designing a class, we view our responsibility in a way that is then only partially important to client code, the class immediately looks like it's doing more than one thing. The thing we want it to do, and then everything else it does. Narrowing the meaning by creating a client-specific interface adds focus, such that the abstraction is precisely what the client needs it to be.

This means you can name it more appropriately – and as we've noted repeatedly, having a useful thing to do and a name that clearly expresses it is what makes high-quality abstraction, and adds up to a clear codebase.

One final note on this principle – as we said, a class may expose several interfaces – each of these interfaces may be specific to certain clients or kinds of clients. This allows a class with a certain responsibility to have that responsibility divided up for multiple clients, such that for each of them, the responsibility is that much more specific and focused. This is the heart of this principle.

In the beginning of this section, I said that there's really a single revelation that underpins this. It is what makes the principle useful – segregation aside. That revelation is that the "interface" (in the general sense) should be specific to the client code.

From practical experience, when an engineer finds themselves taking a class and crafting multiple interfaces to it, the chances are that the conceptual clarity and singular focus that we look for from a unit are lacking. That is to say, the actual segregation might indicate a problem with the unit, whereas the understanding that whatever the shape of the unit's interface is, it should be defined in terms of the needs of the client code.

Dependency Inversion Principle – Our natural instinct – or perhaps simply our level of development as a society of software builders – is to depend on increasingly concrete units as our client code becomes more concrete in its task. The dependency inversion principle would warn us against this – telling us that dependency should always be on the abstract.

The practical example of this is always client code that depends on a closely related interface (often in the same package), from which a concrete class extends or implements. The client code doesn't depend on that concrete implementation.

At the root of this – this principle is a restatement of the purpose of the Interface Segregation Principle. The shape of the unit should be closely controlled by the needs of the client.

This supports the Single Responsibility Principle and thus clarity in the same manner and for the same reasons as the Interface Segregation Principle, so we won't restate all of this.

SOLID understanding

A common phrase with engineers that discover and gain enthusiasm for the SOLID principles is – "don't do that, it violates the X principle." These principles aren't laws – they're principles. They're tools that you can use to think about the shape of your code – leveraging them to ensure that code as clear as possible. The ultimate test for clarity, though, is the reading and comprehension of developers – yourself and others.

So the purpose of going through these principles is to give you a starting point for your own thinking. Start with the target of clarity – and evaluate your own thinking in terms of these principles. Though, as with any art, theory is a lever – it is not the goal.

Crafting software with the first creation

Now that we have a concrete basis for writing clear code, we can step back to the three general parts of any craft.

As a reminder, this craft – software craft – is highly coupled to the behavior craft that we discussed earlier. As we are building behavior, that behavior is expressed and created with software. There are many shapes of software that might create a particular behavior – some more expressive, some less.

Our goal here is two-fold – we want to create our best understanding of the given behavior with the most expressive, most clear, and most comprehensible possible codebase.

So while these two crafts are distinct, their overlap can lead to some challenges. A central part of software craft, though, is overcoming these.

A good first creation with software has two parts – a thinking part, and a technical part. We'll get into both of these, shortly. First though, to get them right, it's important that we are crystal clear about the overlap and transition between the two crafts.

It is this – a singular piece of behavior, say logging into a hypothetical web application – can be viewed as a unit of software. It has input, behavior, and output.

So the move from behavior craft to software craft is really a shift of viewpoint. We make the move when we view the specific piece of behavior as a software unit.

We mentioned above that our first creation with behavior includes three distinct classes of people (executives, behaviorists, and engineers), and represents a shared sense of the direction we think we'll go in. This shared view helps folks to think along the same lines while supporting better, more rapid decisions as the solution hits up against the reality that it exists within.

There's always a point of diminishing returns with the specificity of that first creation. Undoubtedly, we'll have to change much as we experiment and move forward, and there's art in figuring out just how specific to get before our effort begins to represent serious waste. We'll get into more of that when we address people and process.

However, the same is true for the underlying software craft.

Generally speaking, we start with a single piece of behavior. We then view that as a software unit. To get the richness we need from the behavior while keeping the code as clear as possible, the unit will fan out into a hierarchy or graph of abstractions.

As we learn and improve, our ability to anticipate a lot of this will improve. But no matter how far along we are, there is a point after which, without working software in place, our low confidence in our projections will leave us assured that time and energy will be wasted if we continue to make those projections.

Sketching out and diagraming what we think the structure might be is helpful up to that point. For just the same reason as with the behavior. If we have a general idea where we might head, our improvisations and adaptations will be quicker, more appropriate, and take less cognitive effort.

Only one of the three groups mentioned earlier really comes into play as we get into the deeper parts of software craft – and that's the engineers. Though, for the same reason, as many engineers as might be involved, even peripherally, in the areas of code under consideration – these same people should be involved in the first creation.

One of the really bad habits we've had in the industry, historically, has been to try to actually consider the design of the system to be finished before any code hits the hard drives. This is NOT what we are talking about here – we're talking about developing a shared understanding of the general direction to head. As with behavior, the shape of the code will undergo many first creations as we learn, and many modifications as we assimilate those learnings.

So this is part one of the first creation.

Part two is the technical part.

This part can be thought of as putting a technical pin in your intellectual first creation. Since we're looking at this as software craft, our behavior is – to us – a unit of software. At this point, we start a cycle that we will continue as we write code and decompose into layers of abstraction.

1. We write a little bit of automated test – just enough to fail – around our unit of software.
2. We write just enough of the production code to make it pass.
3. We refactor.

Refactoring simply means changing the software without changing behavior [2]. This is where we really drive toward clarity. Three of the most common actions taken when we refactor are pulling out new functions, methods, or classes – that is, creating new units.

When we do this, we recurse into a new instance of this cycle. We write a little bit of test around the new unit, make it pass, then refactor. The depth of the abstraction graph depends on the complexity of the behavior it's supporting. The common pattern is that a method starts to get a bit too long – which will present as a growing lack of clarity. That lack of clarity then implies the need for a new abstraction that will help to hide some of that detail.

The path you take in this and the structure, names, and responsibilities of the abstractions can be brought into focus with a good habit of the intellectual first creation we mentioned earlier. Though much of it also comes down simply to thinking through what has become of the existing abstractions and exercising some creativity to come up with new ones as you carry out the refactor step.

A major, though very common, mistake is to parse out and define these layers ahead of time. It's common practice to even refer to this as designing architecture. Grandiose names for the activity aside – it's premature abstraction. What you actually need from the code will define the types of abstractions that are needed. Some of this might be anticipate-able – but as with any other design carried out before code is written – if it's a straight-jacket and not simply a guide, you're doing yourself a disservice.

The thing to keep in mind is that this is a homogenous workflow from the highest level where we view the behavior as our first software unit. It's a recursive process that flowers through a robust refactoring practice. At each level we peg the vision of our first creation with actual concrete code. This means that the slippery and vague mental processes that accompany our creativity won't subtly change the interface of the unit. This is true for the topmost unit that reflects the behavior we are delivering, or the lower units that represent the domain specific languages in terms of which the higher levels construct their functionality.

Keeping this semantic stability at every level allows developers working on lower levels to shed concern that they might reduce clarity for the higher levels. And it allows developers working at the higher levels to have a deep sense of comfort in the abstractions that they are using – that they will continue to mean and do what they assume they will.

This simple three step cycle is of course commonly known as TDD [2]. Used together with a good intellectual first creation, it allows a measured approach to gradually evolving a software system.

Crafting software by experimenting

The target we aim for when we craft software is comprehension by the next developer that has to change the system.

There are a lot of problems built into this target. Primarily – we can't predict the future – we can't know that the system will need to be changed, let alone who it will be changed by.

We can, however, make some educated guesses about what that person might be like and the kinds of things they might understand readily.

At a bare minimum, we can be assured that, at least at the writing of this book, the person is a human being like ourselves. We might also make an educated guess about natural languages that we share in common, as well as shared cultural background. All of this will be easier to arrive at, if we're working on a local team. There can be complications in this respect if the team is widely distributed. One way or another, these external elements deeply impact the way an individual will read and write abstractions within their programming environment – and it is incumbent upon us to have a sense about them as we are experimenting toward our target – meeting their comprehensibility needs.

One final element of an individual's understanding that we want to have a rough idea about is his technical fluency. What languages and tools will he have a quick grasp on. Further, how quickly can he pick up new languages and tools.

Having this clear picture in our head will help us to collect the people that can serve as concrete proxies for our hypothetical "next developer" as we experiment.

These proxies come in three categories:

- **Myself.** I can't actually change my own cultural perspective, or skillset, but – to a certain extent – I can imagine what it might be like to have a given outlook or capability. As I go through the work of writing code, trying out abstractions, and evaluating, if I keep that sense in the back of my mind, I can evaluate code based on it.

    This isn't quite the same as actually being the target you're writing for. But it's a close second.

    If you do recognize that most if not all of the developers that will potentially be changing your system are very similar to yourself, you're in luck. You can rest a little more fully on simply asking, "does this make sense (to me)?"

Either way, though, you need to develop a consciousness that you're a stand-in for the ultimate reader of the code that you're in the process of writing.

- **Trusted Evaluators.** After you've written code that passes your own test for being quick and easy to understand, the time may come to ask others what they think about the code you've written.

  It's important that you're selective about the evaluators that you turn to for input. They should understand the target that you're after and have the skill to be able to read and comprehend similarly to the target developer you're envisioning.

  This may be more difficult than it sounds. There are some bad habits and practices that have built up in the industry with regard to evaluating code. They tend to be held under the category of "code review." A primary problem is that evaluators tend to examine code solely with respect to their own personal likes and dislikes, without considering the target that's being pursued as the code is written. This may appear at times to work, since in practice, reviewers on the team that owns a particular system will frequently be the actual people that change the system in question.

  Further, at times, certain evaluators can be less than optional.

  Whether they're optional or not, and whether or not a particular reviewer understands the purpose of reviewing code that you bring to them, you have several options. Most importantly, you should keep your purpose clear – that you are looking for feedback in order to make the code you are writing as clear as possible to future developers.

  If you are forced to use a reviewer that can't or won't be brought around to this purpose, this doesn't prevent you from going through with the mandatory review and then finding a reviewer that you trust at a later time.

  The power of the trusted reviewer is that you can get feedback that is of higher quality than you might otherwise. This is a huge advantage in that it makes for more productive experiments. The feedback is then easier to absorb, and it's easier to use as a basis for any improvements.

  All of that being said, it is frequently very difficult to find trusted reviewers. You shouldn't be discouraged if you can't find one or more. Your experimentation will rest more on your own evaluation, and the evaluation from the third category.

- **Interested Developers.** Even if they're not in the trusted group mentioned previously, developers, particularly those that match the target type in terms of background and skillset, can offer useful feedback.

  This feedback can be less explicit – since this type of test audience may or may not understand the purpose of their feedback. The keywords to listen for are along the lines of the "code review" style feedback we mentioned earlier – "I like this," "I don't like this." Personal enjoyment of the code is going to be the indicator that you will get from this group.

As a general rule, even though we disparaged it as less useful than an explicit understanding of our target, the idea that something is pleasing or displeasing to a software developer is a useful indicator of – or at least a hint at – its comprehensibility. So, with some care, the information about the potential comprehensibility to our target audience can be gleaned even from this less-than-ideal audience.

And in reality, it's a natural progression. There are few circumstances where code can stay only in the hands of those we trust entirely. In fact, a less familiar set of developers is the most likely composition of our actual target audience.

So the path forward is clear for us. We build out our software, trying out our ideas around expressiveness with the varying audiences in the same way we try out the nature of the behavior with audiences of different levels of trust and interest.

There is one complication in all of this – at every point in the codebase, there is dependency on the code we are adding to or changing. Up to the top of the stack where the initial layer can be both thought of as a software layer and an ultimate behavior of the system, our dependent is the actual user of the system. As we move layers down – as one layer calls another layer – the dependent more and more becomes the software itself. One unit depends on another – one function, method, or class, delegates to yet others.

In either case, what we don't want is to change the expectations of the higher layers (whether that's software, or people). Small, controlled experiments that change only precisely what we intend – that allows the feedback to be better understood.

That is, if two or three small changes lead to code becoming less readable (according to your audience), then you can be comfortable that you know the changes that need further evaluation. If, however, changes cascade throughout the differing layers and components of your system before readability is recognized as beginning to suffer, remediation will be far more difficult.

Making incremental and controlled changes in this manner and leveraging high-quality test audiences is what will result in powerful experimentation. This experimentation will allow you to really dial in the clarity of the codebase, meaning that, as far as the code is concerned, the team delivering it will be able to move as rapidly as possible.

Ensuring that changes are incremental and controlled rests on the techniques we enumerated above. The individual or team that is pursuing the specific changes must carry out an explicit and thorough first creation. This will not only allow for the adaptation that we described above, but it will also help to quickly determine the increments that should be addressed next.

Following the failed test, passed test, refactor cycle – the TDD cycle – will ensure that even the shape of the increment is becoming as clear as possible in the minds of the developer or developers that are addressing it.

The reason for this is that each line of test code – every time we carry out the first part of the cycle, making a test that fails – is akin to its own first creation for that very small part of the code. Not only is it very small, it's also very concrete. We're specifying in code the thing the very small piece of software that we are building.

The concrete nature of software often works against us. More accurately, that concreteness seemingly makes our abstract thinking work against us. We must think in the abstract and then turn that abstract idea into every single concrete instruction that will be needed to realize the idea. This is where the explosion of effort often happens in software development, because the nature of abstraction is to ignore detail that isn't important in the big picture. To make software work though, all of those little concrete things must be accommodated for.

With a proper development cycle, we leverage the strength of our abstract thought, without suffering its weakness – or at least while minimizing that suffering. We move immediately to spelling out the software's action in the most concrete of terms – other software, viz. the test.

In addition to getting this real clarity about the lowest level concrete detail, we create a suite of tests as we go that ensure that we will be notified if there is a change anywhere other than where we are working. Whether it's at "higher" or "lower" levels of abstraction – if it's in the actual user-facing behavior, or in a low-level module that services database access – or even if it's a peer unit that is at a similar level of abstraction – a good suite of tests ensures that a test made in one unit doesn't change the action or the meaning of another.

So as we work through our development cycle, there should only ever be a handful of lines of code around which there is any uncertainty. Those lines of code are the small increment that we carefully thought through with a first creation and are the focus of making our failing test pass.

Completing the experiment

Once we've written some code, we have an opportunity as a part of every development cycle to integrate changes implied by the generated learnings. The third step, which is commonly called the "refactor" step, is when we do this. Refactoring as an idea in software development is changing code without changing anything about what it does [2].

So whether we've written three lines of code, and been our own test audience, or whether we've written 3,000 lines and we're checking it with an untrusted audience, the findings from those various levels of experimentation can be integrated back into the codebase in the refactor step.

The refactor step is nicely placed because, since all the tests are passing (which is implied by the first two steps), there is a safe platform to change code and have a high degree of certainty that any change to actual action or meaning will be communicated to you immediately by the tests.

And with that, we've completed our experimentation. The next step is to continue the cycle. As we do, we will slowly bubble back up the graph of abstraction we've created until ultimately, we finish the behavior we were targeting.

Crafting software with wisdom

Wisdom is that implicit knowledge and ability to act that comes from experience and regular exposure to the kinds of scenarios that a software developer might come across in "the wild."

Getting a really practiced, intuitive development cycle as well as the habit for a thorough first creation is the first point of wisdom that we come across as we begin to build software. It is always very tempting to "just get something to work" – and to disregard the quieter concern about the comprehensibility of the next developer. With much practice even this temptation can be fought back to a certain degree. I am embarrassed to think about how many times I've succumbed to this temptation only to end up actually being the "next developer" – having to deal with the pile of spaghetti I've thoughtlessly left in my wake.

The other piece of wisdom that will develop as an engineer gets practice building software – is the intuitive understanding about what is clear and what is not. In the beginning, determining this may be a very explicit activity, requiring a lot of feedback. Assuming this feedback is taken and digested and that the engineer continues to practice – to build – in light of that feedback, an intuitive sense will begin to develop around clarity. That implicit knowledge will mean faster delivery and more sophisticated experimentation.

The more this implicit knowledge, this wisdom, grows and internalizes, the more positive will be the impact that a given developer has on the ability of his team to quickly change its software.

SOFTWARE CRAFTSMANSHIP

Overall when we discuss the idea of software craftsmanship, we are talking about two very distinct crafts, viz. behavior craft, and software craft. They overlap in very specific ways, but their audiences and techniques are radically different.

Most importantly, our task is to add value to real human beings with our software. That is, to put valuable software into the hands of our users.

In the real world though, doing this well means experimenting rapidly – which means that the humans that are reading and altering this software have to become first class targets of our craftsmanship. This must be done without sacrificing the dedication to creating value for our users.

We've outlined the down in the trenches technical tools used to make this happen in this chapter. We've left for the next chapter the process tools as well the interpersonal and team context that is so important in real world software projects.

WORKS CITED

1. S. R. Covey, The 7 Habits of Highly Effective People, New York: Simon & Schuster, 1989.
2. M. Fowler, Refactoring: Improving the Design of Existing Code, Reading, MA: Addison-Wesley, 1999.
3. R. C. Martin, Clean Code: A Handbook of Agile Software Craftsmanship, Boston: Addison-Wesley, 2009.

Chapter 11

Areas of competence

People and process

As we've stated and restated in previous chapters, the purpose that we're pursuing is putting valuable solutions to real problems into the hands of our customers. From this, we expect a reasonable return, thus enabling us to repeat the act in the future.

The best way to do this – to put the most valuable solutions into the hands of our customers – is to optimize our development workflow primarily for speed. The faster we deliver, the more quickly we can experiment which gives us the opportunity to more closely meet a given need.

Further, as a matter of basic human dynamics, any solution more quickly delivered is inherently more valuable.

We've repeated this many times as we've built up the underlying philosophical framework for delivering software well. Hopefully, we haven't gotten bored with it because it is the central principle that every practical execution tool rests on.

In Chapter 2, we went deeply into the unique nature of software development. As a recap, we should recall the following aspects of the craft.

Software development is creative.

If we're writing software, we're creatively addressing a new problem. If a previously built solution would meet the need, we might have simply copied that software to the new context [1].

Software development is a team sport.

The members of a software team often have varying interests. They may be related and complementary, but frequently they are not identical to those of their colleagues. Some write code, some think very specifically about how the system will be used, and others consider the problems that the team is looking to solve with its software.

These teams can represent hundreds or even thousands of people and many levels of corporate hierarchy. Or they can be as small as a handful of people working out of a garage.

Software development is entrepreneurship.

Every way that a piece of software comes to life, changes, or evolves alters the business that builds it. Often to build a piece of software is to define the full vision and offering of a business.

DOI: 10.1201/9781003382751-14

It is true that our return is not always in dollars and cents; however, we apply limited resources to create value and reap that return in whatever form it comes.

This means that when we choose to do one thing it often times comes at the expense of something else. If we build the rocket, we can't build the space station.

In typical business situations, judging what we should do comes down to – more or less – a single metric, Return on Investment or ROI. If we invest $100 in Project A, we stand to make $1,000 in return. If we invest $100 in Project B, we stand to make $100,000 in return. Obviously, we will invest our $100 in Project B. We've done something else here that is common in business – we've boiled the time, energy, and inspiration of people down to currency.

This kind of calculation is problematic in software – for reasons we will get into shortly. Decisions of this nature still need to be made. So it's important to have an approach that considers the unique nature of software while still providing for informed leadership regarding the software projects that are pursued.

How we arrange our people and process affects our software delivery in these two arenas. It can speed us up or slow us down – impacting the value that we're putting in the hands of our customers. And it can powerfully improve or radically inhibit our ability to decide where we're investing our resources.

All of this to say, building software well requires getting the right people into the right places. To use Jim Collins' words, we want to get the right people on the bus, and we want them in the right seats [2].

Pulling all of these aspects together and harmonizing them is the topic of this chapter. Taking the varying interests and numerous people and ensuring they row in the same direction in light of these powerful currents is the art of "People and Process" in software development.

THE INTERESTS

Even before we start to examine and direct in this respect, we can categorize the necessary pieces of this puzzle – the interests and role types that naturally emerge when we begin to write software.

The first and most important interest is the problem that we are going to be solving for – that is, the real human beings that we think we might be able to help. This overlaps entirely with the purpose of the business or with the purpose of a segment of the business. The role that aligns most naturally with this interest is the executive leader. Additionally, many organizations create "Product Management" groups to take point on keeping clarity about and understanding the detail of these problems and their solutions. This responsibility naturally connects directly with understanding the way in which the organization is looking to serve its customers.

In reality, anyone, including software engineers, that's involved in the development of software should have a deep connection to the real human problem that's being solved. Unfortunately, though, one of the seemingly natural dysfunctions that often arises in software development organizations is an excessive distance between the purpose of the software and those writing the actual code that fulfills it. This is probably due to the complexity and rate of change of the technology space in general, but there also seems to be a human aspect to the problem. The people that get excited and passionate about writing program code do it for the excitement of working with the machine, often times viewing the actual behavior as a secondary concern.

The second interest – which we've already mentioned in passing – is understanding and bringing clarity to specific aspects of the behavior we intend to create. Many organizations create a Product Management group to really get a grip on this interest. For smaller organizations, software developers often take on this interest. Either way, it's an unavoidable interest that will be dealt with – even if it is somewhat implicitly.

The third interest is simply keeping everything from flying apart and keeping people working together smoothly. The challenge and complexity of building software can bring tension and stress along with it. These, in turn, if not carefully managed, can fray relationships. This interest is usually taken on by managers – managers of engineers, managers of product managers, as well as by higher-level leaders. Additionally, roles commonly referred to as "Agile coaches" or "Scrum Masters" are sometimes hired solely for this purpose.

The fourth and final interest is the technical experts that assemble the computing resources and other technical aspects into a concrete solution for the problem. This interest includes software engineers, data scientists, systems administrators, and others – depending on how the organization divides its labor and the nature of the specific problem set it is addressing.

These are the natural interests that arise and the types of roles that generally deal with them during the course of typical software development. We won't be looking to avoid them so much as to harness and redirect them. When we get in step with the natural rhythm of software development, delivering rapidly and understanding the trade-offs we're making become painless, quick, and natural.

TWO PROBLEMS

For the purposes of arranging our "people and process" – for determining who we put on our team, where we put them, and how they work together – our immediate target is balancing and optimizing for the two problems we quickly outlined above. That is, delivering as fast as possible, while making responsible, informed choices about what we choose to build.

There is a lot of synergy between these two problems, and dealing with one effectively will improve our approach to the other. For this discussion, though, we will treat them as roughly separate problems and we will illustrate how to successfully balance them in a software development practice.

We will start this by diving deep into the specifics of the problem and how it is handled conceptually. We will follow this by the specific aspects of your people and process that, when in place, will carry out this conceptual solution, ultimately balancing these two problems.

The final set of tactical pieces will be arranged such that they do solve for the balance between the two problems, though we will be discussing the conceptual solutions to each separately. This will provide both the principle whose understanding is necessary to be able to adapt solutions to concrete specifics and a good template that will be generally useful and provide a good point from which to start.

SPEED

Unpredictable changes arise regularly in software development.

We seek to meet a subjective human need and because of this neither the humans who potentially have the need, nor we as the product developers seeking to meet it can understand how that need will coalesce once we begin to try to meet it.

In my career, there was a particular experience that illustrated this truth so clearly to me that I've never been able to forget it.

In an organization I had worked with, we began to consider developing a powerful capability that our software hadn't had in the past. We had clients in a number of different types of business. The different businesses had vastly different needs in terms of throughput – though with the current structure of the software, every single request was prioritized and executed the same, regardless the source.

Ten of the most technical folks in the business came together; we were all intimately familiar with the problem and we all knew the kind of solution that would meet our need and better manage our throughput.

It was almost a laboratory environment for analyzing how to identify a need and fill it, because we were for the most part both the customer and the developer at the same time.

The somewhat surprising outcome for me – since I was the one tasked with coding up the first couple of takes – was that our initial design needed massive revision. The capabilities needed refinement as did the user experience.

The group met regularly, and as quickly as I was able to offer rough examples, we made revisions based on the team's experience interacting with them.

The obvious principle I extracted from this is that no matter how well someone knows the domain, or how familiar they are with the problems faced by a given customer type, no one ever knows what will be needed until they begin to use actual, working software.

We should quickly imagine what a world might look like if this principle weren't true. Someone might take a look at the problems that we as humans are facing. They would then locate a software developer – and in a small amount of prose or a quick direct conversation, they might explain the problem and the solution that would work. The software developer would immediately turn that idea into working software and the problem would be immediately solved.

In this hypothetical world, there is zero friction in the process of solving human problems with software. The fact that we might do this as a team doesn't alter our situation at all – because the clear understanding is communicated among all teammates with the same ease that it came from the original individual that discovered the problem – because if it can be communicated from problem finder to developer with perfect clarity, surely the same is true between developers.

Of course, this isn't the world we live in, and those communication channels offer the difficulties that became apparent even in the laboratory setting mentioned above. Adding people to the situation multiplies the problem because it multiplies communication paths.

Using people and process to deliver rapidly boils down, then, to how quickly we can go through this cycle – understanding what value we might bring to a customer, trying something out, revising our direction to more accurately approximate a solution that meets the ultimate, though quite subjective, need.

From the speed perspective, as we lay out the general team shape and delivery process solution, this will be our target to reduce the amount of time in each of these stages.

TRADE-OFFS

It is important as we get into this analysis that we are crystal clear about the implications of the uniqueness of software development on our ability to evaluate the trade-offs we make with our time and energy.

The key component of that uniqueness is that software development is entrepreneurialism. Building software is choosing how the business operates. This is true whether you run the software, or you sell it to someone else.

In the former case, the specifics of the software operation define the workflow of the team that leverages it to serve your customer. For example, if we are a travel company and the software a representative uses to take a phone order requires a particular piece of information, at a particular time – it alters the behavior of the representative, the flow of the call and ultimately the way in which the customer is served.

In the latter case, if we are selling a word processor and we don't include a font that our user might find appealing and useful, it changes the value proposition to that user, alters how we might support it, and means that other capabilities will need to pick up the slack in terms of providing the value that a given individual is willing to pay for.

These are simple examples. There are far more dramatic ones that might be cited – but the point is that every change, no matter how small, to software that our business builds, changes and defines the business itself.

The reason that this is important is because often software development is looked at as an operational concern. Decisions about trade-offs are done as we illustrated in the example above, time and energy are reduced to currency, and compared with a predicted return.

For example, if we spend $100 buying 100 widgets, which we can know we can sell for $5 a piece, we will make our investment back plus a return of $400.

With software development being more like the work of an entrepreneur, both sides of that equation break. We have no idea what the return will actually be, and to be perfectly honest, we don't know how much we will have to invest.

When we start a company, we do research and try to figure out what kind of market there is for our potential solution. We may even ask people how much they'd be willing to pay for it. But the reality – and the reason startups never really predict their return well – is that when we're looking to meet a new need, not even the people whose need we are meeting will be able to explain how they'll respond to a solution for it.

Henry Ford's often repeated famous quip is absolutely on-point in this respect – if he'd asked his customers what they wanted, they would have asked for a faster horse.

A potential user might have a pain point or want something to be better or more streamlined, but they don't know the varying ways that reality will have to be bent and molded in order to get that itch scratched.

Which is the point. We don't know, they don't know. We all have a vague idea but the entrepreneur jumps into those ambiguous, muddy waters and figures it out.

Without knowing ahead of time what the ultimate product or service will look like, and thus, how much it will cost.

This is true no matter how many slide decks, and graphs, and spreadsheets try to get the impression across that he does.

Once a business is in place building physical widgets, where we can obviously make more to match the established demand, we can invest dollars and see the immediate return. This is the part of business that everyone loves, because making more money is just a matter of doing concrete, explicit things that follow obviously from the conditions in the market.

All of this is to say that the creative work of the entrepreneur and the optimizing work of the professional manager are different in kind. Judging trade-offs then has to be done entirely differently.

The story of the evolution of the hard drive in The Innovator's Dilemma is instructive in this. At every stage, when the technology took a real step forward, the company that was selling the last version – they were solidly only in the professional management space. They were optimizing their version of the hard drive, without considering how the actual problem space might be better addressed. Every time, the newcomer ended up beating out the incumbent.

All of this is true of any change that we make to software – even if that software is already being used by a customer.

So one really important question is – why does the entrepreneur jump into the deep waters of creating a business when understanding its return can be so hard to quantify?

They do it for two reasons. On the one hand, they have a passion for a particular problem or avenue for creating value for their fellow humans. Their instinct – in alignment with reality – tells them that a problem being solved will result in reciprocity – in a return for them. On the other hand, years of empirical data show that this is generally true. While not everyone that creates and builds and solves problems finds themselves with a worthwhile return – those who have the humility to really serve the needs of their fellow man and the industry to execute relentlessly do in fact earn returns that make the effort worthwhile.

So we need to make decisions about where to allocate our time and treasure – but ROI in a typical business sense is not really available. The R is potentially off the charts, but unquantifiable, and the I is similarly unquantifiable.

The solution for the software professional is to further follow the lead of the entrepreneur.

We make a couple of important assumptions – assumptions that we can realize with a deep understanding and intentional design of our people and process such that, even in the general case they will bring results.

Assumption #1: There is always a human problem to solve.

Humans always have problems. For every problem we solve, we have ten more opportunities to improve our condition, improve our happiness, or remove discomfort.

Assumption #2: An organization's collective wisdom can reveal a problem to solve.

Even an individual has a pretty good shot at uncovering a problem to solve. A group of folks, assuming they're not hamstrung by any of the thousands of potential interpersonal problems that can arise and prevent creative thinking, not only has a better chance of finding a more important problem – they also bring with them the muscle to more rapidly act on it.

Resting on these assumptions, we are armed well enough to make any decisions about trade-off that we may need to make. The decisions will be qualitative rather than quantitative. It's easy to be wary about a decision that can't be boiled down to a number. Though this is simply the nature of software development and of invention more generally.

So, if you need to decide whether to spend your money on a lease for a new building or on software development, the decision won't be made with a spreadsheet but with a discussion about the qualitative advantages that a building will bring vs. that of the software that might arise from you development effort. The same is true whether the trade-off is software development against an operational investment, or one software development effort against another.

At this point, if you're not comfortable with considering software development trade-offs qualitatively, I'd probably stop reading for a bit and think through that. The rest of the chapter – in fact the rest of the book – will be based largely on the assumptions listed above, and the resulting necessity to make qualitative rather than quantitative assessments about the work that is pursued, particularly when that work is software development.

THE SOLUTION

The intertwined nature of people and process will become clear as we lay out the concrete solution to balancing and maximizing these two interests.

To recap, we want to be as fast as possible putting useful software into the hands of our customers. This means experimenting quickly – going through the cycle of build, try, and adjust with minimal friction. We want to balance that against a qualitative approach to making trade-offs – assuming though that there will always be a problem to solve, and that our collective genius will be able to locate and dispatch that problem when properly applied.

The team

More important than anything else is who we have on our team. A close second to that is how that team is shaped.

The first thing to consider is that the folks on our team are high-quality, high-character people. The conversations that happen throughout the course of a software development project – from determining the functionality of a system to the lowest level implementation details – involve inordinate amounts of detail. This requires deep trust to do effectively, because details of complicated systems become very personal as we work through them. That is, our ownership grows deep because of the extended time we spend absorbed in them.

A person that has character and competence [3] – they are the most highly trusted. They are also most able to trust others. So a team full of high-character, high-competence individuals will be the one that will have the deepest levels of internal trust. This, in turn, means that they'll best be able to work through the detailed, delicate conversations that arise in software development.

The formulation that Jim Collins uses in Good To Great is what he calls "The Level 5 Leader" [2]. We might recoil at this because we're talking about building software development teams. We shouldn't be concerned with leadership should we?

Well to start – the Level 5 Leader is a good model, because the actual traits that define it aren't unique to leadership. The traits – as Collins spells them out – are personal humility and professional will.

Collins' research shows that companies that are led by these types of individuals are the one that go from "good to great." His analysis is focused on top leaders – and leaders that show these characteristics are the ones that really move their companies along most powerfully.

Collins thinks that the two are something of a paradox – that if you're aggressively pursuing your business goals, that humility seems to contradict that.

This is common enough in the business world – success tends to breed arrogance. In fact, it's common enough in the everyday world. The breakdown in logic is easy enough to empathize with. If I've been successful in the past, it must have been my actions primarily responsible for my success. If it's a result primarily of my actions, I am right for dwelling on them – enjoying the sense of superiority my skill and wisdom justify.

To dwell on ourselves is the antithesis of humility. Rick Warren said, "True humility is not thinking less of yourself, it's thinking of yourself less" [4].

This is a fantastic definition and it highlights the power of humility. It frees our cognitive machinery from being tied to the very small fraction of the world that our choices, our skills, and our wisdom represent. It frees us to engage in the broader reality, and ultimately makes us more effective in everything that we do.

That is, personal humility for Collins' Level 5 Leader means that they don't arbitrarily limit their thinking to such a small target as themselves. They open it to broad problems and radical solutions. This, then, enables the "professional will" – the aggressive pursuit of the vision they have for changing the world.

It also enables real, deep integrity. You can be concerned with the interest as it really exists. If our thinking is zeroed-in only on ourselves and our own interests, when a success does come, we might not be able to see when someone else deserves praise, a reward, or a large helping of the glory of that success.

Or even within the context of personal connection, a primary focus on self will short-circuit any attempt at relationship building. Humility more openly looks at all information you might gather, including the interests and passions of others – a notoriously important part of connecting with human beings.

Covey gets at the importance of character and integrity in building the absolutely unavoidable catalyst of business, trust. Collins, then, boils this (as well as Covey's other component of trust, competence) down to just two practical, observable characteristics. These characteristics – personal humility and professional will – on the surface present as a slight paradox, given the behavior of the common man.

So, foundationally, these are the primary characteristics that we need to be looking for in members of any software team that we are building. Trust begets trust and the more these qualities are present in our team members, the more trust will bloom. Trust catalyzes accomplishment – it, more than anything else, drives business forward, regardless the activity.

Professional will in software development will be obvious in several important ways.

The most visible and important way that it will show itself is in a fearlessness when approaching any particular development project. Software development is invention – so by definition it is addressing previously unknown combinations of activities and behaviors. Commonly, individuals can be intimidated by the specifics of the development work that they're doing.

Secondarily, professional will shows through in a focus on purpose. It is easy for software developers to become focused on technology or specific technical problems or solutions. In fact, a big part of the draw to a career in building software is the fascinating technical details involved in a specific piece of software. To put the most value into the hands of customers, though, requires not getting lost in the excitement and the joy of the detail. It means relentlessly seeking to understand what that value is – and how to leverage software to create it.

Probably the least obvious aspect of professional will that we might notice in a software development context is driven by this focus on purpose. The more an individual is hungry to find the most valuable use of software for the organization's customers, the more he will struggle to find the best approaches to building that software. That is to say, using our previously developed vocabulary, it will drive an individual to see and to work on the "people and technology system," as opposed to being content only building the computer.

This is because people and technology systems readily lapse into disrepair. In fact, without intentional effort spent to improve it, the people and technology system will almost immediately begin to break down. Regardless how focused on customer value an individual becomes, if the larger supporting system isn't able to produce that value, it begins to reveal itself as an inhibitor to be fixed.

As we're building our software teams then, our primary points of focus should be personal humility and professional will. Personal humility in software is particularly challenging, because the technologies, solutions, and techniques are so technically detailed that they provide an uncommonly strong illusion that an individual is in complete control of the value that they're creating. We do have a bit of a shortage of humility in our industry and this is likely a large contributor.

Professional will shows itself in three important ways, courageously confronting previously unseen development challenges, focus on purpose, and a growing hunger to make the larger people and technology system work most effectively toward the value we're creating.

No individual is perfect in either of these areas, but as we noted earlier, the better we are in each, the more trust develops on our team. This further enables our ability to put value in the hands of our customers.

Find the best you can, and then continue to develop these fundamental characteristics – and you will have the basis for a world-class software development team.

The team's shape

Once you've got a good set of the right kind of folks, it's important to shape your development team (or teams) properly.

The primary principle here is that a given team should be able to comprehend, build and operate a given software system entirely on its own. No engagement with any other team and no permission should be sought in order to deliver the functionality for which the team is responsible.

As Werner Vogels succinctly put it, "You build it, you run it."

It is important to note that all software is built with the use of other software. Even at the operating system level, the OS software likely relies on BIOS programming. And even lower, while the processor instruction set may not be "soft"-ware in the sense that it can change readily, it is still a programmed system like everything that rests on top of it.

All of that to say – it may be necessary to use libraries or remotely executed procedures. This is not to say that one team is dependent on another team in this instance, even though the software in a strictly technical sense is dependent on the software built by another team.

As an example, we may use Spring Boot libraries as we build our Java application. We may build those libraries into the package we ultimately deliver or run. However, we wouldn't consider the team building the Java application to be dependent on the Spring Boot team itself.

Using libraries like this is so common in business software that we almost don't think about it. We refer to them as dependencies and a medium-sized system may have 100 of them. But we need to be more precise in our choice of words here because there is an important distinction to be made.

The reason there's no team dependency in this (very common) case is that the software being used is packaged and released as a product. The product may be free – but its "interface" (to use a desperately overloaded term from the software world) to the outside world is that of a piece of software that can be downloaded and used. The assumption is that it is complete and that if there are any bugs or feature requests, they will go through a process of review, rationalization, and building that will be far from immediate.

That is, there is an expectation on both sides of the request that an unmet need will not imply immediate action and reprioritization on the part of the team being depended upon – and that for the depending team the wait will be such that it might as well be an immediate "no" to the request. Because of this, neither team affects the workflow or prioritization of the other. That is to say, there is no dependence across teams.

Further, the interest of the depended upon team is solely in the broad reusability of the library or tool that might be needed by other systems. They are not concerned in any specific way with the products that outside teams may be building based on it.

So to reiterate, there are really two kinds of dependency we might talk about in the context of software development. There's technical dependency, where one piece of software uses another piece. Separately, there is organizational dependency, where one team becomes dependent on another, requiring action from the separate team in order to carry out the delivery of the feature set they are responsible for.

Technical dependency presents no problems and is a common, completely normal part of software development. Organizational dependence has a massive negative impact on throughput, though – slowing down all involved teams by orders of magnitude.

To see why this is, it's important to look at organizational dependence in more detail. As we do this, one important thing to notice is that, without a great deal of care, technical dependence can readily become organizational dependence.

Organizational dependence has begun when, in order to put a feature in front of a customer, one team requires concrete work from another. That may be creating database schema, building custom software, or even signing off on a release-to-production workflow. There are degrees of dependence here but the same general forces apply in every case.

1. The team that's being depended upon doesn't have the same interest – that is, they don't have a direct, emotional attachment to putting the feature in front of your customer. Their tool for determining priority is entirely political (for lack of a better term) – against their other priorities, they will determine the importance of yours based on their assessment of how it emotionally impacts those around them.
2. Similarly, in order to avoid the wrong person getting bad feelings, or having to re-address a particular request, the team being depended upon will build defensively.

Both of these results do nothing but add time to the delivery of the software of the depending team.

Eliminating this increase in time means eliminating any cross-team dependency.

Eliminating cross-team dependency can frequently be done simply by the team choosing to do whatever work that would otherwise require another team. So, for example, instead of asking the database administration team – which, for the sake of example, is separate from the team building a particular feature – for a database schema design, the feature team can simply choose to do all database design themselves.

Or – another common case – if the team that's building a feature on a web application needs a REST endpoint created that accomplishes a needed task, they can choose to design and implement this REST endpoint themselves.

In both of these cases, we eliminate dependency simply by taking the initiative – at the team level – to build more of what we need.

Further, both of these instances expose a very general problem in the approach an organization takes to dividing labor. When an organization builds its software teams around technological capabilities or skillsets rather than feature, it makes cross-team dependency a path of least resistance, if not an institutional mandate.

From a high level, the most important thing to do to reduce cross-team dependency is simply to make sure every team is built around a set of features, and not around a capability or technology. So, for example, the following teams push toward cross-team dependency and should be ruthlessly eliminated:

- Scrum Master Teams
- Architecture Teams
- Front-End Teams
- Back-End Teams
- Data (base, warehouse, analytics) Teams
- DevOps (operations) Teams
- … and any other team that focuses on technology or skillset and not feature.

So – to be very clear – everything that your team needs to do that isn't provided by a packaged library or packaged runtime remote call in order to deliver the features that it has chosen to build should be built, performed, and managed by the team itself.

That is, any front-end development that might be needed in service of a given feature should be performed by the feature team, along with back-end development, database design, and architecture. When these begin to be parceled out to other teams, our delivery slows and the value that we are putting in the hands of our customers drops, thus dropping any return we might expect to reap.

As we do this, it's important that we keep tight control on the size of our features. If we aren't careful to break features down in a disciplined fashion, the work involved in delivering them can quickly become more than a single team can handle.

In case it gave you pause, the idea of being "more than a single team can handle" is packed full of meaning. Broadly speaking, there are two contributing factors to what a team might be able to take on – the number of people on the team, and their skill level. There are some challenges with this though. The first is that, while the number of people on a team might be easily quantifiable, their individual skill level is not.

The second challenge is that adding people means accomplishing more only up to a point, past which returns begin to diminish. Both the shared understanding of the feature set and the shared understanding of the technical approach are exceedingly information rich and absolutely unavoidable. This reality means that communication among team members will not only need to be high in volume but high in content.

Further, communication lines increase rapidly as more individuals are added to the team. In fact, the number of communication lines we find ourselves with as we add each individual is proportional to the square of the number of people on the team. A team of 3 will have 3 lines of communication, but a team of 5 will have 10. A team of 10 has 45 communication lines.

Each of these communication lines requires trust, a thorough understanding of each other's perspective, and ultimately a high-quality relationship. Without these characteristics, the kind of deep communication needed simply can't happen.

Further, the responsibility for all of these lines of communication remaining open and healthy is really something the entire team can and should take responsibility for. So as a participant in a given group, I will have an interest in and actively work to remedy any problems with communication lines between participants other than myself. That is, if Joe and Mary are seemingly unable to communicate, their teammate Angela will notice – and she should help bring that communication line back to being healthy.

This all happens pretty naturally on small teams.

The reason that we see this start to breakdown is that it becomes an information overload for team members as the team grows. Again – with a team of 10, there are 45 communication lines. If each team member was concerned with and contributing to the health of the communication lines, they'd be doing nothing else.

What tends to happen is that we naturally spend less effort on particular communication lines, even the ones we're personally involved in (even though that grows only linearly with the number of teammates). The quality of relationship drops, taking with it the quality of discussion, and the level of shared understanding.

Around 10–20 lines of communication is the optimal range for a team. It makes for a large enough team while not over-exerting each member's relational capabilities. It enables every team member to be tracking with each communication line and maintaining a sense of its quality. It ensures every team member can lend a hand to fix a communication line if it's in trouble.

Take a moment to consider this in your own career – when you've been on a team that's had a small number of communication lines, what has been the level of difficulty in tracking all of the individual relationships on the team? What was the depth of understanding of those relationships (even if it was implicit at the time)? How well did you understand the state of your own relationships?

If you're like me, the smaller teams – with fewer communication lines – have always been radically easier to understand. I've always felt more comfortable to help and receive help when any of my connections deteriorated.

Now, to be clear, many people won't think about this explicitly, and they may not even recognize that this is what's going on. While we can actively hinder our relationships, when we're in close contact with people – we have an instinctive desire to come to a peaceful, productive equilibrium. If we're in close, continuous contact with others, it feels uncomfortable and tense when we don't do this – and so the easiest path is often to just get to a place where communication is happening readily.

Obviously, this isn't always the case – people can be offended, and we might choose to run from the problem instead of communicating. Though, very frequently, simply being in close contact – with others watching over us – is just the ticket to create productive communication lines.

So – this rather elaborate discussion of team size is to say that, increasing the size up to about 5 people (10 communication lines) will add productivity without creating communication problems. Up to 7 people or so (21 communication lines) and things won't get too hairy. Much beyond that, and the difficulty we outlined above appears quickly.

To our original question, then, about the amount of work a single team can take on – it is partly circumscribed by a team size that is no more than seven people or so.

The other ingredient is skill level. This is the broader boundary.

Skill level among software developers can vary radically. Further confusing things is the common practice in the corporate world to discuss skill in completely irrelevant terms. We discuss things like number of years of experience with particular programming languages or frameworks or database design. We discuss them because they're easy – because they're concrete – and because they provide a quick way to filter resumes when we're hiring. Unfortunately, as far as predicting the value that an individual might create, they're rather poor.

The important skills, instead, are the four areas of competence that we are in the middle of describing right now – software craftsmanship, people and process, software architecture, workflow automation. Every team member's skill in these four areas will dictate the amount of throughput that a particular team will be able to deliver.

The important thing to note about each of these areas is that there is no end state or top level of skill. We can always be improving, always growing in each of these areas.

This reality is much like we see in any art. While a practitioner will pursue mastery, he recognizes that it is a lifelong journey. It is not a quick trip at which you arrive and then move on.

To return to the original problem then, how are we ensuring that increasing feature size doesn't necessitate a dependency on a separate team by growing past a certain point?

To recap:

- First, we need to make sure the team size isn't too big or too small – between 5 and 7 people is the sweet spot for this based on communication network growth.
- Second, we need to maximize the skills of every individual with the four competencies that we are laying out now. (Software Craftsmanship, People and Process, Workflow Automation, Software Architecture)

The decision then comes down to understanding the state of the team at the time that the development needs to be done. This includes understanding the nature and state of the communication network – how healthy each connection is. It also includes understanding the level of skill in the four competencies that each member has attained.

It should be fairly straightforward to see that no one – save the members of the team, collectively – is in any position to understand from day to day what their potential throughput might be. There may be an identified "manager" on this team who has HR responsibility for one or more of the team members. They don't have any special insight into this throughput – though if they are an integrated part of the team they will have the same contribution to the overall understanding that any other team member will have.

This leads to the unavoidable conclusion – the only way to reliably stay within a team's ability to deliver is for the team itself to choose what it is taking on.

If the feature is too large, it can be further decomposed. Alternatively, it can be put off until it can be addressed at a time when there are fewer needs being simultaneously met.

In doing this, we ensure that we aren't creating any dependence on outside teams.

There are some additional considerations that follow from these realities.

The first is that it is possible that a team simply doesn't have the skillset to pursue a particular feature. That is to say, the collective capability is such that either the decomposition or the actual development is beyond the capacity of the team based on the level of maturity each individual has attained in the four areas of competence.

If the team is small enough, additional, more senior members might be added to bring the capacity up. If the team is already seven-people strong, adding members, no matter how strong they are, will provide diminishing returns, so should be avoided.

At this point, the options are to replace team members with stronger members, grow the existing members before taking on the feature, or choose not to pursue the feature.

Following from this, it's important to always, proactively, be pressing toward the most senior team possible. That means growing every individual as much and as fast as possible. It also means maintaining a culture of mastery within a given team.

As we said earlier, each of the four areas of competence is an unending path along which higher and higher levels of mastery can be attained.

However, it's important that there is a bar of mastery over which 80% or so of the team rests. Particularly important pieces of that mastery include a fairly thorough understanding the four competencies, many years thoughtfully practicing them, and an ability to articulate them and guide others in their application.

Looked at as a ladder, mastery in the four competencies is best evaluated by someone standing several rungs above. This is like any other art or craft that involves mastering detailed skills. It is not possible to recognize the ingrained habits, thinking, and concrete actions that represent that level of mastery if one hasn't attained it themselves.

Having a team that's balanced like this – with 80% mastery – allows for the power of "new blood." New ideas and energy can be brought to the team in a way that doesn't damage the culture of excellence or warp the sense of what the team values in terms of skills.

All of this, in turn, implies that the organizational leader must be of the highest caliber in terms of engineering mastery. Because they will be choosing team members, and because mastery can only really be assessed from above, any engineering team assembled by a given leader will directly limit the throughput of their teams with their own level of mastery. Now for some individuals, this may not be much of a limit at all – for others, they may put a serious cap on throughput simply by their own lack of mastery.

This is of course barring luck. It is possible a leader hire someone that surpasses them strictly out of luck, but it's not wise to depend on luck for the accomplishment of our objectives – and for the impact we want to make on the lives of our customers.

The team's management

As we've discussed in earlier chapters, there are two separate systems we consider when we are building software. There is the computer or software system that we're building – the thing that provides functionality to customers and is the realization of the value that we look to deliver to them. There is also a second system, whose primary output is that software – and this is the people and technology system. This includes the set of interrelated elements necessary to conceptualize and produce the software system. This primarily boils down to putting the four competencies into practice.

The former system is often very implicit and empirical – that is to say, building software is largely an act of trying things, seeing what works, altering your approach and trying again until you've met the need. The latter system is very explicit and a priori. We know the rules for building a successful software practice (or at least you're learning them – which is why you're reading this fantastic book), what we must do is apply those rules with skill. That is to say, building a people and technology system is largely about learning how such a thing works, then practicing it frequently and intentionally.

These two activities require two distinct kinds of leadership.

Building the software requires dynamic leadership. That is, dynamic not in the sense of being charismatic or exciting – but being able to change rapidly in real time. On a software team, anyone that is leading the actual development of the software should be entirely up to speed on the technical details of the feature being worked through and able to "lead from the front" by writing code. The most qualified person, assuming multiple folks working on any given feature, will also change from moment to moment.

Building the people and technology system requires broad influence and the ability to change the shape of the organization. It requires working on a longer time scale – the people time scale – building broad and deep consensus. It can involve separating teams that have long been coalesced as one unit or pulling together teams that have long been separate. It can mean mentoring in specific skills, and it can mean working to ensure individuals on a team have access to the people and information they need to properly conceptualize potential valuable behavior.

These two types of leadership are radically incompatible.

The organizationally defined "manager" is best positioned for the latter scenario – for building the people and technology system. He has an authority that's inherent in his employment in the organization – to varying degrees (depending on the specific title or expected breadth of influence). This means that – at least as a starting point – he has some leverage with which to shape the people and technology system for which he's responsible. The people and technology system that an individual is responsible for almost certainly extends beyond the scope of their "legitimate" organizational control – so there will be change scope that will be entirely influence-based. Though that simply means that expectations around time and the amount of discussion necessary will need to be set appropriately.

The incompatibility really revolves around the time horizons involved in the change that's being led. In the case that the leader is involved in building the software system, the horizon might be minutes, hours, or at the most, days. In building a people and technology system, the horizons might be months or years.

The horizons define both how long it might take to accomplish something as well as an upper limit to the time that might be expected for a leader to respond to a need.

So a leader involved in leading the building of the software system, aside from moving into and out of leadership rapidly, would also field many short-notice (relative to the longer horizon of the people and technology system) interruptions on a regular basis. This would make progress with the people and technology system very difficult.

The only reasonable approach, then, is to dedicate the organizational "manager" to the work of building the people and technology system – and the members of a given team to leading the work of building the specific software that it takes on. That's not to say there might not be input from the team to the manager or the manager to the team. Though in terms of actually leading a given effort, this division is really the only workable solution.

There's a subtle leverage point or advantage that comes along with this division. It means that a given manager can have a much broader scope of responsibility than is normally allocated in software development organizations. Detached from delivery of specific pieces of software, a manager might have as many as 35 or 40 direct reports – compared to the 4–5 reports a manager might be responsible for in the usual case. That is to say, the scope of people and technology system that can be put into an individual's hands is far broader. This reduces the time and complexity of making changes to the system.

The only other blocker to this might be administrative overhead. Commonly, organizations can yolk managers with work that grows linearly with number of direct reports like complicated performance review processes, etc. This is a part of the people and technology system that gets far outside even of the software development organization itself. But nonetheless it is one that, to drive up throughput, should be dealt with quickly.

One other objection that might come up is the "care and feeding" of individual software developers. Commonly, organizations can develop a culture of regular one-on-one meetings – as well as a sense that a manager is automatically a mentor for every developer that reports to them.

With one-on-one, it's important to note that these are largely important when the manager is actively leading actual development of software. They exist in order to keep him abreast of the technical proceedings within the team and to maintain relationship and trust within a mechanism that, for the reasons listed above, is quite sub-optimal.

When the manager is able to step away from building the software system, this need evaporates. Staying abreast of technical developments is unnecessary – and the trust account between the manager and his report is not so easily overdrawn.

The idea that the manager is automatically the best choice for mentor is also one that we can pretty readily dispense with.

As we mentioned before, in terms of mastery, the manager should be among the top for everyone that reports to him. So that qualification, at least ideally, should be met readily.

However, the direction and the focus that a mentee might wish to take may vary considerably from that of the manager. It's for this reason that a mentoring relationship is one that's chosen by both parties – and tying it to the choice to work for a given manager is unnecessarily restrictive. Especially since there's presumably a whole group of folks that work for him that are great options for mentoring.

So while the manager might choose to mentor one or more of his reports – there's no reason to consider it a given, especially considering the energy and commitment that such an authentic relationship requires. There's no reason the rest of his team can't help to shoulder that responsibility. Further, having the additional options increases the chance that a good match is found between mentor and mentee.

All of this to say – increasing expectations around number of direct reports is a powerful, though hidden lever that through decreasing the required participants in larger people and technology system modifications reduces effort, complexity, and ultimately time. This of course multiplies the value that's getting out to the customer.

PROCESS

Our ultimate target is to create a structure that carries ideas – as they form – from the originator, through development, to customer use with only natural resistance. Natural resistance in this system would be the generation of the idea, any experimentation failure, and the skill level of the engineers that are building the system.

Improvement in throughput similarly would then come down to increasing skill and intuition when generating ideas and enhancing the skill level of the engineering team.

This is the ideal.

Approaching this requires a great deal of skill as well – so in the real world, improvement also means pushing process forward so that we are getting as close as we can to this ideal.

This ideal rests on a vitally important – though somewhat complicated – set of relationships.

The more time we spend developing a thing, the more of it will change by the time we're done. Additionally, the more concrete we are about something, the more buy-in we generate. This combination of factors means that the more scope that is in question, the less concrete we can be about it – because the more likely it will be that an increasingly large portion of it will change, creating ever increasing costs as buy-in grows.

That is to say, if we let the size of the chunks of scope that we bite off increase – we are faced with one of two problems. We will be totally vague about the specifics of the development work – meaning our experiments will vary wildly and getting them to converge on a useful need will be difficult. Even as we take feedback from our customer base, the variation that the next experiment might be subject to means we will most likely remain wide of the target.

The alternative to this is that we are very specific about the details of the large chunks of scope. This will mean widespread buy-in – that will grow as a function of the breadth of the scope. This, in turn, means that the cost to change will be high – in terms of conversation, selling, and convincing.

In both of these cases, we thwart our dual purpose – value through speed, and the ability to make trade-off choices as soon as information is available.

The solution to this is not exactly intuitive, but it's straightforward to execute on once we know what it looks like.

This is the key point. The leader needs to have a good grasp on the solution as well as its underlying theoretical foundation. The leader also needs to make sure that this understanding permeates every part of their team – without it, team members can't flex the workflow in an appropriate manner in the face of unexpected circumstances.

To work within this interesting tension, we simply need to adopt one rule – *concreteness of details should be inversely proportional to size.*

That is, something that is trivially small should be entirely concrete. A "50,000-foot vision" should be very abstract.

In this way, change is no longer proportional to scope and in fact, it's cheap regardless breadth of scope.

This seems an easy enough rule to implement until we get practical and try to take the top leader's vision for a new piece of software and hand it off to a development team. This is, in fact, the driver for the overly specific large scope efforts. If we hand off something broad and vague to a development team whose purpose in life is to realize the most concrete form of behavior known to man – program code – we set the stage for endless conversations. These conversations will be driven by the feature team in order to figure out, ad-hoc, all the necessary specifics.

The reaction to that is easy enough to guess, more specificity in the earlier stages. We then find ourselves in a terrible, but predictable spot, where we have long, slow builds that are highly resistant to change.

To solve this, we need three additional tools:

1. Layered decomposition – taking features from vague idea to small, concrete pieces.
2. Differentiated decomposition – taking small concrete features to individual technical decisions.
3. Habit – regularly working through decomposition in a way that doesn't require planning or almost any cognitive engagement.

With these three tools we can keep our commitment to our one rule – *concreteness of details should be inversely proportional to size* – while at the same time not creating the chaos that makes maintaining that rule socially impossible.

Layered decomposition

Taking a broad organizational vision and turning it into software requires at least three levels of definition and decomposition.

Vision – The first of these is the raw idea. What do we think the high-level problem is that a customer might have in the marketplace? How are we going to address that with software? For example, a problem that – since the late 90s – has been recognized and solved with varying degrees of refinement is banking from a computer. It's easy to imagine a company saying to itself, "we notice that folks would love to do some of their banking without having to travel to a branch, and we might use a web application to do that."

A broad vision like this will very often require more than one development team to accomplish. That's fine. At the point of being an expression of vision, very few details will be spelled out and thus the buy-in will be around the abstract idea, which will be easy to change as information becomes available.

Ideally everyone that may be involved in the realization should be involved in conversations around this. The feedback can help to inform trade-off discussions and to refine the idea.

Trade-off decisions at this time are particularly straightforward. We can choose to attack whatever the vision is, or we can choose not to. That may mean we go after another vision or we may decide that we don't want to pursue software development at all at this time. But either way we have that option at this point, without having spent too much time digging into details that would only cloud the thinking.

Feature – Once we've decided we will pursue the raw idea, it can be broken down into a set of features, where each feature can be taken on by a single team. The subset of features that will be directly addressed can be much more specific in details. The additional concreteness is balanced by the fact that the scope is now much smaller. The vision may have been that the organization creates a bank. The feature in question might be something like; create the ability to transfer funds between accounts.

An important thing to remember is that as a part of this layered decomposition – we are decomposing in terms of functionality. In development groups that are dominated by more technically minded people, this can often be a challenge. The alternative, of course, is to begin to breakdown vision by technical implementation details and approaches. So we might have the vision to "create a bank" – and the break down might begin to involve things like, select a database vendor, create a website, or create an API layer.

This kind of decomposition amounts to nailing down a bunch of detail without limiting the scope of the capability. That is, the work of creating an API layer is, without shrinking the scope of the functionality, just as ambiguous as the vision it came from – and at the same time it likely represents a collection of details that have created or will create broad and deep buy-in. So we've gotten the worst of both worlds.

Just to repeat, for that reason, throughout the course of this layered decomposition, it is important to remember that we are decomposing by feature. This is something that can actually be exercised by an end user.

Now, because the individual feature is taken on by a single team, the only people that need to be involved in any decisions about its specifics are those of that individual team. They will have the same target – to deliver the most value to the user with the greatest return to the business. So it will be incumbent on the team to take advice and input from specific customers as well as from experts inside and outside the business.

In terms of defining the details of a given feature, that responsibility will belong to the team – ensuring that the breadth of the buy-in will be contained within those bounds. There will undoubtedly be slight buy-in with folks that contribute thoughts and input to the ultimate outcome. But the difficult and expensive-to-change buy-in will be contained within the team – where the relationships are the closest and the communication lines strictly controlled.

Using our formulation from above, even at the feature level we're still not entirely concrete. We are still covering in abstraction a non-trivial breadth of software development. Because of this, the team – even though they're the most invested – isn't so invested that the specifics of the feature can't readily change. Though that other problems still exist, if we were to try to develop software based on our current level of definition it would trigger confusion, and a steady flow of ad-hoc discussions.

So we need to take the feature to its final state – the trivial feature.

Trivial feature

The feature can then be broken down into one that is so trivial that it can all but directly be turned into software. Where our higher-level feature might have been; "create a capability to transfer money," the trivial feature might be; "create a capability to indicate the amount of money to transfer." Even still there may be increasingly trivial features that might support this one. If there are, you can and should take this down to the lowest possible level.

A heuristic for the trivial feature is that any software developer on your team can look at it and confidently assess it as being a day or two worth of work. The real target is something that has the least possible detail while still being a behavior that a customer would understand and value. The "day or two" bar can always be met – and pretty obviously indicates the limited nature of the scope.

An important note on determining what a customer might value. The measure isn't, "would this be a useful tool all by itself" – it's more along the lines of "would it, from the customer's perspective, materially change the nature of the software."

A method for indicating the transfer amount in our hypothetical banking application, for example, wouldn't be something a customer might go use for its own sake – but without it the transfer functionality that would be usable on its own would not only be materially different, but it would also be unusable.

The point of the distinction is as we discussed above – there are two ways a decomposition might happen, by feature or by technical aspect. Many times this almost seems to come down to a semantic distinction. We could, for example, in our trivial feature about creating the ability to indicate transfer amount, instead break that down to create a text box labeled transfer amount.

The actual code that might come from either of these might be indistinguishable – but the important part here is the human, communication aspect of how we frame these things.

Having the features broken down to trivial allows us to change direction quickly by minimizing buy-in. It also allows us to inform our thoughts about the direction of the overall solution so that we can make trade-offs from the lowest levels of this trivial feature to the highest-level vision.

This is an important part of this decomposition. The truth is, that this decomposition has to happen. If it's not done explicitly and by choice, it will be done implicitly when someone tries to turn higher-level ideas into code. Done explicitly though – it allows those involved at the varying degrees of abstraction to make choices that are as informed as they can be – without multiplying change costs. This meets both of our stated goals, value through speed and the ability to make trade-off decisions as information becomes available.

So as we conduct this progressive, layered decomposition, it's an important discipline to maintain that even when it seems like we might skip over a portion due to it being obvious or uninteresting, that we continue with the breakdown anyway.

This completes the layered decomposition. Once we've taken our vision down to pieces of trivial size, we've decomposed the feature set appropriately.

This isn't a point in time event. At every layer of decomposition, we only really break out enough material that can readily be addressed at the next lowest layer. So while we may take the full vision and start to decompose it into features, we would only do that so far as that set of features can be immediately handled by the team or teams addressing them.

If we work to break out the entire set of features conceivable as part of the vision, we've moved back into defining all of the detail of the vision, which increases buy-in and thus the cost of change. This, again, slows down progress, and makes trade-off decisions more expensive and thus more unlikely to be made appropriately.

Differentiated decomposition

After we've broken our vision down all the way to trivial features, we can begin to work on each of the features to break it down into specific technical work.

Throughout the course of the feature elaboration and decomposition, the involved teams might have been lightly considering possibilities for technical approach. When we get to differentiated decomposition, the time has come to entirely define the technical aspects of the implementation.

For a trivial feature, this will be straightforward and almost feel redundant since the technical folks involved in the conversations will likely have been toying with approaches in their minds.

Now that the feature is clear, unambiguous, small yet deeply bought into, we don't introduce any additional trouble by very strictly defining technical aspects – everything from specific details of data storage, communication mechanisms between components, and even classes, methods, and functions.

Since the trivial features that a team is taking on have been judged to be immediately addressable and since we take that same question to the technical details, we end up with a set of very specific technical work that leaves minimal questions open between the conceptual agreement between team members and the actual code that it needs to become.

At this point then, the TDD cycle begins in earnest as described in the previous section on craftsmanship. We have a well-defined, trivial feature whose behavior can be tested in an automated manner, and a technical approach that will guide the specific work we might engage in.

Habit

The final, incredibly important, piece that comes into play here is making all of this habitual. Everything from decomposition of the vision down to the specific technical implementation details should be habit. Habit ensures that we are minimizing cognitive load. This means ensuring that we're not wasting energy thinking about how or when we might do a certain kind of decomposition. Instead, we're optimizing to spend all available mental energy on the actual task.

The importance of optimizing for cognitive load can't be overstated. The energy that we have available to think and the inspiration we have to create are – from the original idea down to the single line of code – the big limiter on our throughput as we create software.

This decomposition problem is ripe for optimizing in this way with habit.

At each level of the decomposition, we will likely generate far more material than we can immediately address. The two variables in this equation are the number and skill level of the teams we have available to attack a particular vision and the breadth of the vision itself. Both are relatively easy to adjust.

If there's not enough vision, the organization can simply broaden the scope of the problem that it wants to solve and spend the time to do the additional creative thinking.

Alternatively, if there's not enough team throughput to deal with the vision, hiring is the most appropriate solution.

In either of these cases, we get the most value out with a minimized investment by reducing to habit all decomposition from vision to technical detail.

Habit is created by regularly scheduling events to do a certain kind of activity. Everyone who participates will immediately go to the work at hand without coaxing or needing to – at the individual level – prepare themselves mentally.

The habits for larger scope, more abstract decomposition should be less frequent. Smaller scope, more concrete habits should be more frequent. The most concrete activity, for example – actually writing code – should be happening every day.

So to pull this all together, we might have a schedule like this[1]:

- Every six months have a vision casting session that generates broad buy-in around the very abstract notions of the problem space we want to – as a company – be working in, and how we might solve problems in that space. This should include every single person that might be involved in the creation of the solution. It should be a working session – vision is not pushed out, it is forged.
- Every three months have a planning session that breaks out around a quarter's worth of features that your team(s) can embark on toward the mission. Everyone – the same group as in the six-month vision conversation – should be involved in this.
- Every month, for each team, have a planning session that will take that months' worth of features and break them down into trivial features. Only the team members should be a part of this. The buy-in around the specific details should be limited to the smallest possible group to make change as easy and cheap as possible.
- Every two weeks, for each team, take the trivial features and turn them into two weeks' worth of concrete technical implementation details. This should again be limited only to the implementing team. The buy-in around technical approach should be even more strictly controlled, so that change in such a detailed technically sophisticated arena is kept as close as possible. When this kind of buy-in leaks, it can create very difficult to surmount challenges because of the exploding level of detail and expertise necessary to resolve them.
- Every day, talk through exactly what you'll be building as a team and then build it – using the methods outlined in the previous chapter on craftsmanship.

At every point in this schedule we are keeping buy-in under control which allows us to change rapidly and to make trade-off decisions without being bogged down by high change cost. Further the things we learn at every level in this set of habits can feedback into all the others. So if something comes out as we are designing a database table at the two-week planning that speaks to the overall feasibility or cost of the thread we're working, that can feed back up into the overall vision, and direction can be changed as needed with minimal cost.

PEOPLE AND PROCESS

Selecting our people, forging them together as a team or set of teams, and designing the way we work together is a radically difficult problem in software development.

It's important to keep our target in mind when we are doing these things – we want to maximize usefulness to our customer (and thus return to ourselves) while allowing ourselves the flexibility to make trade-off decisions as information arises.

To make that happen, we need a baseline of high-quality people. These people should be both trustworthy and hungry to make a difference with software. Further, they need to be good at and growing in the four competencies of software development.

We then structure the way these folks work together in such a way that they are regularly and aggressively working from vision down to technical detail leveraging disciplined habit.

And finally, as leaders we must be relentless in keeping the best people at the highest levels of mastery. When we do this, nothing will be able to slow us down and the impact we make will be powerful, and ultimately unforgettable.

NOTE

1 The Scrum Framework [5] lays out an approach much like this. It's important to note here the reason why these activities are important, not just that they somehow work just by doing them. In achieving such an understanding, we are better prepared to flex our methodology as circumstances present themselves.

WORKS CITED

1. P. McBreen, Software Craftsmanship, Boston: Addison-Wesley, 2002.
2. J. Collins, Good to Great, New York, NY: HarperCollins, 2001.
3. S. R. Covey, The 7 Habits of Highly Effective People, New York: Simon & Schuster, 1989.
4. R. Warren, The Purpose Driven Life, Grand Rapids, MI: Zondervan, 2012.
5. J. Sutherland and K. Schwaber, "Scrum Guides," 2024. [Online]. Available: https://scrumguides.org/

Areas of competence

Architecture

For the importance of it and the investment frequently made in it, the value and definition of architecture are surprisingly vague. I've served as an architect for a large financial firm – and I've had any number of discussions and asked endless questions about the nature and purpose of the role – and more importantly, of the activity itself.

Architecture – in a large enterprise – often reminds me of electronic dance music (EDM, as it is referred to for short). EDM has no end to sub-genres and sub-sub-genres. There are of course Techno, Trance, and House – probably, depending on who you ask, the highest-level categories. Each of these has a number of sub-genres – for example, under trance we find tech trance, progressive trance, goa trace. Beneath them are yet more interesting and specific categories.

Architecture follows the same pattern – there are enterprise architecture, solutions architecture, software architecture, and security architecture. Under software architecture, we commonly have application architecture and data architecture. The hierarchies and names all seem to have slightly different meanings in different organizations – though there are groups out there that look to standardize on these things.

This has all gotten quite out of hand. When looked at properly, that is when looked at as a means to delivering as fast as possible so that we can deliver as much value as possible, we'll see that architecture as a concept simplifies radically.

As I mentioned, I've frequently asked – as I've gone through my career – what the purpose of architecture actually is. The vagaries that masquerade as answers to this question, and the defensiveness that this often inspires betray the overcomplication of an otherwise perfectly straightforward activity.

By the end of this chapter, you'll know exactly what architecture is, you'll be able to tell others, and most importantly you'll be able to apply it immediately to your organization.

DOI: 10.1201/9781003382751-15

WHAT IS IT?

What is architecture?

Well to start – it's a metaphor. It's a metaphor that relates building large physical structures – houses, high-rises, etc. – to building software.

When we build physical structures, we have many choices to make about the materials we might use and how they might fit together. Bricks, wood, steel, concrete – these are some of those materials. The materials chosen and how they fit together result in the aesthetics and "functionality" that we're looking for.

Building a software system, we have any number of materials that we can use, some of them are what we often think of as technical details – frameworks, infrastructure systems like databases and queues, programming languages, etc. We can also think of the features we are delivering as the material that we are fitting together. And just as in the physical world, how we fit them together determines the aesthetics and functionality.

So far, the metaphor seems pretty solid. We need to fit all these varied materials together in a way that will work along with the reality the end product will exist within. It makes a lot of sense that we'd have a good plan for that, and possibly even carve out roles – that is, divide labor accordingly – so that we can do this as effectively as possible.

WHY DO WE PURSUE ARCHITECTURE?

This is a question that sounds like it would be easy to answer – though it's a little complicated. What we'll address here is the current state of the world. So the question might be what do organizations that exist today hope to achieve by pursuing architecture.

I'd say there are probably two primary parts to the answer to this question.

The first is in line with a principle that we've discussed before – Stephen Covey's "first creation" [1]. Designing software, "doing architecture," is important because it is the first creation. It allows us to imagine what software might look like when it's built, which means that we will build a better thing when we go to actually build it.

One of the reasons we have such an explosion of different types of architecture is that there are so many ways of thinking about the design of a given system. If we look through the lens of data, at all of the various pieces of information we might use, how they might work together, and what kind of storage will be needed, we might look at architecture one way – and we might be inclined to call it data architecture. If we look at our design how it might actually solve a customer's specific set of problems, we might look at the design a different way – possibly referring to it as solution architecture. And of course, if we have a massive enterprise over which we seek to understand the structure of the systems we are building or enhancing, we might call that enterprise architecture.

So, the way we approach our first creation, and the lenses through which our organization views our system (or systems), is largely the basis it has for the activity that is generally referred to as architecture.

The other answer to the question about why we pursue architecture describes a bit more practically how such a specialty takes shape.

Division of labor is a powerful concept that organizations the world over have learned to leverage. Dividing labor allows people to focus on a specific part of the final value so that both they and the folks that they are sharing the labor with can be more focused in their approach. The outcome can be of higher value since the investment is lower based on that increased focus.

Ostensibly, the world of building software seems to be rife with these opportunities. As mentioned above, there is data storage to think about, the specifics of how the customer's problem is being solved, security, and any number of other things.

So focusing on these specific parts of the first creation to the point that we're actually dividing labor is a big driver toward the architecture-focus that is so common in mid-to-large-sized enterprises.

The question then is – with whom are those focused on architecture – the purposefully carved out architects – dividing labor? Who would otherwise do the work of designing the system?

This is where this reason for pursuing architecture gets the most practical.

There are three classes of contributor that yield a part of their work to the architect. We should point out though that these classes cut across a major seam in software development – one we've talked about in earlier chapters, particularly (and most recently) in the discussion on decomposition – that between features and technical implementation details.

First is the software engineering leader. The person that has management authority for an engineering team often finds themselves to have the ultimate authority regarding either or both of the technical implementation details and the feature set.

We know from our previous discussion of people and process that this is a problematic arrangement, but for the time being we are discussing the origins of focus on architecture and the creation of architecture roles.

As an engineering leader, if we do have the pressure to have the final word in one or both of these critical arenas, we can find ourselves feeling a little bit insecure, particularly since that responsibility – somewhat ironically – precludes the possibility of actually having hands on understanding of either. This is because in both cases, even for small teams, there will be multiple streams of material constantly coming at the leader for their "final say."

This of course makes both types of information ripe for "dividing labor" – both for the streams of features and for the streams of technical implementation details. And so, an obvious solution for the leader is to create an architecture role and hand off that responsibility.

The second class of contributor to the labor divisions that architects take on is the hands-on engineer.

There is a lot of software design work done by engineers that are actually writing the code for the system. This work might include software structure, libraries to use, systems to integrate with, and data storage. There are any number of things that might more readily fit into the category of features that engineers design – security, scalability, and actual business functionality.

The more technically sophisticated, the more detailed, the more novel a particular piece of software is, the more challenging it is from an engineering perspective. That challenge often equates to larger design efforts and thus labor that can be divided.

The third class of contributor to labor that the architect can take on is the class that generally takes point on features and product vision. In most organizations these roles are often referred to as product management. But often the same general set of work might be handled by project managers or even solely the engineering managers as noted above. Whatever the role within a given organization, the work that is often off-loaded as architecture is similar. It is defining the shape of the software specifically in terms of features and how it meets the needs of the customer.

So, we use this familiar metaphor – that of designing a physical structure by arranging materials. We apply it, in the general case, to make our software development more effective by offloading the work involved in fitting those various materials together. The more emotional side of this motivation can often be simply having too much work assigned to particular people – followed by the natural impulse to remove whatever work might be reasonably removed that's not core to their competencies or their job description. It can also be related to fear – as particularly noted in the case of the engineering leader – in that the complicated, detail-rich work of software development can readily fail, and providing any available reassurance to avoid failure is helpful. In the case of all three of our potential contributors of architecture work, simply not having the skill to deal with the more technical details of a software project might be the challenge – pulling these sets of details out, considering them separately and assigning them to someone dedicated to the task might also be helpful.

That is, our metaphor gives us a seemingly powerful way to divide labor in order to make our teams and our organizations more effective.

THE PROBLEM

Unfortunately, the metaphor breaks down in some very important places that directly affect this kind of application.

The primary problem is that unlike the physical structure we might construct based on a given architecture, our materials are highly dynamic. Not only do they readily change under outside influence – that is, our "bricks" can be dramatically different from moment to moment, even within the time-frame of a particular effort.

More importantly in software development, every potential material is a candidate for altering and recreating. Unlike the effect of materials rapidly changing from outside influence, this means that the nature of the materials that we are using to build our systems, their very nature down to the most minute detail is on the table for altering or recreating. This would be akin to potentially inventing new kinds of bricks for every building that we design.

Certainly if you go down the stack far enough there are some things that wouldn't get regular explicit thought about reinvention. For example, building a web application, we might not often explicitly consider writing a custom operating system for it. Though that's not to say that this might not be done – or even that it doesn't offer some advantage (performance, security, etc.) – more that, at a certain level because of regular reuse habit, it would keep a team from spending too much time on that particular approach.

The other aspect of this is that – as mentioned above, for certain formulations of the metaphor – our bricks might not be our technical details but features. So "architecture" then might be fitting a set of features or capabilities together in a way that creates value, ultimately, for the customer.

These are even more dynamic because they will change, potentially radically, as we learn – experimenting with them as we write them and as we put them in front of customers. Using our metaphor, this would be like try to change the bricks after we've already placed them in the structure.

So the metaphor breaks down – what does that matter? We know what the real situation is and we can just accommodate the quirks of software development as we go.

The point here is really that the metaphor doesn't work at all. The value of the architecture metaphor is that we fit static building blocks together as an isolated piece of work, so that we can divide labor, and set the rest of the engineering staff free to do their more specific work.

The reality is there are no static components.

As such, dividing labor in this manner introduces more problems than it solves.

Treating the pieces of the engineering effort – be they features or technical implementation details – as building blocks means understanding their nature. With the exception of low-level implementation details like operation system or programming language, these "bricks" are highly dynamic. Even still, if a thing has even the potential to change, this is communication and consensus that must happen with the "architect" and every other player with an interest in the detail. This may not always be the same group. Some folks might have more interest in features, some in implementation details. Either way, even with just one architect and one reasonably sized development team, this is a huge number of edges we've now added to the communication graph. If the organization is the size of organization that typically finds itself beginning to take these kinds of stabs at labor division, with dozens of engineering teams and more than one team of architects, the number of new edges can be astronomical.

"Well we don't need consensus," you might say. "Communications paths might explode – but anytime there's an architectural decision it will be a quick conversation."

First, those "architectural decisions" are legion – every time a detail changes about one of the architecture "bricks" – the nature of the brick needs to be reassessed to ensure it still fits the design. So, even with no need for consensus, simple understanding is a huge deal. More importantly, it is a big consumer of time.

Second, eliminating consensus at these points means that in every situation where architecture decisions are made, an interested party loses its voice. This might be the off-loader of the work or it might be the staff that's taking on the architecture work. In both cases, that loss of voice means less buy-in and thus less creativity brought to bear. This of course, ultimately, means slower delivery times.

To tie this to our primary goal, this means less value in the hands of customers, and less return for the business.

All of that to say – architecture as commonly evolved and practiced within medium to large enterprise creates more problems than it solves.

THE SOLUTION

This chapter is called "architecture" – and all we've done to this point is shown how architecture doesn't work as a metaphor – is that the big takeaway here?

When we discussed leadership earlier, we recognized a key point. To lead well in the software development organization, we must elevate our thinking. The obvious approach to leading is to get out front and make sure software is developed – writing code, designing systems, ensuring tactically that software is built. That kind of leadership is necessary but problematic for the organizationally legitimate leader, or more commonly referred to as, the "manager."

As we elevated our thinking, we realized that there's a broader system that needs broad thinking and influencing – that is to say, broad leadership. Getting the people, processes, and technology aligned according to proper principle and then keeping them there is the more important role for the manager.

There's an analogous elevation that needs to happen here.

Instead of the parallel between the physical structure and software being about the details of specific instances of software systems, we need to realize that there is a general way to look at all software. Ensuring that we achieve and maintain this general structure is the "architecture" that really matters.

With the problems in mind that we've laid out, we can think about where this metaphor might more naturally apply itself.

Let's look at the lowest details – from method names and object relationships, down to the compiler we choose, and even the operating system as we mentioned above. All of these things are blocks that we piece together. All of them could arguably be called architecture.

They all suffer from the problems we outlined above – they're detail-rich and fluid.

If we move up to application servers, database servers, runtime hosts and networks, and even the services that rest on these things that respond to customer requests, we see the same problem. If we were to keep count of every detail, it would have multiplied as all of these things are complex, dynamic systems themselves.

The elevation comes by changing our perspective somewhat. There's a variable that we haven't discussed on which the whole question of architecture turns.

That is the team.

To deliver software with maximum speed, one of the single most important things to do is to keep teams from having dependencies on one another.

This implies a very important aspect of the structure of every possible piece of software that might be developed by a given organization. If there is more than one team – and if those two teams shouldn't have any dependency, they can't share the building or maintenance of any software.

This means the point at which we make a broad structural decision about the software is when it becomes too large for a single team (or in anticipation of this situation). The decision then is simply – and always – to break the software down by feature such that in no longer too large for that single team.

The alternative to breaking software down by feature is to break it down by technical detail. For example, software might be decomposed by frontend, back-end, data storage, etc. If we decompose this way for our teams, it means that – to deliver a given feature – multiple teams will be involved. This, in turn, means that there will always be dependency – if I build a front-end aspect that uses an API from the back-end, I will likely need to be in regular contact with at least the back-end team during development. This says nothing of deployment or operation, which will obviously tie the teams quite tightly together as well. Software and thus teams that are broken down this manner aren't separate teams.

This is the elevation necessary – to think of architecture only as a relationship between software and the team that manages it, and only in terms of a single decision point. That is, is the software of a size that a single team can be responsible for building, maintaining, and operating it.

Again, much like with leadership, this elevation changes our view of the activity such that it better matches reality.

Architecture conceptualized this way fits the metaphor well (which is of course secondary). More importantly, it shines a bright light on one of the most important aspects of running a software development organization properly – keeping teams moving fast means keeping them independent, keeping them independent means not sharing any software.

In software architecture, sharing is not caring.

WORK CITED

1. S. R. Covey, The 7 Habits of Highly Effective People, New York: Simon & Schuster, 1989.

Chapter 13

Areas of competence

Workflow automation

As with the other three competencies, speed is the target. Speed gives us an increased opportunity to experiment – thus a quicker path to meeting an actual, concrete need. Speed also, more basically, just makes a thing more valuable – as humans, we value a thing more delivered today rather than a month from today.

Skill with workflow automation brings a very direct impact to our delivery speed. This is because when we discuss workflow automation, we ask how to remove as much manual work as possible from the task of building and operating software.

A number of terms have a connection to this work – "DevOps" and "CICD" being two of the most common. It's important when we do discuss these important ideas though, that we are dealing with them generally. I believe that the idea of "Workflow Automation" captures this general concept more accurately – even if the name isn't as unique and "techy" sounding.

Again, the important part to remember is why our teams and organizations need this skill. What does it bring to the systems we build and the people we serve?

By skillfully automating everything our feature teams do throughout the course of their work, they increase the speed of their work. That means features in the hands of users quicker. That, of course, means more value and thus more return.

As we get into this, there really isn't much principle to discuss. In the seminal work, "Continuous Delivery" [1], Humble and Larman capture it best: automate almost everything. The qualification – almost everything – is important for two reasons:

1. Ultimately building software is creative and subjective, so there are sets of things which don't offer themselves to automation. Writing the software itself is one of these, as is uncovering needs, or – even at a high level – designing the system to meet these needs.
2. There are points where manual – that is to say, human – intervention is actually desirable. This may be a sign off that code has been examined by a second party, or a go ahead for a production release.

DOI: 10.1201/9781003382751-16

That's not to say that either of these are things that must be done, but there are, frequently, interventions that might make sense to a given business.

Those caveats aside, the real key to this – and it really is as simple as it sounds – is to take the set of tasks that developers do and build software systems and leverage existing tools to automate them.

That is – in the effort to deliver the features – the value – that the customer is looking for, we're writing some software.

If that sounds like business as usual for software developers, you're right. The work to automate workflow is exactly the same kind that a developer would be engaged in otherwise.

In fact, many projects even begin their lives fairly automated if only because the development team that is building it is so used to a particular part of their workflow being automated.

For example, it's not a given that every software project uses source control management (SCM). Even still – since so many teams across the globe have been using SCM tooling for decades – it might seem shocking.

This is true across many of the aspects of development workflow. As individuals and teams become accustomed to those types of automation, it can become easy to just assume that they've always been there, and folks have always used them. This is as true for build servers, SCM tooling, and deployment scripting.

So "automate everything" doesn't start from absolute zero. Further, it is important to view even the things we've come to assume (such as SCM) as aspects of the design and implementation of our workflow automation. Knowing how and why they work – and the reason for their existence – will enable more sophisticated approaches.

All of this boils down to a very simple mental model. The motions we make to take our software from idea to running system represent a use-case in our system – just like any other use-case. There's concrete user value that we can realize by writing code.

While software developers tend to be the most direct user of such code, the value to the customer and to the business arises from the speed it creates.

To further focus that, the various aspects of workflow automation are identical in nature to any other features we might build. They are a part of the same architecture and follow the same process through to completion.

WHAT CAN GO WRONG

This all sounds very straightforward. What could possibly go wrong?

Two main reasons underpin the problems that organizations might have with their workflow automation.

Laziness

The first is that they just don't do the work – beyond what is implicitly obvious.

As we mentioned earlier – if a particular type of workflow automation is sufficiently common practice – many organizations will do it without even realizing. The lack of it will strike folks as odd and its implementation won't be questioned. The example we used earlier is a great case-in-point – almost no enterprise of any size would question the use of a source code control system.

The same organization, though, if even the slightest bit of unfamiliarity is attached to a given aspect of workflow automation, might balk completely.

While the heading here is "laziness," the perception that workflow automation is for the internal staff and that their comfort is consistently at the bottom of the list of priorities is also often a common root cause for this choice.

This is disappointing on the surface – an organization that places so little value on its own people deserves the challenges that this bad attitude will provide.

More importantly though, choosing not to invest in workflow automation betrays poor understanding of the overall (people and technology) system. This is the reason that the refrain has been repeated with such regularity throughout the pages of this book – speed leads to value which leads to return.

Slowing a team down with manual development workflow defeats the purpose of the business and reduces the return that leaders and engineers alike are able to reap.

Specialization

The other challenge that stands in our way when it comes to workflow automation is specialization. This is when individuals and teams begin to focus only on the workflow automation aspects of a system or set of systems.

Specializing around technical aspects of a given system comes with unavoidable problems. So whether it's specializing around front-end web development or data transfer or – in this case – workflow automation, the results are the same.

Whether it's the team or the individual, focusing only on a certain kind of technical work means that there will be times when the amount of work is insufficient to keep the specialist(s) busy. Further, the individual or team will be less connected to specific needs. These two things combine to drive toward over-engineering (or gold-plating as it is often called). Every bit of effort that goes into building beyond what is actually needed is value that is being taken away from the customer and return that is being lost.

Specifically with workflow automation (as opposed to other kinds of technical specialization), once the programming is done to automate the workflow, the maintenance load it creates is small. So if the specialist is an individual on a single team, that person will be unoccupied. This will potentially end with extreme gold-plating. More likely, though, it will lead to taking on workflow automation work for other teams. This will then lead to the creation of a separate team, since one feature team creating build automation for another will be awkward.

However, we end up with the separate specialized team, the problems are the same as with any other technically specialized team. That is, the short-term incentives for the team become centered around delivering the technology rather than around delivering value – and the interpersonal communication network necessary to deliver actual value explodes in size.

On a feature team, the motivation and the center of discussion is around a given feature. That feature, in turn, is – as directly as possible – something that we believe will be valuable to a customer. This may turn out not to be true, but that result would only mean that we would spend time refining the approach and correcting the direction we were headed. The point though is that our team and its discussions are always centered around things that represent either direct value to or experiments that lead to direct value to our customer.

A technologically specialized team (like a database team, or in this case a workflow automation team – more commonly called a "DevOps team") may deliver small pieces and it may view those small pieces as experiments. They are not however directly connected to user value. This can be seen as multiple feature teams request workflow automation from the specialized team. These feature teams become the customer of the specialized team, and the specialized team measures its success by its delivery to this customer.

That is, the specialized team is only indirectly concerned with the actual feature set that is being delivered. Practically speaking, this indirect concern is really no concern at all, because the sense becomes that the feature team has it in hand.

This may not seem like something that will slow things down at all.

It does and the mechanisms that it uses to slow throughput are subtle. The first of these is simply the energy of the team. The general sense of accomplishment and purpose that lends energy to work is attached to the technical aspect that the team is delivering – again, workflow automation in this case. This means that often the energy and passion of the team will be directed at the accomplishment of technical work that doesn't support a particular feature.

This might present as over-generalization or simply as unnecessary technical capability. Either way, the energy and gratification of delivery have come from the technical capability. This is all effort that could have been more directly applied to the feature. The feature then will be delivered more slowly. The value delivered will be lower than it should have been.

In addition to these misaligned incentives, prioritization becomes indirect and similarly misaligned.

As we mentioned earlier, a specialized team of "workflow automators" will need to serve multiple teams in order to fill their time. This means that they will have multiple "stakeholders" as a team – that is, multiple streams of requests. Those requests must be prioritized – if they're addressed out of order, ultimately the customer will be getting less value. So it behooves the organization to figure out and deliver in order for every feature.

If we stopped here – we might just say, well yes – this is a challenge, but we just have to do the work to make sure we're delivering in order.

The problem is that this work ... is work. Every team – given their perspective – will imagine that every feature and thus every request they make is the top priority. This is because they are working the list of priorities that they have view of (which is limited from the overall organizational perspective) – and they're working it top to bottom. The natural conclusion is that they've done the work to figure out what the priority is featurewise, and they should have immediate response to whatever they might ask for.

For the workflow automation team, bringing in the broader organizational perspective means assessing every priority that comes into the team on an ongoing basis (since priorities will be shifting continuously for feature teams). Even if this were a one-time event, it would be somewhat overwhelming. There will need to be a collection of stakeholders as with a feature team. That collection of stakeholders will bring a case about the relative value of a given piece of work. Difficult discussion will ensue to synthesize priority from those cases.

Even if this were all that was involved in judging priorities, it's clearly a lot of work – a lot of time and cognitive bandwidth that's been sacrificed. That is, it represents a great deal of value that will be unrealized.

But it gets worse.

The feature team has no concrete measure (such as money) with which to express their sense of priority in terms of a concrete trade-off. Feature teams can judge their own priorities by what the customer will likely pay the most money for (even if we don't always think explicitly in those terms).

Which means that in the (fairly likely) case we have an instance where the collective synthesis of the several stakeholders doesn't result in a serialized priority list, we must bring in leaders with broader perspective. The time that it takes to schedule this represents a great deal of value lost.

But isn't this just division of labor?

A popular defense for specializing around workflow automation is that it represents division of labor and division of labor is a known lever for efficiency. In fact, division of labor is cited frequently when any kind of technological specialization is pursued.

It's a fair argument, but it breaks down quickly in the way we mostly outlined above. Division of labor works when there's a clear interface between two parties. If I am able to concretely and precisely define my need and what I will provide in exchange for it, I can hand that off to my colleague (or even to another business). Further, I will be able to quickly and trivially ensure that the finished product meets my needs.

If – as the requester – I must be constantly engaged during the course of the creation, due to rapid and un-anticipatable evolution, then division of labor ends up costing more than it saves. This turns out to be the case since workflow needs are connected closely to the overall system. As a part of this, the human communication network grows rapidly, as laid out above. The numerous decisions to be made multiplied by the size of the communication network is a huge cost that is not offset by specialization (which of course are increased skill and focus).

All of this to say – the idea of division of labor doesn't apply with workflow automation specifically – or with technological specialization in general. On the surface, it does seem like this should offer advantage, but on a more careful inspection, the problems we've outlined here end up costing more than the technique offers to save.

WHAT THEN SHOULD WE AUTOMATE?

As Jez Humble says, we should automate almost everything [1]!

Almost everything that we might automate in a development workflow is fairly straightforward. This is the reason that we laid out the challenges first. Avoiding both of those pitfalls – whether it's simply choosing to pursue workflow automation or choosing to refrain from specializing – will put your organization in the place it needs to be in order to mature in its workflow automation.

It is useful, though, to look at the specific areas available for automation. It can help to guide thinking, inspire new approaches, and make the connection between the tools and technologies and the ways we might put them into use.

As we explore these different areas, we will do it in a somewhat linear fashion – to make the analysis as straightforward possible. Obviously, though, in real-world software development, many of these tasks are ordered differently or even accomplished in parallel.

The beginning of any software change is "The First Creation" [2] – conceptualizing it mentally in the mind's eye.

Design

At least for the time being, this first creation is probably the least automatable aspect of a good development workflow. It involves understanding the potential human need and synthesizing a potential approach for meeting it.

Writing code

After that, we move on to writing code. There are two distinct things we do when we write code – we decide what code should be written, and then we enter that code into a computer. In both of these cases, we can get a great deal of help from automation.

Tools:

- *Deciding on the code to write* – This activity can be assisted with search engines like Google, or more comprehensively with generative AI tooling like ChatGPT or GitHub's CoPilot. Both of these classes of tooling are constantly being enhanced and will likely offer more and more automation with this early development task.
- *Entering the code into the computer* – There are a number of high-quality "Integrated Development Environments" (IDEs for short) that offer automation from syntax highlighting to code formatting to rapid building and testing capabilities.

Sharing code: Mutual modification and version management

Once you've written some code, the next thing we frequently find ourselves doing is sharing it with others. This may be to get the opinion of a colleague (or to impress them with your skill), or even to let your colleague take the next development step after you've completed your work.

A further complication arises if you not only hand off one piece of development work to your colleague but also keep one for yourself – such that you are modifying the codebase at the same time.

Before I continue, I want to reiterate that calling out some of these specific types of automation might seem a bit remedial to many development organizations. As we laid out earlier, this is the case with workflow automation – some practices have become or are becoming so ubiquitous that even reflecting on their purpose seems backward. It's important though to look at the obvious streamlining so that we can get a good sense of the general value that comes from eliminating manual work in our development workflow.

Getting back to our scenario, my colleague and I both making changes to the same codebase. Let's assume that we are both working out of a local directory on our own computers and that when we make our changes, we send each other the changed files. In this scenario, as soon as our project grows beyond a handful of source files, we will find ourselves grinding to a halt. Modern projects can easily get into the range of hundreds or thousands of source files. Changes can often cut across a pretty broad set of those files, depending on how well the task is broken down and how modular the codebase is.

The automation around this has evolved from command line tools to locate changed files to full featured systems to manage source code. These systems not only track the changes you've made they offer the ability to "merge" in changes made by others. That is the exchange of code that is being change simultaneously by multiple parties is handled entirely by software. The huge possibility that exists that we might forget to share a particular file or share the wrong file is all but eliminated. In modern development shops we don't really even think about this anymore.

Another important aspect of source control systems that has developed over the years is an ability to have ready access to a specific set of the source files. So for example, last Friday I made several changes to a shared codebase, then my colleague made several changes to the same codebase, and then we both tested the changes together. Having a quick handle on the full set of code allows one to quickly pick up the line of thought – with confidence that only the changes we expect will be there. This is particularly important as teams grow and the number of contributors to a particular codebase increase. Overall, it is powerful automation that allows us to think and act more quickly.

Simply leveraging a modern version control system powerfully automates the sharing of code. Though, again, many of us have become so accustomed to this automation that it's almost difficult to imagine a world without it.

Suboptimal workflow often begins to feel like it's the fastest way to get work done. This can make for a challenging people problem when you do begin to put focus on optimizing workflow. The transition from sharing by hand to using SCM systems like CVS, Subversion, and git is instructive in this respect.

Looking again at the pre-SCM setup above. We edit files locally and transfer files through email or ftp as we are finished with them and want others to use them.

Let's assume that the project consists of two developers and five files.

The process is manageable – I have to tell my partner what file I'm working on – and when I'm done, I just package it and send it along.

We've been doing this for years. So the habits around our workflow are well ingrained.

And then my partner tells me he wants to make the move to git. That means installing and learning a new tool, as well as allocating a computer to hold the shared repository. More painfully, it means changing all of my habits.

For absolutely no return.

This scenario likely seems ridiculous on the surface – most of us start with an SCM system without even thinking about it. But bear with me and imagine that you've been on this team for years, you've been collecting a paycheck to maintain these same five files. You've gone through the quick routine of communicating about the file you're editing and sharing when you're done.

It's practiced and it's easy.

This is the challenge with most workflow automation – what is in place is practiced and (seemingly) easy. The return comes in the shape of the (very incremental) additional cognitive load available to apply to the software you're maintaining – and in the ability to handle additional head count.

Really, this is sort of the problem with all of software. Henry Ford's famous quip – that if he had asked people what they wanted that they would have asked for a faster horse – applies powerfully. In general, people can't see the value in something new until they use it. Add to that the human disinclination to change, and we can clearly understand Ford's insight.

When we build software for customers, we're in Ford's position – separate from our customers, looking to put something new in their hands, and ready to do the work to convince them of the power of it once it exists. When it comes to building software for ourselves – workflow automation – the desire for a faster horse can short-circuit the natural energy to really break new ground.

This is of course a big driver toward the first of the two primary problems (laziness – just not doing it) with workflow automation in many organizations.

The trick is to see past current habit – and simply imagine that things can be even better.

Technique: Trunk-based development (or "TBD")

So what we will begin to see as we move in to one of the primary "techniques" involved in workflow automation is that at the core of this competency is not so much putting the right technologies in place but properly using those technologies to our advantage.

We will notice several things as we look closely at source code version control tooling.

One of these is that the capability for having a ready handle to a specific set of source code has evolved from simple file-based revision numbers, to tags that can be applied to the whole codebase, to automatically created revision numbers, and even to revision hashes based on the content of the codebase.

Further, an early and powerful capability that rose to prominence was the branch. Much like the tag, the branch operated on the entire codebase. Instead of just marking it though, it even allowed the mechanics of the tooling to apply only to that version of the codebase. So when you create a branch, it would really be like a branch on a tree in that you can continue to apply changes to the branch that don't apply to the trunk. They might be merged in at a later time. Until that time though, it is possible to completely disregard work that may be happening in the parallel version of the codebase.

To add to the fun, branches can be created off of branches. Approaches to branching can have varying degrees of complexity. For example, each individual might have a branch that they merge to a testing branch at a certain time. This testing branch might allow only fixes and no features – releasing might be a matter of then merging that testing branch into the main line of development. Among other names, this might be called trunk or master or head – depending on the particular version control system.

Complex branching schemes like this arise to alleviate the challenge of having multiple streams of development work happening on the same codebase. Married with an accompanying process, it takes all of the complexity of getting things to work together ... and puts it at the very end.

There are some problems with this – problems that lead to making the organization slower.

First of all, it moves the working-together complexity – that is, the complexity involved in merging changes – to much later in the process. When we address them, we're far less familiar with the codebase. This is a serious challenge even if we leave the changes for only a couple of days. Though organizations with branching schemes like this often go for a month or longer.

That lack of familiarity means that we're adding a serious amount of time for relearning when we need to correct "merge conflicts."

Second, we're leaving one of the most fraught activities for the time of highest pressure – when we want to get our system out into the hands of the customer. This radically increases the chances of additional misstep. It also further reduces throughput, since human creativity does not flourish under high pressure.

Finally, developers that might fix a merge problem are likely to have moved on to other development work. This means that those merge problems now have to be prioritized against that new work. The effort to prioritize the problems reduces speed and value simply because of the time necessary. The additional negative effect, though, is the unpredictability that it streams into the follow-on development. Building software is already really unpredictable, but to take the most unpredictable part of it, package it up, and then send it forward into the next sequence of changes takes it to another level. That of course ups the adaptation cost (in terms of everyone's time), lowers morale, and damages relationships. All of which has a horribly detrimental effect on actual throughput.

The real secret here is simply to do away with branches and push regularly – at least several times a day – to the main line of development (again trunk, master, whatever your tool calls it). What this does is it makes merges radically smaller. You're merging in a handful of lines of code rather than hundreds. You're also very familiar with the changes you're currently making. And you're resolving the unpredictability long before you get to the high-pressure time of delivering to a customer.

It's difficult to overstate the impact that this seemingly straightforward change can have on the rate at which you and your team will be able to move.

There are a couple of challenges to be dealt with – though – before moving your teams to TBD.

A little reflection will reveal these problems quickly. First, by pushing code immediately into the mainline of development, it's possible that one developer's changes might destabilize the work being done by another developer. Second, the probability that all development that is undertaken prior to a release is finished at exactly the same time is low. That is, when using TBD, it may frequently be necessary to deploy code that serves a feature that isn't yet ready to be put in front of customers.

The first of these rests on two very related techniques.

Technique: Automated build and test

Ensuring that a newly published change doesn't destabilize ongoing development for a colleague means building and testing every time something is shared. When this is accomplished, every developer on the team can have reasonable degree of confidence in the state of the code. Any breakage they see – even if they've pulled all the recent changes – is due to their change. Or somewhat less likely, the breakage might be due to semantic evolution against incoming changes. Even in this latter, worst case – running down the semantic divergence and accommodating it will be quick and painless because there will be few changes to look through. This is even more true because any conversation with its creator will be on the basis of recent knowledge. That is, both developers, as they are resolving this conflict, will be very familiar with the small set of code in question.

There are any number of tools available to take care of this. Really all that is needed though is an ability to either poll or be notified of changes to the source control repository and to do a little scripting to perform the build and test. The tooling then can be as simple as using the ubiquitous cron utility and some shell scripting.

Of course, there have been a number of free and commercial tools available to simplify and streamline this work offered from all corners of the software world. Jenkins was one of the early tools – but now both hosted apps like GitHub and GitLab provide highly sophisticated platforms.

The tooling is less important though than the technique – every time code is shared, it's compiled, packaged, and tested – from the use-case down to the method/function level. Functionality shouldn't unexpectedly change and neither should semantic relationships between grains of abstraction.

Of course, this raises its own interesting challenge – ensuring automated tests are written at every level of abstraction.

Technique: Test-driven development (or "TDD")

As a part of crafting great software in Chapter 10, we covered how to write code with a proper TDD workflow. This technique is also key in our desire to achieve Trunk-Based Development – and to move the merging of our code back from the last minute to when the code is actually written.

Ultimately, our need here – as we laid out in the last section – is to always have a good suite of tests that cover the functionality as well as the meaning of our abstractions from the highest to the lowest levels.

The alternative to driving our development with tests is to write code, get it working and only then to write the tests.

The primary challenge with this approach is based in the reality that the code we're testing (we'll call it "production code" from now on) must be structured in a fairly specific way in order to keep tests small and easily maintainable. It must be modular, the modules must be small, and overall the cyclomatic complexity – the number of paths through the code – should be as low as possible. Even after many years of experience and with a thorough knowledge that this is the target, it's a difficult target to hit without having quick feedback. That is to say, if we write code without driving it with tests, we will likely have some – probably much – refactoring to do to get the tests into place.

This profoundly slows development. It also creates a powerful incentive to simply avoid testing.

Since by the time tests are pursued the primary payoff ("getting it working") has already been achieved, forgetting about the tests can seem like a solid choice. It will speed things up, reduce the frustration of refactoring something recently written, and generally get value into the hands of the customer more rapidly.

The cost of course is that Trunk-Based Development – early integration – will be precluded. Merging will be pushed toward later in the release cycle, risk will be increased, and troubleshooting time will shoot up. That is, all the advantages we could have had fly out the window.

So, to have your cake and eat it too – to both eliminate that refactor time and enable Trunk-Based Development – TDD is unavoidable.

Technique: Feature flags

Once you've gotten your TDD discipline in place and you're build and test happening automatically, there's one final piece that you need to enable Trunk-Based Development – feature flags

This will solve the second of the two problems enumerated above – handling the release of incomplete feature work.

The idea of the feature flag is fairly straightforward – it's the ability to turn a particular feature on or off. As with automated building and testing, there are plenty of tools available to do this – but even a simple configuration that is built into the software package is sufficient to get the effect.

The purpose of the technique though is to ensure that even if the development of a feature was incomplete when the software was released, the feature will be unavailable.

So between the feature flag, automated build and test, and TDD, we can be assured that unstable or un-useful features won't be put in front of a customer while simultaneously allowing a developer to share code into the repository at any time.

Sharing systems: Mutual execution and version management

The next part of a development workflow happens when we want to execute our complete system. Just like our approach to our codebase, these complete systems might be shared across a team or an organization and executed in different manners with different user bases or different purposes.

So while with our codebase we might be sharing with other developers to get feedback or to allow them to make modifications or improvements to work we've done, sharing our systems is done for a different purpose. It is with the intent to get feedback on the running system to determine its level of usefulness to differing degrees or even to put it into full use by our target customer.

Developers might "bench-check" a system on their local computer, there might be a common area for judging against acceptance criteria to which the system is published, or there might even be an environment that attempts to mirror the full usage environment as much as possible.

All of these situations demand a concept analogous to the source code version control identifier.

When we package up a complete system, we attempt to eliminate as much variability as we can – even including aspects of the operating system and hardware configuration in the packaging. Sometimes, with certain tech, we can even include the operating system and the hardware themselves in the package.

The identifier, then, gives us a point to which we can connect our testing, observations, and expectations about performance.

Concretely, some of these packages might be – in the Java environment – .jar/.war/.ear archives. In the JavaScript world they might be an NPM package. Or in the Dot-Net environment it might be a Nuget package.

These packages eliminate code and dependency variability to differing degrees. That is, if we use the same packaging, we will know we haven't recompiled (which can subtly vary in certain cases), and we haven't re-"linked" – rediscovering dependencies (which can change less subtly).

To further restrict the variability, we might use container technology like Docker. Packaging a docker image includes with it much of the standard operating system configuration, including networking, basic operating system tooling, as well as basic infrastructure software like application servers. If you use a docker package, you have all the guarantees from above, with some added control.

Container technology shares operating system duties with the underlying host. So there will be some variability still.

We can begin to eliminate that with cloud configuration scripting. We can configure our hosts and networks with scripts that we store in our source control system.

We might even package cloud virtual machine instances with all of our software and manage them as the packaged software. In addition to that, there are any number of specialized services that are offered from managed cloud providers that offer manifold methods for restricting variability.

Whatever the tech, the point is that we package our software such that we can connect our expectations about its operability to a given package and communicate that easily to others as they execute – potentially in parallel.

In the Java and Dot-Net worlds – Maven and Nuget have version numbers that are associated with a given package. Released versions can be immutable in the service to provide additional assurance of the meaning of the package.

Docker images have an identifier hash much like git's.

Again, the point is to attach our expectations reliably to the binary packaging.

Technique: Continuous deployment

Once we've laid out how we execute and review our systems, the key technique that removes any potential for error or slow-down while allowing both review and usage in a controlled manner is continuous deployment.

If TDD is done well – and the lines of communication on the delivery team are few and operating well – much of the "are there bugs" testing will be automatic. The acceptance criteria of each piece of work and thus the feature tests will all be concrete and well-formulated and so regressions should be all but non-existent and any disconnect with the acceptance criteria should be readily caught in review and before context is lost to time.

That is to say, the only sizable bit of "testing" is the review that ensures that what was asked for is what was delivered. Assuming healthy process, this will be done within a week or two of getting that nailed down and within days of it being developed.

Subsequently putting the capability in front of subsets of the ultimate user base might be the only other validation prior to full production usage.

What those reviews look like and who the customer subset is are all business questions. That is, taking any actual action requires bringing in the fuzzy context surrounding the overall business – necessitating the participation of an informed human actor. Everything else, though, can be automated.

So ideally, the developer might share their code to the code repository, it would be built and compiled, and deployed to a basic validation site. There it might be checked by the user "representative" – the product manager. When that review is passed, that specific package that was checked (since we have an identifier for it) might be pushed along to the customer subset site. This selection procedure could be manual to allow the product manager(s) to make the choice – though the actual push to the environment could be completely automated. But once it's sent along, we have confidence that it's the exact same software in the new environment as was validated in the more limited environment. The same can be done prior to pushing out to the entire customer population.

The different types of validation are something that would be specific to a given business, but the basic procedure can be generalized from this.

There were a number of caveats that we mentioned along the line here – we're assuming good test coverage, Trunk-Based Development, etc. If these things aren't in place there may be some manual testing needed, there might be complicated merges, and rebalancing of priorities in the face of merge conflicts. Obviously, if an organization's procedure makes manual steps like this necessary to avoid major harm, they should be taken.

The point though is to eliminate the need for them as quickly as possible because they radically reduce throughput, the possibility for innovation, and ultimately the value that an organization is able to put into the hands of its customer.

Technique: Observability

Things are going to go wrong in production.

To troubleshoot you need to be able to deduce from information that comes from your systems what was happening at the time of the problem and thus what action should be taken to repair it and prevent future occurrences of it.

There are two sets of information that are interesting in this respect, telemetry – the metrics and other quantitative data you can gather from the system from the application layer down to network and CPU, and logging, the more subjective messaging that comes from all of the running software (including the application software that you've written).

On a single system, this might be easy to grab simply by logging into a given system.

However, single-system applications are no longer the norm. A service like Datadog or another logging and metric aggregator is an indispensable tool for finding and fixing problems.

Further with functionality distributed potentially over multiple types of sub-system (e.g., front-end, API-layer, and database), correlating the activity becomes important. Including a correlation ID in calls across systems is an important technique in this regard. This is an identifier that passes from system to system as a particular capability is carried out by a user. This identifier can be put in a log to make actions and their effects easier to follow and thus troubleshoot.

AUTOMATING WORKFLOW

Automating workflow, then, from typing the code into the IDE to operating it for users is largely about managing two separate modes of sharing – sharing code and sharing systems.

As an art software development is complicated by the fact that there are so many different folks with so many different interests involved in putting that value into the hands of the customer. It's no surprise then that much of the thinking about how to do it well lands on how to accommodate multiple people and multiple teams leveraging the same software in different states.

In one sense, it's not at all complicated and Jez Humble's exhortation to "automate almost anything" is really enough to get us to where we need to be. In real-life organizations, though, the two problems we looked at when we began start to stand in our way.

We need to be careful to be aggressive and not to devalue this particular programming simply because the immediate beneficiary is the programmer himself. As we've pointed out, looked at more broadly, the customer benefits by the development team maximizing the value delivered.

We also need to be careful not to fall into the specialization trap – a trap that infects much of software development. Workflow automation is simply another set of "stories" [3] for your system – that just happen to start with (very legitimately) "As a developer ...."

If we're careful about both of those pitfalls though, we'll have no problem getting to the place where our workflow is radically automated and the space between idea and value is made as small as possible.

The only ingredient you'll need to add is a healthy dose of discipline.

WORKS CITED

1. J. Humble and D. Farley, Continuous Delivery: Reliable Software Releases through Build, Test, and Deployment Automation, Boston, Addison-Wesley, 2011.
2. S. R. Covey, The 7 Habits of Highly Effective People, New York: Simon & Schuster, 1989.
3. J. Sutherland and K. Schwaber, "Scrum Guides," 2024. [Online]. Available: https://scrumguides.org/

Bringing it all together

Chapter 14

Starting the new development shop

It's thrilling – starting a new development shop from scratch. Not only is the software entirely green-field – so is the team itself. There's nothing like a completely blank slate on which to build out the practices, the technical approach, the ways that issues get debated, and even the type and personality of the team itself.

I started my technology career at the Federal Reserve. I had been programming for quite some time, since I was very young. While I didn't yet have the (seemingly) required Computer Science degree or any professional experience, I did need a job. After plastering the northeast United States with my resume, an opportunity presented itself. It was a job in information security. This was in the early 2000's – so this field was not yet the developed, well-understood one that it is today.

I'm still not sure why my boss at the time hired me. Perhaps it was that in addition to being green and (hopefully) moldable, I was also a bona-fide computer geek.

I had no idea what was involved in computer security. I knew that I loved to program and to fiddle with computers in general, and that the team had a sweet automated single cup coffee machine (a novelty at that time). I also got the impression there would be programming involved somehow ... and a paycheck.

I was sold.

I'm sure it was already in the works at the time I was hired, but within months after being hired, my boss told me that he was being tapped to lead a new group that would manage incident response across the entire Federal Reserve System. This was the Federal Reserve's National Incident Response Team, or NIRT as it was affectionately called. He asked me to come along. I liked the guy a lot and had no other basis for the decision – so I said, why not!

Next, he asked that I build the incident response notification system that would track and manage the state of the Federal Reserve's information security posture.

I didn't know it, but at this point I was starting a software development shop. Of course, it was just me in the beginning. It did include some consulting from my boss. Though this was mostly to fill in some of the gaps in my

DOI: 10.1201/9781003382751-18

software development knowledge. Some of the more "enterprise-y" aspects of software (relational databases, among other things) had gone into my too-boring-to-think-about bucket in my younger years. I might have paid more attention if I'd known they'd be such a staple of my career.

Throughout the early life of the "NIRT," we hired some consultants to work on the project, building different aspects of the system that I simply didn't have the time for. As we grew from the initial team of 7 to dozens of geographically dispersed staff, we also started to run into some of the more typical interpersonal challenges – misunderstandings about scope, prioritization, etc.

So, to combat these I began to (in my complete ignorance of any thinking done prior to my entry into the industry) develop procedures to ensure we were communicating well and prioritizing and planning properly.

Building this system and the procedure that surrounded it was one of my all-time favorite professional experiences. It was broad enough to be interesting every day, and directly connected to meeting a need such that everyday felt purposeful. Whether I was installing a new server in our data center, purchasing new application server software, writing code, or troubleshooting a bug, the variety supported by clear purpose made every day exciting and fun.

Little did I know that in all of these things, I was stumbling into precisely the right way to build up a software development shop. The aggressive way we pursued our business objectives (thanks, largely, to my boss – I didn't really understand this at the time) created the right tension against gold-plating anything, be it process, architecture, or code.

The hunger for excellence (that I largely shared with and learned from my boss) maintained the other side of the tension. We may be building and building fast, but we really want to build well or it's not going to make a difference.

This particular shop didn't grow to any huge size. The high-water mark was probably two full-time staff, and maybe three high-level consultants. It didn't need to be huge though. With the small staff we met the need, supported the mission, and were flexible enough to evolve as the larger infosec team and the mission rapidly expanded.

So if there's one secret – one take-away for building a software team from the ground up – that I've seen repeated throughout the course of 2+ decades in this industry, it's to create that tension. You should have excellence on one side and aggressive build-out on the other – and then mix in a healthy portion of do whatever it takes.

I was lucky enough at the NIRT to not know that developers are "just supposed to code" – or that development teams "always need a hands-off manager that assigns tickets and instructs in specific aspects of development." I was lucky enough to be completely unaware that operations teams are the ones that are supposed to install hardware and infrastructure software like application servers, queues, and web servers – and that you should have a separate testing team to test your software. Mostly, I was lucky enough to have a brilliant boss that gave me a great vision and then told me to get it done or be subject to ridicule.

So that's the equation – the one take-away:

$$success = (aggression + excellence) \times doWhateverItTakes$$

If you're anything like me – that equation is just dripping with fun. Which is why starting a development shop is so fun. I believe, though I haven't done an extensive study, that it's also why folks will put up with the pain and agony of dealing with venture capital and the other dysfunctions of the independent tech start-up world – simply because they understand the dynamics of this equation – and how much fun it is.

To be clear, just as in my experience – starting a new software shop doesn't have to take place in that excessively high pressure, silicon-valley-esque environment that many of us think of. Though that is a common scenario, because building software takes money.

What we will be talking about in the coming pages, though, will be the general case – regardless where funding might come from, and regardless the existing (or not existing) organizational structure.

So to start, let's boil that take-away down to some general principles.

CAPITAL

The first principle of the new development shop is that capital – whether it's the political capital of the host organization, or the financial capital of the funded start-up – is always short. Those supporting the build-out have no reason to be sure it will be successful, and funds for starting a build-out always have an upper limit.

The proper – and fairly natural – response to this is the aggression that we called out in the success equation above. Obviously, this aggression needs to be tempered with the human need to keep "our saw sharpened" [1] (to use one of Covey's metaphors). So, provided we keep ourselves personally well-cared-for – sharp and able to do the thinking and acting our endeavor requires – aggressively pursuing the build is the starting point.

Stopping here is the first major problem folks run into.

BALANCE

The next aspect is to have a deep hunger for excellence. Jim Collins calls this out in "Good To Great" as an important part of any business [2], but it's especially important in the early stage development group, because the limited capital means limited scope for redundancy or other safe-guards.

The aggression and the hunger for excellence must be deeply held values across the entire team. The leader certainly must have them – because the leader will set the tone for the group. But if every single individual doesn't take to their work with a passion to build as much as possible as well as possible, the development shop will fail to blossom.

PEOPLE

These two traits are difficult to find – and in fact the third trait from the equation above (doing whatever it takes) needs to be an integral part of the personality of every single person you hire in a shop that's just taking off. Again, all of this generally applies to software organizations of any size – but every individual has an outsized impact when the shop is small – so getting every hire right is of extreme importance.

There are three big challenges that organizations face in this respect.

The first is over-focus on technology. A quick survey of start-up job postings will give you a sense for how badly folks trip on this error. Posts ask for specific frameworks and languages and even certain architectural styles. They even ask for experience in the specific domain that the start-up intends to do business in. All of these things are largely irrelevant – even though they seem like they might be useful at a surface glance.

More importantly though, they are a distraction, wasting time and energy that might have been spent filtering for the things that do matter; aggression, hunger for excellence, general engineering aptitude, and a desire to do whatever it takes.

The second challenge – is that even when we have a good idea about the traits we need in our team members, we often look for proxies we can test for that we believe imply those traits. It's hard to see how aggressive someone is in an hour or two interview. So we might ask about other things that might be the results of that aggression or accompany and indicate it in some way.

Using a proxy isn't a terrible idea – because there's some truth to that reasoning. The choices for proxy though are the things that tend to bring in the real problems.

Again, specific languages are often used to gauge general engineering aptitude – so a job may require "10 years of C# experience." A better proxy might be something like – "10 years of programming in an object-oriented language." Even the object-oriented qualification might be unnecessary. Even 10 years in a procedural environment would reveal a high degree of aptitude.

Though years of experience is something that can fail, itself, as a proxy, on occasion. The pithiest formulation of this that I've encountered is that someone "might have 10 years of experience – or less appealing, they might have one year of experience 10 times."

The point in all of this is that thought should be applied to any proxies used, not leaning too heavily on any specific proxy.

And the third and most important challenge that people run into when they are looking to staff their up-start development shop is knowing what they're looking for.

Now – since you're reading this, and I've repeated it a number of times so far, hopefully you're pretty solid on what you're looking for. To reiterate once more – you're looking for aggressive folks that are focused on excellence and will do what needs to be done to build out the organization and its software.

As with these traits themselves, the knowledge of and hunger for these traits in others needs to be held by all members of the team, since hiring always includes more than the top leader.

To say it once again, all of this really applies more broadly to any organization that's building software. The lack of any guardrails around the way the team works though makes it even more important as the team is starting. Not only is there more damage that can be done by folks that aren't up to the work, but there is also less time and money available to absorb replacing them.

SIMPLICITY

A corollary to the fact of limited capital is simplicity.

Our solutions in all cases should be as simple as possible but no simpler. That is, our sense of excellence should be the boundary to trying to find the minimal solution to whatever the problem is that we're looking to solve. And I'm not just talking about the software we're building. This could be process or architecture or even support tooling.

It's important to always be looking for the simplest possible solution to the problem that solves it in an excellent, compelling way.

So if your customer needs a straightforward use-case for a new piece of software and there is nothing that makes sophisticated architecture or framework necessary, building the front-end with vanilla JavaScript and forgoing the Onion or Hexagaonal architecture for later in the lifetime of the software might very well be the best solution.

Similarly if email with a professional-looking custom domain is required, a simple hosted email provider might be preferrable to an on-premise architecture that includes email servers and domain servers, etc.

There are times when solutions can be overly simple such that they don't meet the need. At that time we can step up the complexity (as incrementally as possible) – staying as simple as possible for the new less simple need.

As with the hiring practices examined above, this isn't bad advice for any kind of software development shop. The shortness of capital though means that a little extra energy spent being as intentional as possible about this is energy well spent.

SOWING AND REAPING

Stephen Covey uses another great metaphor when he explains something he calls the production/production-capacity balance – the "Golden Goose" [1]. For an individual our production – our output, our contribution – is performed with the same time and energy we have available to invest in our ability to produce. That is, we have to decide to either allocate our time and energy toward learning about a particular technique or technology, or toward leveraging what we do know to produce what our or organization needs.

The story of the Golden Goose is that there was a goose who was laying golden eggs. Every day, there was a new golden egg. They were valuable. The farmer took each to market every day and made a small fortune.

Greedy for gain, the farmer came up with a scheme to make as much money as fast as possible – so he slaughtered the golden goose in an effort to get all the eggs at once. Finding that, all said and done, the goose didn't contain the eggs – she was making them every day.

In an effort to deliver as much as possible, we slaughter the Golden Goose if we under invest in our growth and development. If we over-invest, we don't produce anything and thus we can't put food on the table.

The balance again is the key.

This same principle applies to software development organizations.

In the case of the up-start, it's important to pay close attention to this balance. The lack of capital will lead to extreme pressure in some cases on the production side. Even if we're being really sharp on the simplicity principle mentioned above, the temptation can be strong to kill the golden goose.

In addition to focusing on the simplest possible solutions, it's best to try to err on the side of production capacity in this balance, since the pressure will generally be quite strong in the other direction. Though again, it is a challenging balance.

Production capacity isn't just a long-term play either. Laying groundwork, improving the group's ability to deliver pays immediate incremental dividends as well as profound ones in the longer term.

I remember joining an organization who had recently left the "new development shop" phase. The founding developer was transitioning out, and the business was growing a sort of second-round team to take it into the future.

One of the profound challenges this team was having was that it was starting to slow a bit. This rested on two bits of groundwork that had ended up being lacking – process and code-craft.

Looking at the latter briefly, when I started working – and this was in the days of JSPs and Servlets in the Java world – we had JSPs that were thousands of lines long containing vast swaths of the business processing. There was little abstraction, vast subtle duplication, and poor variable naming. In short, the codebase was a heaping pile of ... spaghetti.

This was undoubtedly a big source of throughput decline. But the problem started years before in quick, hacky choices made to get the immediate problem solved and to move on.

Over the years that I was there we started to dial this back a bit – but it was far more expensive to be doing it at that time, when the staff was larger, and the expectations of quality operation were higher.

They hadn't quite slaughtered the Golden Goose, but they were definitely in the process of strangling it.

It bears repeating a number of times – production and production capacity are a balance. Everyone on the team needs to have this truth under their belt – and feel good about investing in the latter as much as they can sneak in, because the pressure will be so strong toward the former.

The more that groundwork can be laid while delivering just enough production to be bringing in additional capital (through revenue, goodwill, or investment) the better the team will be in the short-term and particularly in the long-term.

THE FOUR AREAS OF COMPETENCE

Having these principles laid out, let's take a close look at how this bears out in each of the four areas of competence. We've touched on a couple of these in giving examples for each of our principles, but the principles play out powerfully in each one of these areas of competence.

Software craftsmanship

Software Craftsmanship is expressed in the details of the code that we create. Variable names, the abstractions we choose, and the specific way we express the behavior we desire all combine to create either clarity or confusion.

The way we think about these things, the discipline and depth of understanding we apply to the mechanics of our development, and our passion to make our code as easily understood as possible all add to this.

The craftsmanship that we bring to the construction of our software is a prime place that the balance between aggression and excellence plays out.

The reason for this is that the problems created by missing clarity are quiet and subtle. It's hard to notice a codebase that's slowly rotting – becoming difficult and slow to work with. This is multiplied by the healthy but adrenaline producing aggression that we take to our work in the newly formed development shop.

In many cases, that adrenaline – that excitement – can cloud the challenge we face in difficult code. It can feel the same as fighting through any of our more legitimate problems, such as understanding the domain or discovering the clearest way to express something. In fact for many of those common problems, that excitement is often leveraged to push through them when we might not have otherwise done so.

In more sober moments – with a rotting codebase – we might step back and notice that we're dealing with unnecessary hardship. We're trying to run a highly competitive marathon with a weighted vest on.

This is where the focus – the obsession, even – on excellence balances out this challenge and our aggression. By determining ahead of time that we will follow the path of excellence even when the excitement we feel might be masking its advantages (which, again happens continuously in development projects in general) we will make better choices out of the thousands of decision points we face every day.

Whether that's spending a little extra energy to formulate a clearer and more concise variable name, or whether it's maintaining a properly test-driven workflow – the focus on excellence even in the face of the excitement of aggression will pay off powerfully.

The pay-off can be clouded in the short-term by excitement (though it's definitely there). It is, however, most notable in the longer term as we take a more sober accounting of the impact of the codebase.

People and process

Having the right people in place makes a difference that multiplies value from each of the four areas of competence.

The most important part of the people and process competency during the early life of a software development shop is being able to distribute authority well. Often when a shop is smaller and there are fewer people, individuals – particularly leaders – take on more varied work than they might in their larger counterpart.

If a leader – and almost everyone in a small development shop is a leader – can't trust the folks around them to do the things they need done then overload, burnout, and general failure will accompany his enterprise.

We treated it as a core principle earlier in this chapter – and it bears repeating here in this section as we dive into people and process. Selecting and bringing to the team the right people – aggressive, focused on excellence, and willing to do whatever it takes – are important. Engineering acumen is necessary as well – though, as explained earlier, discovering it can be challenging. It's important to understand if and when you use proxy measures to uncover this ability that they actually do imply the particular attribute that you are looking for.

Those attributes are primarily in the four competency areas. So instead of looking for ability to write Java code, look for the ability to craft code in general, regardless the language.

A high-quality software developer will have familiarity with more than one programming language – judging their usefulness to the team isn't about how well they know a specific language. If your team really wants to write C# code for the build they're engaging in, the best predictor of success as a part of the team isn't necessarily previous experience with C# – it's previous experience crafting high quality software.

Further, we should note that there's not much difference between a software developer and a team leader or manager. In the early stages it is unnecessary to have any kind of technical management layer other than maybe a single individual to oversee the entire shop. For such an individual, you're still looking for almost the same traits that you would be for any other software developer.

They may have a little bit more depth of experience, perhaps an increased comfort dealing with interpersonal concerns, and particular skill with leadership. But in general the same traits that make a good software developer make a good leader. That is, aggressive focus on excellence combined with high and growing skill in the four competence areas.

Now to be clear, commonly, organizations will hire developers that don't have much in the way of people or leadership skill – who don't have a good grasp on the people and process competency. This is either carelessness, another example of a bad proxy, or just the result of an excessive demand for engineering talent. When people look to hire, they do so with the hopes that the engineer will help to make their team successful. A common view of the software development team is that the individuals are carrying out simple, technical sets of tasks with little need to collaborate. Thus in their hunt for success, they downplay the need for the subtle interpersonal skills that really make a social activity like software development work.

Practically, what all of this means to the new development shop building out its team is that every hire should be pursued with great care. Additionally, everyone involved in the hiring should have the highest degree of understanding available in the four areas of competence. It's impossible to evaluate levels of mastery in these areas above what the evaluating individual has attained. So – in a way – you're limited in what you might select by the people doing the selecting.

Conveniently, if you do this well, you will be anticipating the additional management needs that arise as the organization grows. Your organization will be ripe with folks that expertly balance all four areas of competence and thus are able to do and to lead well.

The other question in this competency is how people work together – what processes and workflows are chosen and how do they fit together to meet the organization's needs.

The key principle here is simplicity.

It's important that process should be as simple as possible and no simpler. Aggressive team members working to build as fast and as well as possible will find excess process grating – and they should. Any workflow steps that are put into place without meeting a definite need are wasteful. That waste is in terms of the limited capital we discussed earlier in the chapter.

Similarly, too little procedure will mean that team members will likely work on things that are thrown away or that don't matter, or even that work at cross purposes with their colleagues.

So the underlying point is, much like with finding the right people, the energy in the process side of the question should be put into finding the right balance between too little and too much. Understanding that this is an ongoing question.

That's the hard part – especially as a development group is starting, there should be regular thinking done by some or all of the team about the most applicable, helpful, and appropriate workflow. That workflow should then be slowly and thoughtfully put into place.

If this is done well, it will anticipate many of the more sophisticated tools that will be needed as the team expands.

How do we do this well; this goes back to earlier chapters. First, we need to understand the forces at play in software development. This is particularly important in the current case because they will only be initially developing. Some forces will therefore need to be dealt with more urgently than others.

For example, if only one or two people are engaging in software development activity – including any leadership duties – there are two major traps that don't apply to such a team yet. There's no real worry about keeping a team marching in the same direction, nor is there much worry about a developer getting lost in the weeds and not staying in touch with the direction or vision of the product. The former will readily be dispatched with normal, informal conversations. The latter will be taken care of by the fact that the product visionaries – whether that's the CEO or a delegate like a product manager will likely be in regular direct contact with the one or two folks that make up your software engineering practice.

Because of all of this, the daily standup – a regular practice that's often of a great deal of value to larger organizations – doesn't need to be implemented yet.

That may change rapidly – or it may stay the same for years – after all great software can be written by really small teams.

The point though is that you understand the principles that drive the practice, you are regularly evaluating where you are at in relation to those principles, and you change the practice as soon as your context makes it necessary.

Your CEO might have closed a large funding round and as a result might task you to add 10 software developers over the next three months. As you added those members to your team, you will almost immediately notice the shift in context. Without a daily standup, some development work will languish, some will be out of step, and some team members will appear to be disconnected. It is definitely time to add the daily standup to the mix.

With just one engineer (and perhaps one product visionary) back of the napkin discussions and then directly jumping into code can be a perfectly workable "methodology."

Though regular weekly cadence, thorough feature decomposition, and broad forecasting all become increasingly important as the organization grows.

Again, the key being to keep a close eye on process – keeping it as simple as possible but no simpler. For example, adding thoroughly developed long-term forecasting at the very start of the shop would be wasteful but not engaging in thorough feature decomposition when there are 3 or 4 team members will create real problems.

Architecture

Architecture is ultimately any software design that cuts across multiple teams. The main thrust of designing good architecture is to keep teams as independent as possible – by making technical dependencies as few and well-designed as possible.

The work to do in this space for the software development organization that is just forming is therefore very little. It will likely take at least a little bit of time before there are even multiple teams to worry about.

The things that can be done when thinking about architecture at this point though are straightforward.

First, don't anticipate. Don't try to leverage fancy architectural patterns. Don't even spend any time worrying about accommodating multiple teams.

Often, folks when they think of architecture, they think of things like queue platforms, or database design, or interactions between services. Again, don't bother with any of this. Unless of course your use-case dictates it.

If your use-case needs parallelization that goes beyond what you can get out of a modern multicore CPU with the threading libraries provided by the language and the OS, then by all means use a queuing system.

To throw big, bulky tech like this at a problem before either the use-case or the organizational structure make it useful is waste. It's a waste of that limited capital that we mentioned in our guiding principles.

The question, then, is – but shouldn't we be planning for our growth?

Well yes – and to start with, you are. You're planning to not waste money on things that aren't likely to help you at all with your growth.

Second, though, the biggest pro-active thing you can be doing to anticipate your future architecture is to pay attention to your craft. Clear, crisp abstractions that are well-named, well-tested, and most importantly, modular, will allow rapid moves into the world of multi-team software as soon as you're in the space to be needing it.

So that's really it – there's not much balancing to be done for architecture between aggression and excellence. At the beginning stages of a software organization you can, for the most part, ignore architecture. Though the biggest way you can be preparing for your growth is simply to focus on the excellence of your craft.

Workflow automation

By the time I started my senior project in college, I had been working a number of years in professional software development. At the time, there were a lot of basics and techniques that weren't taught well in higher education.

One of these was source control.

I remember going over the initial stages of the project with the project lead, showing how I had gotten things set up in CVS and prepared the basic structure of the project before getting some of the basic code in place.

The project lead was a full-time student – and not an industry veteran by any stretch of the imagination. Our customer was a local business. He complained that we shouldn't spend our time on things that didn't matter to the "customer."

I was more shocked than anything at the time – it was my first real contact with the "let's save the patient money by not washing our hands" attitude. I went along with it – and we got a passing grade, largely because I'm sure the folks evaluating our project weren't really industry veterans either.

We didn't, though, leave our customer with a buttoned-up codebase with history and the capability for a team to pick it up and readily change it. I didn't feel particularly good about what we were delivering. Though it wasn't really worth battling about.

In one sense, a take-away from this might be, but Kyle, this sounds like your project lead was doing well to focus on our limited capital (in terms of our customer's buy-in to our ability to deliver) and on aggressively getting something into his hands? Isn't he just subscribing to the principles we've just outlined?

In a sense, yes – and you're right, his heart was in the right place.

There is a real balance to be maintained in workflow automation – much like there was in process. It's very easy to gold plate how the technological support of our development is implemented. We can spend thousands on build servers – whether they're hosted or on our own infrastructure. We can layout intricate branching strategies and release validation signoffs.

However, even if we have only one developer – so long as they're not their own customer (and we'll ignore that case, since we couldn't make money that way and this, after all, is an executive guidebook) – having an intentional and controlled way to take a line of code through development and testing to operation in an automated way will increase throughput.

Source control is a basic, and today almost trivially implemented, building block. Add to that cron (or the background, timed processing tool of your choice on your platform) and some shell scripting and you've got what you need to make that happen.

As you involve additional developers, further problems are solved with this – keeping conflicting changes from derailing progress, etc. Though, even with one developer these tools provide for the automation that will maximize your throughput in this respect.

I love the illustration presented in Growing Object-Oriented Systems Guided by Tests [3] – the Walking Skeleton. This approach is absolutely ideal – before starting any actual use-case development, get a basic skeleton system that will go through the workflow that you are interested in using – all the way out to the production operation environment. This controls all of the mess and confusion and risk that accompanies figuring out these problems for the first time by addressing it as early as possible.

WRAPPING UP

The shortage of capital – whether that's in confidence from the broader organization or it is actual financial capital – drives a lot of the considerations appropriate for the kick-off of a new software development team.

In every area, it means that we intentionally allocate time to balancing what we're producing against what we're doing to improve our capacity to produce. Whether this is delivering a feature while intentionally spending the time to pick great, communicative variable names within the code that will result in that feature. Or whether it's choosing to forgo specific process sophistications until later in our development.

This is real work, and it will take real time. So preparing for this means putting ourselves in the frame of mind to be investing into it in both of these ways.

If we do though, we'll be far more likely to build something that really makes a difference to our customer. And further, we'll be best prepared to handle the success that follows that.

WORKS CITED

1. S. R. Covey, The 7 Habits of Highly Effective People, New York: Simon & Schuster, 1989.
2. J. Collins, Good to Great, New York: Harper Collins, 2001.
3. S. F. a. N. Pryce, Growing Object-Oriented Software, Guided by Tests, Boston: Pearson Education, Inc., 2010.

Chapter 15

Enhancing the existing development shop

Often, we find ourselves in an existing development organization that is simply not performing to the level we believe it to be capable of. In fact, this is probably the most common scenario we may face in today's software world. The organization may not seem to be as innovative as it should be, relationships may be strained, or it simply is not making the expected impact in the lives of customers.

Every single individual in a given development organization will have a unique perspective on its ability to carry out its mission. This is why we've made such an effort to clarify and elaborate the primary skill set of a team member – the four areas of competence. Knowing these and being skilled in their application is the responsibility of every single team member. Of course, organizational leaders will have particularly broad visibility and will more readily be able to make change in certain aspects of the practice – such as broad organizational realignment.

Similarly, changes to other aspects of the practice are more directly and immediately effected by those writing code – things like craftsmanship and process.

All that being said, moving the organization forward is a team effort. It's also one that takes constant diligence and unceasing effort.

That is to say, the four areas of competence are areas of mastery. They are not things you either do well or you don't. A team of practitioners will continue to grow in these so long as they continue to put in effort. There is no "arrival"; there is no final state in which a team can rest in the assurance that they can no longer advance in their skill.

WHERE TO START

Speed.

How quickly the organization can take an idea from the napkin to customer use is our goal. We've explained repeatedly why this is – so at this point it's more important to recognize that it gives us a single, clear guide in our efforts.

DOI: 10.1201/9781003382751-19

The things that we do that make us faster are what we are looking for.

The four areas of competence are the complete set of the general skills needed. Learning and applying them properly in a given context is the whole duty of the software professional.

Improving is straightforward. We take a look at our existing practice and find the long straw, the aspect of our practice that is slowing things down. A good hint here is to look for things that make people uncomfortable. Good candidates for closer examination are things that seem unpleasant, or that software developers deride as "un-cool" or "inelegant." These intuitions shouldn't be relied on for solutions but are absolutely priceless for getting at the problem.

One example that we'll revisit several times is the daily standup. Often standup time can become a drag that everyone dreads – with frequent cynicism being directed at it. If this is the case, it's a pretty good bet that starting our thinking here will be profitable. This discomfort does not, however, imply that we should simply remove the standup.

Following discomfort should sound familiar at this point. Using the vocabulary we outlined in our discussion of thinking tools, what we're talking about is examining the way we work with implicit thinking. Implicit thinking often presents itself as a feeling or even discomfort, a subtle hint that our reality isn't aligning with our invisible, implicit logic. Implicit reasoning can readily get us to what's wrong. If we're doing something wrong, though, it's unlikely that we know how to do it well – otherwise we would have already changed our method. So, the improvement will then need to be more explicit, after which our intuition can be trained sufficiently to be able to guide us in the right way.

I told a doctor once that it hurt when I tapped on my head in a certain way. He told me, then don't do that.

Simply stopping or throwing out a technique often seems like it will stop the discomfort based on this very basic mode of intuition. Though to repeat, it's likely our intuition simply isn't well-enough trained to offer us any more productive solution.

When we do realize our intuition isn't bringing us anything more useful than "well just don't do that," it's important that we transition to thinking through things explicitly. Of course, there are situations where this intuition is helpful – when the cost of continuing is particularly high.

At any rate, as we are looking to enhance our practice, the likelihood that our intuition is adequately trained is low, because we're looking to do things we've not done before (if the things we've done before got us to where we wanted to be, we'd already be there).

So explicit thinking will be your dominant mode here.

After we've found what we think is our bottleneck, we find an incremental improvement that we can use to enhance it.

We then consider what it would look like to make that fix. If it raises other pre-requisite changes, we put this change down and select one of them, repeating it until we find a change that doesn't require any other changes.

Then we make the change.

If this sounds familiar, it's because it's basically the Mikado Method for refactoring [1] applied to refactoring your software organization. The same principle works because changes that seem incremental often aren't and incremental changes are the only safe and effective way to move your organization forward.

Once we've made the change, we let it run for a little bit to make sure it's stable and doesn't have any follow-on effects that might need to be dealt with.

Then we start from the top; find the slowdown, find the incremental improvement, implement, repeat … forever.

TYPICAL SLOWDOWNS AND POTENTIAL FIXES

Throughout my career, I have come across largely the same sets of symptoms. These common symptoms generally have very similar types of fixes.

The oversized standup

Probably the most common symptom I come across is the oversized standup. More than 6 or so people in a daily standup, or a meeting that takes more than 5–10 minutes are both big indicators here. To highlight how intuition connects here, if you have an oversized standup, it's likely folks are annoyed by the time taken, or even cynical about the meeting or the entire process.

The lack of collaboration here is the massive impact on throughput. This problem is definitely a legitimate slowdown.

So as we proceed in Mikado Method fashion and pick up this first stick, we might ask ourselves simply, how do we make the standup(s) smaller?

The stick that likely shows up here is that standups can't be made smaller because we'd end up excluding legitimate team members. That is, the reason our standup is large is because our team is too big.

So putting down the standup stick and picking up the team size stick – how do we make the team smaller, we ask ourselves.

A common answer is that we have six developers and six manual testers in addition to a product manager on the team.

Several potential solutions present themselves here:

1. We might move the manual testers off to a separate team.
2. We might simply make 3 separate teams with 2 developers and 2 testers on each.
3. We might automate the testing and gradually eliminate the manual testing roles.

Solution 1 worsens the situation because the hand-off queue that was in the team is now deepened by the team separation.

Solution 2 is potentially workable if the system is parceled out feature-wise to each of the new teams. If this doesn't happen, the additional coordination will make the old team setup desirable. It's also challenging because the bandwidth is possibly so much lower. The real possibility is that the teams don't produce enough software to justify being separate teams.

Solution 3 is probably the most workable solution – though it also implies a lot of upskilling for a team that has depended historically on manual testing. It's unlikely they've been engaging in a good TDD workflow, or that they are even yet capable of it. So the incremental solution would then be – get everyone up to speed with TDD and then slowly phase out the manual testers.

If we do select solution 3, the problem reduces to a substantial, though typical leadership challenge. Learning TDD, choosing to engage in it, and taking responsibility for the operational state of the software ("quality," to use the common, though somewhat ambiguous buzzword) all represent deep change for the individuals that must make it. The leader guiding this transition will need to invest great energy and initiative into persuasion and into maintaining momentum.

The status meeting standup

Closely related to the oversized standup is the status meeting standup. This dysfunction is obvious within about 30 seconds. It's accompanied by the same negative effects as the oversized standups. People talk at the group instead of questioning and collaborating with one another. It's a thing they've been told to do, and they carry out the letter but not the spirit of the practice.

Similarly to the oversized standup, the lack of collaboration is the very real sap on throughput here.

There are several things that might be giving rise to this.

The first is that it is in fact oversized. It's hard to collaborate effectively if there are too many people in the room.

The second is that the organizational leader – the individual with HR responsibility for much or all of the team – is choosing to control the details of the work that individuals take on. This can include everything from what to work on, how to implement it, or when it will be completed by.

Controlling these details instantly removes ownership from the hands of the team members doing the work. The status meeting standup is the most immediate and obvious symptom. This is because the team knows instinctively (even if they aren't able to verbalize it) that they are accountable to that manager for every detail of their work and not to one another.

The fix for this one is easier than the potential fixes for the oversized standup. It's simply that the manager stops controlling the details of the tactical implementation. The way to make sure that this happens is to remove them from the standup and instruct them to stop providing input on tactics. The only legitimate business they'd have in the standup is to ensure the process is working well. By micromanaging in this way, they're doing the opposite.

Spaghetti code

This is a fascinating one because the problem isn't generally felt across the organization until it's already pretty bad. The delivery rate radically slows. As a result of this, morale drops. Non-technical leaders wonder why, when things were going so well before, did we magically start to slow down. Senior team members might start to jump ship.

There aren't a lot of sticks to pick up here. A healthy team is regularly (and very incrementally) refactoring their codebase as they go.

So similar to the micromanaging team leader, the solution here is easy in a sense – just ask the team to start cleaning up, with maybe additional urgency at the beginning until the team starts to pick up speed.

The habit of cleaning as features are being delivered is a learned one though.

More importantly, cleaning as a team delivers requires good test coverage, and it requires a good workflow that accommodates regularly reviewing and refactoring. Both of these rest on a good TDD process being under the fingers of every team member.

So there aren't a lot of sticks to pick up. Though since this will probably be new, and since educating in TDD workflow is a long-term, deep, challenging activity, these particular sticks might be a little heavy.

Though, obviously, they're worth it.

Non-modular teams and non-modular architecture

We touched on the oversized, non-modular teams when we started picking up the sticks for the oversized standup. Which is appropriate, since frequently an oversized standup is in fact an indicator that the team itself is oversized.

In that previous section, we discussed the option of splitting the oversized team out into three separate teams. In the specific case above, there was a real blocker in that it would have left each team with only two developers.

Let's consider a similar situation where the test automation is in place, but we have a standup that is 12 developers and a product manager. At this point, we would have picked up on the same oversized standup as at least one of the symptoms that the organization was presenting with.

Since we aren't saddled with figuring out what to do with all those manual testers this time, we might readily break this down into three teams of four developers.

A side-challenge might be finding product managers to add to the two addi-tional teams. For the sake of this analysis, though, let's assume that the one product manager can handle all three teams or that the organization immedi-ately hires to fill the need.

The next stick to pick up in this case is that the teams will each need a separate section of the system to manage, by feature. Separating the team by technical aspect or not providing separate systems at all will result in coordination overhead that will ultimately have the teams acting as one. This reflects the powerful "Conway's Law" [2].

So we decide to assign different segments of functionality to the three different teams.

The speed impact in this case will be notable.

There are some subtleties to this – the teams must be independent – so they shouldn't obey the programmer's impulse to reuse things if those things belong to other teams. That is duplication should be encouraged in the case that the team takes on the needed thing and evolves it to meet their needs.

There can be a sense that sharing things among teams is "more efficient," since we're not duplicating code or resources. We should remember that code is cheap, thinking and communicating are expensive. Sharing takes much more of the latter.

This is all an effect of Conway's Law – as you split out the teams to be independent, you will feel a discomfort if the architecture is still non-modular to pull the teams back together. This is a specific point where intuition should be ignored. Or better, you should let the intuition drive you toward splitting out the application more deeply at the points where the teams are split out. This will reduce the tension and leave you with the result you want – speed.

Internal hand-offs

On a single development team, it's common find an internal hand-off from development to testing. In teams with two-week iterations, it's not uncommon for there to be an effort to perform any programming in the first week and any testing in the second.

Intuition should serve well even if you've never witnessed it – it feels as awkward in person as it does reading it on the page. What are the developers doing for the second week? What are the testers doing in the first? What happens if something takes longer than a week – do we stop it and not test it and put it over for the following development week?

We hit on this a little bit in the oversized-standup case, and the two scenarios often go hand-in-hand, because manual testing often implies that you have many more individuals on a team than you would otherwise have as well as that we begin to see internal hand-offs.

The solution here is what we called out in that section – adding automated testing and gradually eliminating manual test roles. The same sticks follow – the team needs to learn TDD and it needs to get the coverage up on existing software.

This is another important spot where intuition can deceive.

The tension that's created by these internal hand-offs is often dealt with by separating the two activities into separate teams – e.g., one team for development and one team for testing. This deepens the problems created by the hand-offs and creates coordination and load balancing problems that require additional management. Further, it reduces the ownership by each of the teams on the end-product – developers: "oh it still needs to be tested – who knows if it's good enough for the customer," testers: "I can't change it – so I may have found the bug – but who knows when it will be fixed."

The reduction in ownership, the hand-off cost, and the coordination radically reduce throughput – so while creating separate teams for the developers and the testers might alleviate short-term tension it will make everything far worse in the long term.

FIXING AN ORGANIZATION

So as you begin to examine your own organization and ask what you can do to move it forward, you should remember several things.

Remember that you'll never arrive, so you should pace yourself. You're not as good as you might one day be, but you'll quickly be able to figure out how to move past where you were yesterday.

Remember that the algorithm is straightforward; speed is the guiding light, find the thing that's slowing you down – use intuition as needed, find the incremental fix (using The Mikado Method), make the fix, start the process over again.

We've tried to lay out several of the common starting points and some of the sticks you might pick up to give a starting point and a template for how to think about your own enhancements. But remember the work here is thinking through these things – starting from the principles about how software development work and within the framework of the four areas of competence.

WORKS CITED

1. O. E. a. D. Brolund, The Mikado Method, Shelter Island: Manning Publications Co., 2014.
2. M. Conway, "Conway's Law" [Online]. Available: https://www.melconway. com/Home/Conways_Law.html. [Accessed 2024].

Chapter 16

Scaling the small development shops

Growth is something we're always hungry for in business. It means greater impact for our customer – and it means greater return for us.

As we look at growth more closely, we realize it's a bit of an ambiguous term. The real value that we look for with whatever we mean by growth is just that – our ability to conduct more business. In past years, this can almost directly be translated to more people. In operational work, having more hands always means more business conducted.

So in days gone by, for all but a few specific activities, conflating business growth with headcount growth has caused no problems. The distinction has been unnecessary, because for the practical purposes of running the business, they were the same thing.

Unsurprisingly, for us as humans, this has been deeply embedded in our collective intuition.

So much so that even as the fundamental nature of business has shifted as a part of the information age's reliance on software, huge numbers of business leaders attempt to continue to apply that age-old intuition.

As we discussed in earlier chapters, when we find that intuition begins to fail us, we have to make the switch from implicit thinking to explicit thinking, concretely examining the facts that we find until we our intuition is updated.

We'll do that in the general case here – as we start to examine how we think about scaling in the age of software.

So as we started the chapter, we need to continue to keep in focus our ultimate goal – increasing the impact we're making on the customer and the return we're reaping from that impact. At the same time, we need to call into question how that connects to how we add people to the team.

If we've gotten a stack of cash and told scaling is our next step, or if we've in another way implicitly come into the idea that we need to scale, that is fine. The impulse to add people isn't a terrible one – doing it effectively just isn't as simple as it seems on the surface. So, starting from our real purpose explicitly will help us to reason through our scaling and reduce the chances that we trip over any of the difficult parts.

DOI: 10.1201/9781003382751-20

A BABY IN A MONTH

So to make this as clear as possible, simply adding people to a software development team doesn't necessarily speed up the development.

As Warren Buffet pithily put it, nine women can't deliver a baby in a month.

However, to continue with that idea – nine women can create nine babies in nine months. That is, the outcome we're looking for (nine babies) offers us opportunity to parallelize so we can gain advantage with additional "staff" – reducing the project timeline from 81 months (well, you get the idea) to 9.

An identical principle is in play in software development.

If the outcomes we are looking for are inherently parallelizable, then adding staff will improve throughput.

Sometimes this possibility comes through with ease in the way that a need is articulated. "I need a banking system and I need a carwash automation system." The two systems are clearly different purposes even at the most unsophisticated level. So at worst, two people will be more effective than one.

More often though – and even really in this contrived example case – we can make the software systems we are building more parallelizable.

That's the secret to leveraging headcount "scaling" in software – shaping the systems properly so that the additional folks add to and don't detract from throughput.

We'll get into that in more detail shortly, illustrating exactly how to do this and how to build the team in a way that you can readily keep the outcomes shaped properly and continue to gain the advantage from the added folks.

SCALING WITHOUT ADDING PEOPLE

Before we do, though, let's step back to the two types of scaling. There's adding impact to our business – and there's adding people (with the assumption that it will add impact to our business).

To state this more directly, we can add impact without adding people.

In fact, if you're not simply being instructed to increase head count, it's a good idea to start with focusing solely impact. It's cheaper and will multiply the effect of actually growing the team.

Let's, then, take things back even further. Ultimately, in software development, impact is improved by moving faster – by taking things from idea to solving a problem for a customer in less time.

This speed is the result of expertise in the four areas of competence. So to scale business prior to growing the team, focus on improving expertise – from the top leader to the most junior developer.

As you're doing this, you will come to a point where improvement slows (the higher up you get in the competency areas, the slower continued progress becomes). At this point, then, consider beginning to adding people.

In this way, you can be scaling your business without the huge expense of extensive hiring.

MINIMIZING COMMUNICATION

The real secret to "headcount scaling" is minimizing the communication network.

This boils down to minimizing the size of the working group that addresses a given piece of software development. This is because if the working group size is 5 and we add one person, we're adding 5 communication paths. If the working group is 25 and we add a person, we add 25 new communication paths.

Such a working group must come to equilibrium on the many decisions that are made every day throughout the course of development. Every communication path is going to be active for almost every decision. This is very difficult after a certain point – at about 7 or 8 team members. Every individual maintaining 8 lines of communication is about the maximum that can be handled effectively.

So, the largest number of people we can have on a software team then is about 7 or 8 people. We can scale by growing the team to this point. Within the team, they will be able to manage their own work (assuming a reasonable level of skill), break it down in such a way that it might be shared, and then work it in parallel.

I packed quite a bit into that "reasonable level of skill" caveat. The team should have a process that breaks their work down into successively smaller pieces and they should have a good TDD workflow which is highly automatic. As a group, they should have a decent mastery of the four areas of competence.

After 7 or 8 people scaling head count can be accomplished by creating additional teams.

This seems straightforward enough. There's one important point to keep in mind though.

The teams need to be independent of one another. If one team needs work from the other, then both teams must become aware of the priorities and technical choices of the others. The communication network ends up being as complex as it would have been if the two teams were one team. In fact, for all practical purposes they are just one team, no matter how they are viewed by the organization.

There is one exception to this. This exception is the case where one team can view the other as the customer – funneling its development needs in alongside the team's other customers. If it can follow the same basic contract that any other customer might have with that team – that is, it can make a request for functionality, make its case for priority, and then judge the finished software as either having met its needs or not, the communication network won't explode in the same way.

That is to say, the process infrastructure and the mental model should be such that the requesting team is identical to any other customer that the team might be serving. This is expensive and a little clumsy – but it makes sense in some specific, important cases.

One of these cases that frequently comes up is the coalescing service.

A particular web application, say a banking system, might have several large subsystems that wrap up into a single (from the user's perspective) experience. There might be a deposits subsystem, a withdrawal subsystem, a login subsystem, etc. Each of these might be separate systems built by separate teams. To have them look and feel like a coherent system, we might create a coalescing service that basically provides look and feel and pulls in the separate subsystems as if it were a client to each of them.

There's distinct user-value in the coalescing service (presenting an ostensibly unified system to the user) and it would place certain requirements on the various services – like the connection points it might use to integrate things.

Other than that special case, in order to minimize the communication networks, the teams must be small. For the teams to be small, the systems that they take on must be carved out such that they can be built, operated, and maintained without engaging any staff outside of the team.

This implies on the technical side (for a typical web application, though the principle applies to any software domain) that from the front-end html and JavaScript all the way back to the database, the system should be entirely isolated. The database should be separate, the source control should be separate, everything should be separate. Any overlap creates the possibility that the two teams will begin to share and engage each other throughout the development of their systems.

This may create duplication. That's ok. The return that we're getting from the separation will far out-strip any extra typing or thinking that might be a result of duplication.

It may involve two teams having two pieces of code that might be generalized, but instead evolve in separate directions. Again, the return from the separation far more than makes up for this.

MANAGEMENT STRUCTURE AND MINIMIZED COMMUNICATION

One of the biggest, most unnecessary challenges to scaling well that presents itself is simply management structure. The most noticeable challenge –and the biggest lever that can be pulled to make positive change in this regard – is the number of reports that an individual manager is assumed to have the capacity to direct.

For a variety of reasons, this number is almost always far too low. I've observed development organizations that assigned around 5 developers to a manager, and yet fewer managers to their bosses, the directors.

One of the biggest reasons for this is something we've covered to some depth already. The prevailing mental model assumes there's really just one system to be building – the computer system that the developers are actively coding. This model tends to view the manager of the development team as a one who coordinates and instructs in specific task completion (with directors, if present, being their backup in this task). To be fair, this, like some of the other ideas we've discussed so far, is an intuition that has been applicable and powerfully reinforced over centuries.

This breaks for several important reasons. The real work of software development is cognitive – a manager that is controlling the tasks and the implementation details becomes a bottleneck for all work. Even if the manager doesn't explicitly ask for this control, if he is too present, has too little to work on, or has too few reports, and especially if the team is junior, the team might start to make the manager the bottleneck themselves. Either way, this minimizes the ownership level of the team. They'll be less energized, have less concern for, and take less initiative with the development of the system. After all, they have the manager to fall back on. Finally, the manager – getting pulled into tactical delivery – doesn't have time to spend on the people and technology system – the system that builds the computer system. This people and technology system (as we've discussed in previous chapters) falls quickly to entropy. The strength of the team in the four areas of competence erodes if there is not active focus on progress by the leader.

So this defunct model – that views the manager as the guide to getting work done – must change. It is this model, though, tends to result in the small teams.

The causal relationship happens to go in both directions here – which is useful.

In addition, then, to instructing managers to focus on the people and technology system and to let that system take care of building the computer system, we can also just bump up the number of reports that our managers have. This will make managing tactical details difficult. Now again, I've witnessed managers that will try to just take on all the extra tactical control to the point that they do damage to themselves personally – so we can't just take this latter step without some instruction in moving focus to the people and technology system.

Ultimately, the ceiling to this should be with a manager having around 40 reports. So if you're just starting to scale, and you have a handful of engineers and a manager – do not even think about hiring another manager until you've got 4 or 5 teams in place with plans to continue to expand. That's a pretty big development team, and assuming you've hired solid engineering talent, this will be a lot of development bandwidth.

A common objection to this is that there simply isn't enough time for the weekly one-on-one meetings that every manager is "supposed" to have with their subordinates.

To that objection, we should simply ask ourselves why our folks are spending that much time on pre-planned one-on-ones.

The first reason often cited is that the leader should be building relational ties in order to facilitate accomplishing the work that is on the group's agenda to get done.

There's an important aspect of this that needs to be examined. If we've truly moved our manager out of tactical delivery, the quantity of input and other relational drain they'll be engaging in will reduce significantly. They will need to make some moves with regard to the people and technology system – to keep it moving forward. Those changes however are so much fewer and further between that, again, the manager simply won't be drawing as regularly on his relational capital. Further, those kinds of moves often have such positive impact with team members across the board that they almost immediately coalesce as deposits of relational capital.

One-on-ones in this case are far less necessary.

Think of the friend that you haven't seen for 10 years, and you pick right back up where your relationship was at that time. You haven't imposed on their time, irritated them with small personal habits, or otherwise drawn on your relational capital – so your account is right where it was. Now think of life with your spouse or other close relationship. It's absolutely necessary, if you value the relationship, to spend time listening and empathizing, and doing all the things that add to your relational capital on a regular basis or before you know it, you're overdrawn, and the relationship is over.

Another challenge is administrative overhead. In some organizations each report represents significant administrative work – HR, performance tracking, and other work of this nature. The solution here – the details of which are outside the scope of this book – is to simplify these demands on the manager.

Getting the manager out of the tactics of software creation, and bumping up his reports, we've both improved the speed of the team – which means more return coming in, and we've eliminated a great deal of (potential) expense in terms of middle-management salaries.

In our journey to scale so far, we've shaped our software and our teams such that communication is limited to groups of around 7 or 8 people. We've also streamlined our management structure so that it consists of just enough heft to keep things on the tracks and moving forward without adding to the communication network or otherwise slowing up the independent small teams that report to them.

HOW TO ADD PEOPLE

The next consideration is making sure that when we add people, we do it in a way that doesn't diminish our overall throughput.

The first really important part of this is that we add people slowly, preferably one at a time. It often becomes (financially) possible to expand headcount very quickly. This temptation should be avoided. If there's anything that should be done carefully and with intention, it's hiring.

There are several reasons for this. Firstly, finding good people is difficult to begin with and simply takes a great deal of planning, thinking and discussion to get right. Secondly, it's important to make sure that each hire absorbs the culture and ways of working that you (and your organization) have spent precious time and energy arriving at. And finally, the architecture has to keep up with the team structure – remember, each team should have a completely isolated system. If you add two teams all at once and haven't separated out the appropriate systems, you're going to create some mischief for yourself.

We've already discussed hiring at some length, so we'll not get into that any more deeply here.

Though with regard to each hire absorbing the cultural norms and working methods there are a few things to say. This isn't about overriding someone's personality or eliminating what makes them unique as an individual, but there are important standards that, especially as your organization matures, should be expected from individuals. Much of this is really the level of skill in the four areas of competence. At the higher ends of mastery in each of these areas, there are habits and ways of working that will need to be assumed.

A method I've seen work well for this is simply having a class or series of classes that introduce folks to these things.

Now to be clear, it's not that the things that are a part of this shared culture can't be discussed and modified if better working modes are discovered. It's more that there will be a common, shared starting point from which those conversations can be taking place. Further, that work can immediately move forward without having to spend a lot of time getting retail equilibrium in the culture.

This will minimize the disruption – it will minimize what would otherwise be a ramp up of the whole organization to the new individual – so that there's no drop in throughput as the individual is absorbed.

Every time you get close to creating a new team, a couple of things should be done. First of all, a system should be identified to be given to the new team. Then the team from which the new team will be formed should be identified – creating the new team should be more of a splitting of an old one. This allows the existing team to seed the new one with its habits and relationships to minimize the chaos that happens when completely new people come together.

The system identification – finding a partition for the team to own – should be straightforward. That is, so long as a key practice is followed even when not scaling. Each team should have two fully separate systems. If it inherits a single system, it should split that system immediately. That will allow scaling to happen seamlessly at any time.

SCALING FOREVER

If you implement each of these practices – basically in the order outlined here – you'll be able to scale seamlessly forever. You'll be able to add people and then teams, ramping up your throughput from building simple systems to building the most complex things imaginable. Further, you'll even be able to descale well, drawing down staff and throughput as the business situation demands.

To review:

1. Recognize there are two types of scaling: improving the business and increasing headcount.
2. Start by improving the business without increasing headcount.
3. Prepare the existing team structure and architecture to be independent and decoupled.
4. Prepare the management structure by having managers take on appropriate headcounts and get out of the tactics of building computer systems into the strategic work of building the people and technology system.
5. When you add people – add them carefully and slowly – teaching them about your culture as you bring them in so they're not a drag on throughput when they start to contribute.

ANTIPATTERNS

Now that you have the algorithm under your belt for seamlessly and painlessly scaling your software development organization, we should look at a handful of antipatterns that you will want to be careful to avoid.

Scaling with bad team structure

One common approach in the industry is simply to add people to a team until they cry for mercy. Teams as large as 15 or 20 people aren't uncommon. As we've discussed, the communication networks drive down their throughput. This will become apparent. One of the techniques used to attempt to get past this is relying more and more on the people manager or a project manager to assign and monitor small pieces of development work. As we've mentioned, this creates a bottleneck around the individual that monitors these tasks – and in the case of project managers, the lack of technical understanding can often make this bottleneck even more tragically damaging to throughput.

Of course, the ownership drops pretty rapidly as these kinds of solutions are attempted.

And none of this solves the problem that you'll still have to create another team at some point.

Scaling with bad architecture

Often following from the bad team structure antipattern is a bad architecture. When a team grows to large, the pressure to split can become powerful. One of the easiest ways to (at least apparently) split a team is by technology – so we might separate out a front-end and back-end team – (ostensibly) bringing our team sizes down, significantly.

Though as we mentioned in the previous section, the problem will come in the fact that neither team will be able to deliver a feature on its own. This means the communication networks will still all need to be in place. And while the daily standups or other meetings might include additional people, those people still have an interest because, again, they can't deliver anything on their own.

Further, there are a finite set of lines across which we might separate when it comes to our technical delineations. So even if we can manage the massive communication network (which will likely be handled by even more coordinators – project managers, people managers, and the like), there will come a point where there are no more splits that can be made.

This is scaling with bad architecture because every time we split our teams in this manner we're creating a new technology-focused architectural component (as opposed to the feature-focused architectural component we laid out above). Though to be honest, we probably thought of them as such even before we split – which enabled that thinking in the first place.

So the communication network will continue to grow, coordinators of all kinds will step in and bottleneck us in manifold ways. Our speed will evaporate. Our stakeholders will marvel at our lack of innovation and our morale will drop precipitously.

Scaling with coordination

Now in the previous antipatterns, we've discussed how one of the unfortunate results of these naïve approaches is coordination. There are, however, a number of commercially available development process frameworks that are if nothing else at least honest about their approach to scaling.

The pattern we see here is simply starting with coordination. The single upside is that compared with the previous two examples, at least we don't have to go through the chaos of discovering the need for coordination to compensate for our unfortunate team or architectural structure.

The downside is of course that we end up in the same place – slow. We have low value – which means low innovation – which means unhappy business, unhappy customers, and unhappy builders.

While there's a certain amount of refreshing honesty in simply starting with coordination – it's like the honesty of the thief telling you he is going to steal all of your money.

Even if we recognize a bit of our organization in these antipatterns, it's possible to repair our position by simply going back to the algorithm listed in the previous section and getting our house into order. It's never too late, but you do have to choose to make the change.

SCALING THE SMALL DEVELOPMENT SHOP

We framed this scaling conversation around scaling a small development shop. It should be clear though that this approach applies to any arbitrarily large software development organization – even to hundreds or thousands of developers.

If you find yourself stuck in some of the antipatterns we've listed here, and you're already a fairly large organization, getting things into order will require some time and energy. Though these principles carefully applied will get you to where you need to be.

Of course, it is better just to start your journey preparing to properly scale. That's not always possible though.

Chapter 17

Simplification

Continuously starting, enhancing, and scaling

In previous chapters, we've looked at the major lifecycle steps for a software organization individually. In a lot of cases, we can have a pretty good idea where we stand – and what the next step for our organization might be. As with building the software itself, as we get into it, we may need to adapt or even rethink how we're approaching a given step.

The real target for the engineering leader should be to handle these steps in a continuous fashion. Dealing ad-hoc with improvement or scale is a decent step in the right direction. Though, as with the habits we build into our software teams at the delivery level, we free up cognitive bandwidth when we take one off improvement of the people and technology system and make it a habit we live every day.

Freeing up that bandwidth allows a fewer number of leaders to enable and empower increasingly complex and productive people and technology systems. Those increasingly enabled people and technology systems, in turn, will deliver software that is orders of magnitude more valuable.

Further, turning the growth of the people and technology system into a continuous habit will mean that when a shift is needed, the ramp up time will be all but eliminated.

For example, when many organizations desire to scale, they need to stop and plan several very different sets of activities: training, hiring, and architectural planning at a bare minimum. When growth is continuous, the organization will be ready to scale whenever it is needed. That includes scaling down if necessary. When economic conditions dictate scaling down, there is often a huge planning expense (however hidden it might be) that adds to the pressure. Eliminating that means no break to value delivery and minimal additional cost – so that calculations about how much relief is needed become far less (ostensibly) dynamic.

The habits that we'll outline here require a leader.

A leader is needed whenever people must change. The "people and technology system" in a software organization will always be changing, either for the better or for the worse. There is no real equilibrium since the forces of entropy are simply so strong. Shooting for status quo is a recipe for decline and destruction.

DOI: 10.1201/9781003382751-21

So, to ensure that the system is growing, constant leadership toward improved circumstances is a requirement.

These habits, then, are speaking to the leader – to the individual who will maintain that pressure against chaos and toward as much value as possible.

They apply across any leadership circumstance we might find ourselves in.

If the organization is large – even representing hundreds of engineers – whether the leader's scope is broad or narrow, the same sets of habits can apply. If the organization is small, and there is only one leader, then the situation is equivalent to the narrow-scoped leader in a larger organization. In all cases, the same habits apply.

Of course, every leader lives within a larger context. Whether that is leaders above him, a board directing him, or the market dictating his path, it is possible that this broader context short-circuits some or all of these habits.

That is probably the ultimate leadership challenge in software development – removing these barriers. This becomes so specific to the organization though and to the nature of the relationships in question that there's no general guidance to be given within the scope of this book.

Where we will start though is to lay out the approach that the leader can be using to turn growth from an ad-hoc interruption to a continuous operation that requires minimal cognitive bandwidth.

STARTING A NEW TEAM

Starting a new team is almost as straightforward as it sounds – though as we discussed in Chapter 14, there are some caveats.

Of particular importance as we place this into our continual growth habit is to recognize that the vector we travel as we are starting a new team might be in a completely new organization (as was the implied model in Chapter 14), or we might be adding a team to an existing collection of teams.

Ideally, action from both of these vectors is identical.

Independence

Before we start a new team, we should ensure that every existing team is independent with respect to its peers. For the brand-new organization, this is trivial.

In the non-trivial case, this independence boils down to two things.

First, the new team should be assigned to a set of functionality that it can build and release with no assistance from any other team. This is primarily an architectural question. Prior to starting the new team, a segment of the system (that is a set of features) should be put into the purview of the new team. If the features the new team intends to build don't exist yet, this is trivial, the new team will build the system out independently from the start.

If the team, however, is assuming responsibility for part of an existing system, things are slightly more complicated. The coming section on scaling discusses the need to prepare for a new team by slicing off a separate system that it might assume. This is essential – a new team must have a system to take on.

Secondarily – to keep a team independent, the team should – among its members – have all the skillsets necessary to deliver its feature-set top to bottom. When this is lacking, the team will either slow down considerably or it will (more likely) look for help from other teams. That is, they will cease to be independent. This may range from simply asking questions or looking for advice to asking for aspects of their work to be done for them. In any case, it means the team can't be independent.

Third, other teams shouldn't depend on the new team. This may be a hard situation to imagine if you're starting your team from scratch. Though, if you are assembling the new team from existing teams there may be relationships or interpersonal dependencies that if not taken care of can harden into inter-team dependencies.

Finally, one of the biggest challenges with independence in organizations that have existing teams is the specialist team. This might be an operations team, a "DevOps" team, a database administration team, or any number of other specialties that crop up in the software development world. These teams create dependencies on themselves by their very existence. The principle here is that for starters, these types of teams simply shouldn't exist, and most importantly any work that might have been pulled out into technically focused specialty teams should be done by the feature team themselves.

Culture

Another important consideration as we start our new team is the culture that we are setting it up for. Culture is kind of a squishy, poorly defined idea in the corporate world many times.

For our purposes here, the aspects of culture that we are interested in are that the team – as a group – understands and embraces mastery in the four areas of competence. Further, to any extent that their mastery is lacking, they should be open to and aggressively pursuing attaining it.

The higher the mastery and the more aggressively the team pursues additional mastery, the better. Though there is a line beneath which you should reconsider starting the team. If the team won't be able to operate its software development activities on its own – you should reconsider assembling it. If the team takes a lot of prodding to enhance its own mastery – or worse still, views attainment of mastery skeptically, you should reconsider starting it. The time and energy the leader will need to invest prodding and convincing is effort they can't be spending on broader structural enhancement. This is very problematic because – as we said earlier – the people and technology system will quickly devolve if active attention is not paid to it.

That is to say, beneath a certain level of competence and active learning, the team will cost more than the value that it will create.

Management

The final consideration to be observed when starting a new team will be that the management staff are in place to be able to handle it.

As we've laid out earlier, the ceiling for a development manager's report count should be around 40. So if your new team will put your staff over 40, a second manager will be needed.

A common but wasteful practice current today is for development managers to take on only 5 to 10 reports. The same with the manager of managers.

This all leads to terrible bloat as well as a tendency for managers to be overly involved in the day-to-day building of software and unable to effect the structural change that should more appropriately be their focus.

With the culture structured as we've noted here, and the scope of a manager's responsibility being reasonably broad, ensuring that proper management is in place should be a far simpler activity than it might otherwise be.

Creation

So with these caveats taken care of, the leader can assemble the team and set it to work.

The leader's responsibility to the team after creation then is to keep an eye on structure as well as the team's overall level of mastery (as judged by its practices) – then to act as the catalyst to move them forward as needed. Again, the better the culture that has been assembled to start, the lower this load will be, though it will never altogether vanish.

ORGANIZATIONAL ENHANCEMENT

The way to maintain the ability to continuously start (and stop if necessary) teams is to constantly be enhancing the people and technology system.

Not only does continuous enhancement provide that capability, but it also directly improves our throughput. The better we are structured, the higher the level of mastery in our teams, the more value we will put into the hands of our customers, and the more return we will reap.

This is probably the single most important aspect in the continuous growth habit. If we build teams – or if we scale teams – with low levels of skill, we do ourselves no favors. I've seen an engineering team with around 100 people that delivered incredibly slowly. It wasn't a surprise after seeing the hiring practices. The organization practiced a technique I call "warm body engineering." This is where instead of viewing skill as the most important factor in throughput an organization begins to view headcount as that factor – if we just hire more people we can move faster.

To be clear though, headcount can in fact allow you to move faster. But it must have some very important structure and skill in place. Otherwise, it will do more harm than good.

The role of the leader in enhancement is three-fold:

1. Ensure that the culture of the team continues to be of high-quality and improving. This is where software development begins to reduce to good, old-fashioned management. This might mean hiring, firing, counseling, inspiring, or generally guiding people into the space that you will be needing in order to be producing at the highest levels.
2. Ensure that the skill level in the four areas of competence is high and improving. Yes, this is redundant given our definition of culture. But it bears repeating – the leader should be doing everything within his power to grow the skill level of the team he's stewarding, even if it means replacing members.
3. Ensure that cross-team structure is improving. Both the architecture and the teams should be entirely independent. Of course that's the ideal – though there are often a number of details that can be improved even when the structure is mostly in shape. Though, in less mature cases there are any number of small steps that can be taken to decrease the distance between the current state and the ideal.

All three of these represent change – and for the most part – broad change, which is why the leader is so pivotal.

SCALING

If we've been careful about how we've started our teams and if we've been pushing them toward further enhancement, scaling should be all but trivial.

Scaling comes in two flavors – adding people and adding teams.

To add people, we simply find and hire a person that when added to a particular team doesn't bring the culture below the problematic threshold we've identified. That is, team members should have enough skill in the four areas of competence that they are able to maintain independence and deliver well.

This shouldn't be all that tricky.

If we've started our team well with a good culture, and we've enhanced it beyond that minimum, the team should be able to absorb a wide range of skill levels and learning velocities. That judgment call needs to be made by the leader that understands well the maturity of his team and gets a good sense of the impact a given individual will have on that maturity.

The only additional question is that of management, if the added person exceeds the 40-report ceiling that we have outlined above, we'll need to add a new manager to the mix and separate out the reporting structure somewhat.

The second flavor of scaling is adding a team – which in our continuous growth habit that we're developing simply means looping back to the "Start A New Team" phase.

Before that, we have a small punch list to take care of.

First, we need to ask ourselves if we need to create a new team. The instinct that leads to this is a drive toward additional throughput. However, we may still have a lot of advantage to be gained simply by growing the people we already have. If that's the case, we should instead move back to the "Organizational Enhancement" step – putting additional emphasis on mastery in the four areas of competence and on minimizing any structural shortcomings.

Further, do we have enough scope to justify the new team. Sometimes short-term pressure can inspire immediate scaling action. Verifying that there is enough supported product vision to give purpose to a new team for the foreseeable future is the step to take here.

Second, we need to ask ourselves if we are able to create a new team. To create a new team we have to have an existing team or teams that can contribute people such that the new group will have the level of culture that we desire. Or we need to hire to that end. If we hire, we are ultimately carrying out both flavors of scaling simultaneously.

There also must be a system available for the new team. This means at least one of the existing teams not only isolated their features architecturally, but also created a secondary isolation – a secondary system and set of features – that can be readily handed off.

If either of these things are not true – if we don't have or can't get the people or if we don't have a system to hand to the new team – then we need to go back to the "Organizational Enhancement" step with an eye toward fixing our shortcoming.

The target is to have the ability to scale long before we ever really think we need it.

ONE CONTINUOUS LYRICAL MOTION

In music, frequently, musicians learn a piece of music or a style piece by incremental piece. A scale might be practiced or passages from a full work of music. After piecewise comfort is attained, the musician steps back, attaches all the little increments together and they slowly merge together into a song.

This should be our goal here – and its why we took a close look at the specifics of each of these steps. As we say in music, we should get these parts "under our fingers." Once we do this, we should then step back and play it as one continuous song, striving for smoothness and the lyrical, story-like quality that makes for good music.

What that means practically for the software organization is less distraction from the work of development as we are steadily and powerfully moving forward in the capability that drives that work.

Chapter 18

A complete mental model for the engineering organization

Building a software development organization is a challenging, and as we've seen, ongoing process. It's not something that we reach the end of and can move on from. Because of this, it's problematic to think of the life of our software development organization as something we start, build out, and then set loose to create software systems for our businesses and their customers.

In Chapter 17, we reached the culmination of what it looks like to build a software development organization. We saw how it is basically an infinite loop of starting a team, enhancing our skills, and then scaling.

A primary part of this model to take note of is the fact that it is the same in its essentials no matter the size or state of the existing organization.

We spent 17 chapters getting to this point. In the earlier chapters, we discussed just how unique software development is – the aspects of software development that make dealing with it a special kind of challenge. This is really why we've spent such great effort building up the model used to grow an organization.

The greatest damage done out in the wild to an organization's ability to deliver software is naïve or careless handling of the capability itself. Many organizations will grind their own delivery to a halt over poor architectural choices or bad coding habits. I've seen it repeatedly in the two and half decades I've been working professionally. I would venture to guess that if you've made it to this point in the book, you have witnessed a similar pattern.

Up until this point, the delivery of actual software has been treated almost as a side-effect. In a way, it almost is. If you develop a well-considered approach to growing your organization, if you and your people are growing individually and corporately in the four areas of competence, you will deliver increasingly potent software.

Though it is understandable, in a book dedicated to understanding how to deliver software, that we might question why we've so far spent so little time talking about how that activity should actually occur.

It's a fair question – though to restate, the answer is that the hard part about building software isn't the act itself. It's maintaining a delivery system that will continue to work and even improve across the timeframes that matter to stakeholders, businesses, and ultimately to customers.

DOI: 10.1201/9781003382751-22

With all of that being said, in this chapter, we will be adding the final piece to our model. In addition to the complicated, ongoing work of maturing our practice, we will add the work of delivering software.

To use the vocabulary of Chapter 4 ("The Two Systems"), the focus of our model so far has been building up the "People and Technology System" that builds the "Computer System." What we will layer on now is the work of building the Computer System.

The distinction and the care that we are taking with this are to ensure that we don't make one of the other primary mistakes made by development organizations. That mistake is made when we confuse the two types of work. The work happens at different speeds, depends on different actions, and leverages different sets of skills. To confuse them often means using the wrong tool on the wrong job – which, in the best case, just causes confusion delivering the Computer System.

In the worst case, it damages the People and Technology System, multiplying through reduced capability, decreased output.

THE TOOLS

The first thing to talk about is the tools that we bring to bear as we layer tactical software delivery into our mental model.

In Chapter 3 ("Ways Of Knowing"), we discussed a set of thinking tools that are appropriate at different times throughout the course of operating our software development organization.

As a quick recap, there are basically two dichotomies that we choose from every time we exercise our cognitive muscles.

Explicit vs. Implicit

We can think about things explicitly. When we use this paradigm – we can usually put things directly into words and have a direct sense (and ability to verbalize) the data and syllogisms we use to reason through a thing.

This method is far less prone to error – though it is also significantly slower than the alternative. It should be chosen when our error tolerance is low, or we simply don't have intuition in that will serve us.

Alternatively, we can think about things implicitly. In practice, we call this using our "gut" or our "intuition." It is still thinking but the conclusions present as feelings that are often very difficult to distinguish from other unrelated passing emotion.

If we've trained our intuition well, this can be an extremely fast way of making even complicated decisions. Though again, it is error prone because of the reality that the way it communicates with us feels so similar to unrelated emotional context.

As we said, if our intuition is untrained or if our error tolerance is low, we should avoid relying too heavily on this procedure.

Deductive vs. Inductive

Deductive reasoning is the act of taking data and known rules and making a conclusion about the situation. We take general information and make it specific to our circumstances.

Inductive reasoning, however, is gathering a number of examples and then determining what the rule is. We take a bunch of specifics and arrive at a general rule.

The real choice here is whether we have a set of applicable rules (that we trust) that we can work from. If we do, it lowers the energy, time, and cognitive bandwidth necessary to reach a conclusion to use deductive reasoning.

If we lack applicable rules, the best that we can do is to carefully gather data and then extract rules.

Leadership

The last tool we need to discuss before we lay out the model in full is leadership. We covered this in detail in Chapter 5 ("Leadership").

Leadership is important any time that change is necessary. Whenever humans need to take action that differs from that they're already doing, it becomes necessary for one human to influence another.

As John Maxwell says, "Leadership is influence, nothing more, nothing less" [1].

There are two distinct types of leadership that will come into play.

Type 1, Direct Leadership – This type of leadership is based solely on interpersonal influence. Managers, team members, executives – everyone can exercise this kind of leadership. It's simply the ability to influence someone else's behavior without the leverage of a position.

Type 2, Positional Leadership – This type of leadership is leverage that a given organization grants a specific individual. It puts an individual's pay or even employment on the table as leverage to realize the influence.

Both of these types of leadership have their place and are important. Type 1 takes a lot more effort and skill on the part of the leader, but even with a high degree of this type of leadership, there will be times that raising the cost of non-compliance is an important part of realizing the best possible outcome for an organization, particularly when a given change makes people very uncomfortable.

THE MODEL

The short version of the full model (as seen in Figure 18.1) is that we're layering the ongoing work to build the Computer System on top of the ongoing work to build the People and Technology System. The complication to this

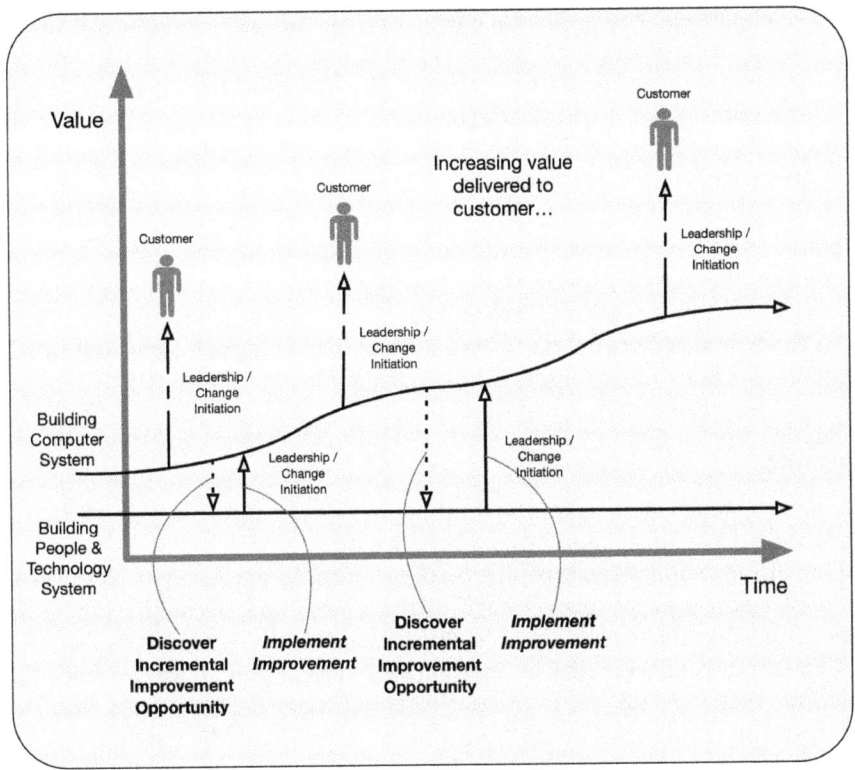

Figure 18.1 The figure shows the relationship among all aspects of software engineering, on a graph that puts time on the x-axis and value on the y-axis

being that the work that we do on the People and Technology System raises our capability delivering the Computer System.

So the Computer System delivery – the actual building of the software – is dynamic and changing with respect to our work on the People and Technology System.

At the same time, both activities are constantly happening as soon as we begin the work of building software for people.

Day-to-Day, building the people and technology system

As we modeled in Chapter 17, there are basically three parts to the infinite loop that represent our work to grow our People and Technology System:

1. Start a team – create a new team, with a given set of scope, and set them free to build.

2. Enhance our teams – for each team and for the organization as a whole, find the long-straw enhancement that can be made and incremental improvement immediately realized. The Mikado Method applies much the same way it does to code, here.
3. Scale our teams – add people, until a new team is needed, then start over at step 1.

Since the two systems are continuously building and evolving their objects, as we said, it's easy to forget that the work on the two systems is distinct, leveraging different tools and techniques.

So to the end of keeping things separate and applying the right tool to the right job, we'll lay out very specifically what we bring to this task.

Thinking

There are three primary axes for thinking in this system – whether to start a team, what to enhance, and how to enhance it.

One of the primary goals of this book has been to put into your hands the rules that you need to answer each of these questions without recourse to induction – that is to say, without having to conduct the experiments yourself.

That being said, even if I haven't entirely earned your trust yet with the solutions that I've laid out in this writing, rediscovering the truths that I've presented on these pages (or proving a better way) should be straightforward and shouldn't require regular experimentation. That is to say, once you've found the solution, you'll likely have to keep an eye on it. But you won't need to re-derive the rules each time you see the problem.

So, worst case – that is, if you trust none of the specifics you've read here, you'll be proving out a small set of problems as you grow, and then thinking through them deductively as you see different specific examples. That is, pessimistically, the ongoing effort to grow your capability will be primarily the fast, relatively low-cost mechanism of deductive reasoning.

A note should be made here – and we will highlight again later – this is the opposite as compared to actual creation of the Computer System. Building software is almost entirely inductive or empirical – it rests primarily on experiment. This is one of the big areas that creates confusion – software developers, when they begin to work on the organization itself, can often be caught in the fact (even if they don't recognize it) of using experiment to do everything. This is a huge waste of time, but understandable. Some care is needed here, if this is a habit that you've developed.

So whether you trust the rules elaborated in this book, or you go through them yourself, your thinking will be explicit until you develop deep habits around the techniques it takes to run a good software development shop. That is perfectly fine and expected.

What it means though is that the more you use these tools, the better you get at intuitively leaping to the right answer.

Just like with any sport or musical instrument (or really any human activity), practice will make you proficient.

Leading

Adding people and adding teams are both highly disruptive. They change peoples' daily experience and potentially threaten their jobs or the responsibilities they've gotten used to. This begs for Type 2, positional leadership. A high degree of Type 1 leadership will soften many of these challenges, but that softening can last a long time and become very expensive without some Type 2 leadership to simply make the change happen, to change the reality, and then to guide people through it.

The powerful part of this type of change is that these kinds of structural enhancements will have such positive effects for everyone involved that the leader will end up growing in influence as a result.

This is an important difference as compared to building the Computer System. If Type 2 leadership is regularly used to direct minute decisions about software creation, the result will be a sapping of the influence of the leader – a situation that's often compensated for by overly frequent one-on-one meetings. This is huge waste. Type 2 leadership is helpful for infrequent, specific structural changes – though tactical software delivery is another story.

It's also important to look at the "enhancing" step closely. This one is a mixed bag – a lot of the process questions, particularly those within a single feature team – and can be handled strictly with Type 1 leadership. The same goes for particular questions of craft – e.g., where does the team need to improve in terms of writing clearer code.

To the extent that it can be, these issues that are local to a team should be left to the specific team to handle with its own Type 1 leadership. In fact, even the presence of someone with positional authority can be problematic and create an implied directive from that individual. If possible, positional leaders – managers, directors, etc. – should keep some distance from the actual development of software, for just this reason.

However, it can be that a team can become comfortable with sub-optimal delivery practices. The positional leader, the team's manager should have an eye on this and be ready to step in, if the team gets stuck in a situation like this. This could include a team getting overly comfortable with bad variable naming or tight coupling – or skimping on their TDD practice.

Additionally, one of the useful aspects of the positional leader is that they often have a broader perspective – having second-hand (through their followers) interest in larger parts of the organization. Because of this, issues that cut across individual teams are going to be more visible to that leader.

Not only that, but those cross-cutting issues are more likely to be neglected by team members. The positional leader has the option to exercise his Type 1 leadership – to try to ensure the team members are seeing the bigger picture and begin to buy-in and make the choice to do the more advantageous thing without leverage. Or, if that becomes too expensive or time consuming, it's a perfectly understandable opportunity to exercise Type 2 Leadership.

Some of these cross-cutting issues might be the shape of the architecture, the way that features are parceled out across teams, or even whether or not teams are broken down by feature over technical interest.

So, much of the leadership exercised in the building of the People and Technology System can be Type 2 – Positional Leadership, though not all should be. This is an area that is fairly nuanced and will take some practice as a leader to get right.

Day to day, building the computer system

The challenge with building the Computer System is that it is done from a moving platform. One day we may be doing thing one way, and the next day our way of working might have changed – hopefully for the better.

One of the important things to keep in mind through all of this is not to be too judgmental about the way we were working in the past or the way we are planning to work in the future. Not only that, but it's also important to realize, even in the small details, that we'll never "arrive" at an end-state.

The evolution of the ability that the team has to build its software should be improving at a comfortable pace with as little attachment as possible to current state or next state.

Part of this rests with the method that is being used to enhance the People and Technology System. In Chapter 17, our target was to evolve toward a nice smooth, continuous but not disruptive, process of growth and enhancement. That's the contribution we make as we build the People and Technology System.

The contribution on the side of actually doing the work to build the Computer System is to be flexible and expect the change.

A great example that I've witnessed a couple of times in my career is the move from an ad-hoc system of work assignment to a single pipeline with a (several week) time-limited delivery cycle. In the ad-hoc world, every team member is assigned work from any authority that might need it. There's habitual priority arbitration, other than the team member's sanity and his readiness to run down all interested parties for a decision.

The move is an important one in the life of a software development organization. It not only speeds up delivery but makes the life of that poor team member that was pulled in every direction far better. More importantly, it increases the likelihood that this team member will continue to work for the organization.

As the transition is made, an organization doesn't simply stop what it's doing and make the transition. Sometimes with good planning the change can be pretty cut and dry. But often, there's a transition period where we play by both the old rules and the new rules.

This is where leadership becomes so important. Every team member should be striving to find the best direction and then influencing his fellows. Momentum is easily lost – the leader will ensure progress is made even amidst the ambiguity of transition.

Another situation that might be faced is change to a development practice. This might be something like a team starting to use TDD after not having used it in the past.

As we've mentioned before, if the technique is new, time must often be allowed for learning. So, working in both ways, or tolerating yourself and others as the technique is gradually learned and adopted is a powerful part of making the constant growth smooth and sustainable.

The same need for leadership should be called out here – transitions are full of momentum sapping ambiguity. The more every team member is exercising leadership, the more the organization will be able to continuously grow even through those confusing times of transition.

This challenge aside, the actual work of building the Computer System is to:

1. coalesce the needs of the person whose need we're potentially meeting
2. decompose those needs into nearly trivial enhancements (each that are actually meaningful to a potential user)
3. decompose those into technical aspects of a potential system
4. write technical instructions for the computer
5. operate the system in such a way that use can be gotten from it.

Thinking

Every single one of these steps requires experimentation. There are no rules that will result in the right way to meet a need, or how to technically compose that solution. The computer program may be based on rules and deductive reasoning once it is written, arriving at it is anything but deductive.

That being said, many of the small decisions that are made from discovery of need to the way code is formulated can be very intuitive.

The way the necessary experiments are conducted can often be very similar. So it is possible to build up intuition about the experimentation and thus make our reasoning more implicit, and thus faster.

We should note again – since the big snare we want to avoid is mixing up the tools and techniques that we apply to building each of the different systems – that building a People and Technology System is deductive in that there are rules that can be derived that don't change over time. Once we understand the rule, the reasoning about the People and Technology System is entirely deductive. Building software is the opposite.

Though the similarity between the two is that if you do them enough, both become intuitive and implicit – that is to say, faster.

Leading

Ideally, the group of people building software are on a single team. As a part of the People and Process competency, this should be a primary target. In fact if this isn't true, this should be one of the first things on your People and Technology System enhancement to-do list.

Until this is true, Type 2 leadership – coercive leadership may be needed. Interests in the running software might be held by two separate teams with little relationship between them. Because of this, interpersonal influence – that is to say Type 1 leadership – will be, at best, very time consuming. Likely, it will simply be impossible, due to the lack of relationship between team members.

Once teams are independently building and operating their own small set of features, this changes though. The faster (and much more fun) Type 1 leadership – direct leadership – among the team members should become the norm. Once the team is mature and operating well, Type 2 leadership – and even inclusion in development of leaders with the possibility of Type 2 leadership – positional leaders – should be avoided.

That is, any decision within the team can be made and championed by someone on the team. Since the team is working together day-to-day, they will have the relational bonds that will make influence possible.

WHAT IT MEANS

So we've brought together the difficult but continuous work of the building of the software development capability and the building of the software itself.

They require different tools and a different focus, but as activities they stay the same throughout the course of a software development organization's life. So once we learn how they operate, all that remains is to do them and constantly work to get better at both of them.

As a reminder, the work of building our capability alters the path of our software building. It's important as we do that work, that we're keeping that in mind, and working to make the enhancement as smooth as possible. Similarly, as we do the work of building the software, we must understand that there will be discontinuities as the system is improved that will require patience and leadership. That leadership drives through the ambiguity while continuing to deliver valuable software.

As we carry out both of these important pieces of work, we will as an effect of that work be delivering increasing impact and radical improvement to the life of our customer.

That ... is what it's all about.

WORK CITED

1. J. Maxwell, The 21 Irrefutable Laws of Leadership, HarperCollins, Nashville, 1998.

For Product Safety Concerns and Information please contact our EU
representative GPSR@taylorandfrancis.com
Taylor & Francis Verlag GmbH, Kaufingerstraße 24, 80331 München, Germany